A PORTRAIT OF CHRIST: The Tabernacle, the Priesthood, and the Offerings

David Cloud

A PORTRAIT OF CHRIST:
The Tabernacle, the Priesthood, and the Offerings

This edition April 20, 2014
ISBN 978-1-58318-178-2

Published by Way of Life Literature
PO Box 610368, Port Huron, MI 48061
866-295-4143 (toll free) - fbns@wayoflife.org
www.wayoflife.org

Canada: Bethel Baptist Church
4212 Campbell St. N., London Ont. N6P 1A6
519-652-2619

Printed in Canada by
Bethel Baptist Print Ministry

DEDICATION

I dedicate this book on the tabernacle, the Old Testament's peerless portrait of Christ, to Pastor Wilbert Unger. I am thankful for the privilege to have known many godly saints who have brightened this dark world, and Pastor Unger is one of these. He has lived a Christlike example before me for the nearly quarter of a century I have known him. We understand, of course, that any godliness that a believer has in this present world is a mere dim reflection of the perfection that is in Christ. He is Second Man who is *full* of grace, and His people receive imperfectly and in part from that fulness (John 1:14, 16).

Table of Contents

A PORTRAIT OF CHRIST:
The Tabernacle, the Priesthood,
and the Offerings

Importance of the Tabernacle

The tabernacle with its priestly system has been called "God's masterpiece of typology."

Nothing has helped me better understand the Triune God and the salvation that He has purchased for man.

The tabernacle's importance is evident by the amount of space it occupies in God's Word.

Whereas the record of the creation of the universe takes up two chapters of the Bible and the fall of man takes up one chapter, the tabernacle, with its priesthood and offerings, takes up 50 chapters (13 in Exodus, 18 in Leviticus, 13 in Numbers, 2 in Deuteronomy, 4 in Hebrews), and references to the the tabernacle in other parts of the Bible occupy many more verses!

It is sad that this important part of the Bible tends to be so neglected.

The very details of the tabernacle teach us that God wants us to meditate on it and learn from it in all of its facets.

An Old Testament type is not the same as a biblical parable. A parable has one main lesson. The details are given to support that one lesson. Consider Christ's parable of the widow and the judge in Luke 18:1-5. The one lesson of the parable is stated in verse 1 - "that men ought always to pray, and not to faint." The details of the parable are there only to support the one lesson.

But an Old Testament type has multiple lessons.

> "We have it upon the highest authority, that, not only in its grand outlines, but in all minutest details, everything was to be made 'after the pattern' which God showed to Moses on the mount (Exod. 25:9). And so we also read in Acts 7:44 and Hebrews 8:5; 9:23, teaching us, that Moses was

shown by God an actual pattern or model of all that he was to make in and for the sanctuary. This can convey only one meaning. It taught far more than the general truth, that only that approach to God is lawful or acceptable which He has indicated. For, God showed Moses every detail to indicate that every detail had its special meaning, and hence could not be altered in any, even the minutest, particular, without destroying that meaning, and losing that significance which alone made it of importance. Nothing here was intended as a mere ornament or ceremony, all was symbol and type" (Alfred Edersheim, *History of the Old Testament*).

The tabernacle creates peerless images in the believer's mind about Christ.

Once understood, the images linger in the mind and are brought back repeatedly by the Holy Spirit.

> "The Types are, in fact, a set of pictures or emblems, directly from the hand of God, by which He would teach His children things otherwise all but incomprehensible. In the Types, if I may be allowed the expression, God takes His Son to pieces. By them does He bring within the range of our capacity definite views of the details of Christ's work, which perhaps but for these pictures we should never fully, or at least so fully, apprehend. The realities which the Types represent are in themselves truths and facts the most elevated, facts which have taken place before God Himself, facts in which He has Himself been the actor. These vast and infinite objects He brings close before us in emblems, and presents them to our eyes in a series of pictures, with the accuracy of One who views these things as they are seen and understood by Himself, and in a way in which they may be seen and understood by us" (Andrew Jukes, *The Law of the Offerings*).

God's use of illustrations reminds us of their importance.

God has filled the Bible with illustrations. Indeed, God has filled the universe with illustrations of spiritual things. Men need examples and illustrations, and every preacher and teacher must remember this.

Charles Spurgeon said that a sermon without illustrations is like a room without windows. When one of his students remarked that the difficulty was to get illustrations in any great abundance, Spurgeon replied,

> "Yes, if you do not wake up, but go through the world asleep, you cannot see illustrations; but if your minds were thoroughly aroused, and yet you could see nothing else in the world but a single tallow candle, you might find enough illustrations in that luminary to last you for six months" (Spurgeon, "Sermons in Candles").

While we can and should draw illustrations from everywhere in life, the very best illustrations of spiritual truth are found in God's Word. Since the Bible is perfect and it is able to make the man of God perfect (2 Tim. 3:16-17), it contains perfect teaching as well as perfect illustrations to support the teaching.

The tabernacle sheds light on the Gospels, and the Gospels shed light on the tabernacle.

The teaching of the tabernacle and the teaching of the Gospels fit together in divine perfection, giving us an astounding revelation of Christ.

For example, consider the offerings presented "before God" and offered unto God and burnt as a "sweet savour unto God." These depict Christ's relationship with the Father in a most fascinating manner. This gives deeper understanding to New Testament passages such as John 1:1-2 (of the Son being the eternal Word and dwelling with the Father) and of John 1:18 (of Christ being eternally in the bosom of the Father).

This aspect of the offerings also gives us a deeper understanding of what transpired on the cross, when the Son offered Himself as the perfect sacrifice and the Father had to forsake the Son because He was bearing the sins of mankind and the Son cried out in agony, "My God, my God, why hast thou forsake me?" a statement so important that it is repeated three times in Scripture (Psa. 22:1; Mat. 27:46; Mk. 15:34).

This aspect of the offerings also shines light on the Son's prayers to the Father when He was on earth, such as the prayer of John 17 where Christ spoke of the glory He had with the Father before the world was (John 17:5). In these lessons we will see how that such things are better understood by the tabernacle.

The believer grows in his comprehension of the lessons of the tabernacle as he grows spiritually in Christ.

When we are baby Christians or carnal and disobedient, our spiritual understanding is weak.

> Hebrews 5:12-14 For when for the time ye ought to be teachers, ye have need that one teach you again which *be* the first principles of the oracles of God; and are become such as have need of milk, and not of strong meat. 13 For every one that useth milk *is* unskilful in the word of righteousness: for he is a babe. 14 But strong meat belongeth to them that are of full age, *even* those who by reason of use have their senses exercised to discern both good and evil.

> 1 Corinthians 3:1-2 And I, brethren, could not speak unto you as unto spiritual, but as unto carnal, *even* as unto babes in Christ. 2 I have fed you with milk, and not with meat: for hitherto ye were not able *to bear it*, neither yet now are ye able.

The first time I studied the tabernacle was in Bible college in the mid-1970s as a new Christian, and though I was impressed with the beauty of this divine illustration, my understanding was very elementary. As I continued to look at this portion of Scripture every year as I read through the Bible, I grew a little in my understanding of its lessons, but the next time I gave serious attention to the tabernacle was when I prepared the first edition of my course *Bible History and Geography* in 2002. By then I had been walking with the Lord and devouring His Word for about 30 years, and the tabernacle meant more to me.

In 2013, when I was 40 years old in the Lord, I decided to do a much more serious study of the tabernacle, using about 40 different commentaries and books and devoting weeks to this pursuit, and this time the teaching of the tabernacle opened to my understanding in the most wonderful way and was much more precious than ever before.

For one thing, I saw the relationship between God the Father and God the Son in the offerings in a way I had never seen before. I had read about this, but the beauty and power of the teaching had never settled on my mind as it did this time. At the same time, I know that I have only barely begun to understand these things.

> "The real secret of the neglect of the Types, I cannot but think may in part be traced to this — that they require more spiritual intelligence than many Christians can bring to them. To apprehend them requires a certain measure of spiritual capacity and habitual exercise in the things of God, which all do not possess, for want of abiding fellowship with Jesus. The mere superficial glance upon the Word in these parts brings no corresponding idea to the mind of the reader. The types are, indeed, pictures, but to understand the picture it is necessary we should know something of the reality" (Andrew Jukes, *The Law of the Offerings*).

We will continue to learn from the tabernacle.

Just as offerings will continue to be presented in the millennial temple on an 18-foot altar as teaching lessons to the whole world, so we will continue to learn from the tabernacle in future ages.

> Ezekiel 43:17-18 And the settle *shall be* fourteen *cubits* long and fourteen broad in the four squares thereof; and the border about it *shall be* half a cubit; and the bottom thereof *shall be* a cubit about; and his stairs shall look toward the east. 18 And he said unto me, Son of man, thus saith the Lord GOD; These *are* the ordinances of the altar in the day when they shall make it, to offer burnt offerings thereon, and to sprinkle blood thereon.

The writer of Hebrews said there are lessons about the tabernacle and the priesthood that are not presently revealed or understood.

> Hebrews 9:5 And over it the cherubims of glory shadowing the mercyseat; of which we cannot now speak particularly.

The tabernacle reminds us that God's people need teachers.

Every believer has the indwelling Spirit of God to help him, but if we could understand everything in the Bible on our own, God would not have given teachers (Eph. 4:11-12).

I have been a passionate Bible student since the first day I was converted in the summer of 1973, but the teaching of the tabernacle was largely closed to my mind until I had help from teachers via commentaries and churches and Bible College. I thank the Lord for the wealth of sound teaching material that is available in the English language.

Design of the Tabernacle

The tabernacle was a sanctuary where God dwelt among His people.

> Exodus 25:8 And let them make me a sanctuary; that I may dwell among them.

From the tabernacle, God spoke to His people and guided them in their wilderness journeys.

> Exodus 25:22 And there I will meet with thee, and I will commune with thee from above the mercy seat, from between the two cherubims which *are* upon the ark of the testimony, of all *things* which I will give thee in commandment unto the children of Israel.

> Exodus 13:21-22 And the LORD went before them by day in a pillar of a cloud, to lead them the way; and by night in a pillar of fire, to give them light; to go by day and night: 22 He took not away the pillar of the cloud by day, nor the pillar of fire by night, *from* before the people.

The tabernacle is called

> "the tabernacle of the congregation" (Ex. 27:21) (133 times)
> "the tabernacle of testimony" (Ex. 38:21) (4 times)
> "the tabernacle of witness" (Nu. 17:7) (5 times)
> "the tabernacle of the LORD" (Nu. 17:13) (10 times)
> "the tabernacle of the house of God" (1 Ch. 6:48) (1 time)

A brief description of the tabernacle can be found in Exodus 40:1-8 and Hebrews 9:1-5. A full description is in Exodus 25:10 - 27:19.

> Exodus 40:1-8 And the LORD spake unto Moses, saying, 2 On the first day of the first month shalt thou set up the tabernacle of the tent of the congregation. 3 And thou shalt put therein the ark of the testimony, and cover the ark with the vail. 4 And thou shalt bring in the table, and set in order the things that are to be set in order upon it; and thou shalt bring in the candlestick, and light the lamps

> thereof. 5 And thou shalt set the altar of gold for the incense before the ark of the testimony, and put the hanging of the door to the tabernacle. 6 And thou shalt set the altar of the burnt offering before the door of the tabernacle of the tent of the congregation. 7 And thou shalt set the laver between the tent of the congregation and the altar, and shalt put water therein. 8 And thou shalt set up the court round about, and hang up the hanging at the court gate.

> Hebrews 9:1-5 Then verily the first *covenant* had also ordinances of divine service, and a worldly sanctuary. 2 For there was a tabernacle made; the first, wherein *was* the candlestick, and the table, and the shewbread; which is called the sanctuary. 3 And after the second veil, the tabernacle which is called the Holiest of all; 4 Which had the golden censer, and the ark of the covenant overlaid round about with gold, wherein *was* the golden pot that had manna, and Aaron's rod that budded, and the tables of the covenant; 5 And over it the cherubims of glory shadowing the mercyseat; of which we cannot now speak particularly.

The tabernacle was composed of a court area within which was the rectangular tent of the tabernacle itself.

It was made according to a pattern that was shown to Moses (Exodus 25:40; 26:30; Acts 7:44).

The description of the tabernacle in Exodus 25-27 begins with the ark of the covenant in the most holy place (Ex. 25:8-10) and ends with the gate entrance into the court (Ex. 27:16-17).

Thus the description begins with God. It is described from God's perspective rather than from man's. This is always the correct perspective. God is the heart and soul of creation and of life, so to speak, and when we put God first, everything else falls into its rightful place. The first law is to have no other gods before God. To put God anywhere but absolute first place is to commit idolatry. Jesus taught us to seek *first* the kingdom of God and his righteousness, promising that all things would be added to us if we do this (Matthew 6:33).

Here we will give a brief overview of the design of the tabernacle. Later we will look closely at each part.

The court

The court was surrounded by tent walls (Ex. 27:8-18). It was 100 cubits* (150 feet or 45.7 meters) long by 50 cubits (75 feet or 22.8 meters) wide (Ex. 27:11-13). The curtain walls of the court were five cubits (7.5 feet) high (Ex. 27:18). The curtains hung on 60 wooden pillars. (* The standard Jewish cubit was 18 inches.)

> Exodus 27:8-18 Hollow with boards shalt thou make it: as it was shewed thee in the mount, so shall they make *it*. 9 And thou shalt make the court of the tabernacle: for the south side southward *there shall be* hangings for the court *of* fine twined linen of an hundred cubits long for one side: 10 And the twenty pillars thereof and their twenty sockets *shall be of* brass; the hooks of the pillars and their fillets *shall be of* silver. 11 And likewise for the north side in length *there shall be* hangings of an hundred *cubits* long, and his twenty pillars and their twenty sockets *of* brass; the hooks of the pillars and their fillets *of* silver. 12 And *for* the breadth of the court on the west side *shall be* hangings of fifty cubits: their pillars ten, and their sockets ten. 13 And the breadth of the court on the east side eastward *shall be* fifty cubits. 14 The hangings of one side *of the gate shall be* fifteen cubits: their pillars three, and their sockets three. 15 And on the other side *shall be* hangings fifteen *cubits*: their pillars three, and their sockets three. 16 And for the gate of the court *shall be* an hanging of twenty cubits, *of* blue, and purple, and scarlet, and fine twined linen, wrought with needlework: *and* their pillars *shall be* four, and their sockets four. 17 All the pillars round about the court *shall be* filleted with silver; their hooks *shall be of* silver, and their sockets *of* brass. 18 The length of the court *shall be* an hundred cubits, and the breadth fifty every where, and the

height five cubits *of* fine twined linen, and their sockets *of* brass.

The gate

There was only one gate into the court, and it was on the east side (Ex. 27:14-16). It was a cloth gate made of four pillars and a curtain 20 cubits (30 feet) long.

Exodus 27:14-16 The hangings of one side *of the gate shall be* fifteen cubits: their pillars three, and their sockets three. 15 And on the other side *shall be* hangings fifteen *cubits*: their pillars three, and their sockets three. 16 And for the gate of the court *shall be* an hanging of twenty cubits, *of* blue, and purple, and scarlet, and fine twined linen, wrought with needlework: *and* their pillars *shall be* four, and their sockets four.

The altar of sacrifice

The brazen altar or altar of sacrifice was made of wood covered with brass (Ex. 27:1-8). It was five cubits (7.5 feet) square and three cubits (4.5 feet) high and had horns on the four corners. The sacrifices were killed on the north side of the altar (Lev. 1:11) and the ashes were placed on the east side, which was the side facing the gate (Lev. 1:16).

Exodus 27:1-8 And thou shalt make an altar *of* shittim wood, five cubits long, and five cubits broad; the altar shall be foursquare: and the height thereof *shall be* three cubits. 2 And thou shalt make the horns of it upon the four corners thereof: his horns shall be of the same: and thou shalt overlay it with brass. 3 And thou shalt make his pans to receive his ashes, and his shovels, and his basons, and his fleshhooks, and his firepans: all the vessels thereof thou shalt make *of* brass. 4 And thou shalt make for it a grate of network *of* brass; and upon the net shalt thou make four brasen rings in the four corners thereof. 5 And thou shalt put it under the compass of the altar beneath, that the net may be even to the midst of the altar. 6 And thou shalt make staves for the altar, staves *of* shittim wood, and overlay them with brass. 7 And the staves shall be put into the rings, and the staves shall be upon the two sides of the altar, to bear it. 8 Hollow with boards shalt thou make it: as it was shewed thee in the mount, so shall they make *it*.

The laver

In front of the entrance to the tabernacle was the laver for washing (Ex. 30:17-21).

> Exodus 30:17-21 And the LORD spake unto Moses, saying, 18 Thou shalt also make a laver *of* brass, and his foot *also of* brass, to wash *withal*: and thou shalt put it between the tabernacle of the congregation and the altar, and thou shalt put water therein. 19 For Aaron and his sons shall wash their hands and their feet thereat: 20 When they go into the tabernacle of the congregation, they shall wash with water, that they die not; or when they come near to the altar to minister, to burn offering made by fire unto the LORD: 21 So they shall wash their hands and their feet, that they die not: and it shall be a statute for ever to them, *even* to him and to his seed throughout their generations.

The tabernacle

The tabernacle itself was a rectangular tent that sat inside the court area. It was 30 cubits (45 feet or 13.7 meters) long, 10 cubits (15 feet or 4.5 meters) wide, and 10 cubits high.

The side and rear walls were made with boards covered with gold (Ex 26:15-30). The boards were 10 cubits (15 feet) high and 1.5 cubits (2.25 feet) wide (Ex. 26:16). There were a total of 48 boards. Each board fit into two sockets of silver (Ex. 26:19).

> Exodus 26:15-30 And thou shalt make boards for the tabernacle *of* shittim wood standing up. 16 Ten cubits *shall be* the length of a board, and a cubit and a half *shall be* the breadth of one board. 17 Two tenons *shall there be* in one board, set in order one against another: thus shalt thou make for all the boards of the tabernacle. 18 And thou shalt make the boards for the tabernacle, twenty boards on the south side southward. 19 And thou shalt make forty

sockets of silver under the twenty boards; two sockets under one board for his two tenons, and two sockets under another board for his two tenons. 20 And for the second side of the tabernacle on the north side *there shall be* twenty boards: 21 And their forty sockets *of* silver; two sockets under one board, and two sockets under another board. 22 And for the sides of the tabernacle westward thou shalt make six boards. 23 And two boards shalt thou make for the corners of the tabernacle in the two sides. 24 And they shall be coupled together beneath, and they shall be coupled together above the head of it unto one ring: thus shall it be for them both; they shall be for the two corners. 25 And they shall be eight boards, and their sockets *of* silver, sixteen sockets; two sockets under one board, and two sockets under another board. 26 And thou shalt make bars *of* shittim wood; five for the boards of the one side of the tabernacle, 27 And five bars for the boards of the other side of the tabernacle, and five bars for the boards of the side of the tabernacle, for the two sides westward. 28 And the middle bar in the midst of the boards shall reach from end to end. 29 And thou shalt overlay the boards with gold, and make their rings *of* gold *for* places for the bars: and thou shalt overlay the bars with gold. 30 And thou shalt rear up the tabernacle according to the fashion thereof which was shewed thee in the mount.

The structure was roofed with four cloth coverings. First was a covering of linen entwined with blue, purple, and scarlet, and engraved with images of the cherubims (Ex. 26:1-6). This was the covering that could be seen from inside the tabernacle.

Next was a covering made of goats' hair (Ex. 26:7-13). Over this was a covering made of rams' skins dyed red (Ex. 26:14). Finally, there was a covering made of badgers' skins (Ex. 26:14). This was the covering that was seen from outside the tabernacle.

The Tabernacle Coverings

Exodus 26:1-14 Moreover thou shalt make the tabernacle *with* ten curtains *of* fine twined linen, and blue, and purple, and scarlet: *with* cherubims of cunning work shalt thou make them. 2 The length of one curtain *shall be* eight and twenty cubits, and the breadth of one curtain four cubits: and every one of the curtains shall have one measure. 3 The five curtains shall be coupled together one to another; and *other* five curtains *shall be* coupled one to another. 4 And thou shalt make loops of blue upon the edge of the one curtain from the selvedge in the coupling; and likewise shalt thou make in the uttermost edge of *another* curtain, in the coupling of the second. 5 Fifty loops shalt thou make in the one curtain, and fifty loops shalt thou make in the edge of the curtain that *is* in the coupling of the second; that the loops may take hold one of another. 6 And thou shalt make fifty taches of gold, and couple the curtains together with the taches: and it shall be one tabernacle. 7 And thou shalt make curtains *of* goats' *hair* to be a covering upon the tabernacle: eleven curtains shalt thou make. 8 The length of one curtain *shall be* thirty cubits, and

> the breadth of one curtain four cubits: and the eleven curtains *shall be all* of one measure. 9 And thou shalt couple five curtains by themselves, and six curtains by themselves, and shalt double the sixth curtain in the forefront of the tabernacle. 10 And thou shalt make fifty loops on the edge of the one curtain *that is* outmost in the coupling, and fifty loops in the edge of the curtain which coupleth the second. 11 And thou shalt make fifty taches of brass, and put the taches into the loops, and couple the tent together, that it may be one. 12 And the remnant that remaineth of the curtains of the tent, the half curtain that remaineth, shall hang over the backside of the tabernacle. 13 And a cubit on the one side, and a cubit on the other side of that which remaineth in the length of the curtains of the tent, it shall hang over the sides of the tabernacle on this side and on that side, to cover it. 14 And thou shalt make a covering for the tent *of* rams' skins dyed red, and a covering above *of* badgers' skins.

The entrance into the tabernacle

The tabernacle had one curtain entrance on the east side called the door (Ex. 26:36-37).

> Exodus 26:36-37 And thou shalt make an hanging for the door of the tent, *of* blue, and purple, and scarlet, and fine twined linen, wrought with needlework. 37 And thou shalt make for the hanging five pillars *of* shittim *wood*, and overlay them with gold, *and* their hooks *shall be of* gold: and thou shalt cast five sockets of brass for them.

The two compartments of the tabernacle

The tabernacle was divided into two compartments. The first was *the holy place*, which was 20 cubits (30 feet) long, 10 cubits (15 feet) wide, and 10 cubits (15 feet) high. It is also called the sanctuary (Heb. 9:2).

The inner compartment, *the holy of holies,* was a perfect cube 10 cubits (15 feet) long and wide and high. Sometimes the holy of holies is called the holy place (Lev. 16:2; Heb. 9:25).

The holy place

The first compartment contained the following three objects:

There was ***the golden candlestick*** with seven lamps (Ex. 25:31-39). It was made of solid gold and was on the south side of the room (Ex. 26:35), which was on the left side as the priest entered from the court.

There was ***the table of shewbread*** made of wood covered with gold (Ex. 25:23-30). It was two cubits (3 feet) long, a cubit (1.5 feet) wide, and a cubit and a half (2.25 feet) high. It was on the north side of the room (Ex. 26:35), which was on the right side as the priest entered the tabernacle. On the table were placed 12 loaves of bread in two rows of six each (Lev. 24:5-6).

There was ***the incense altar*** made of wood covered with gold (Ex. 30:1-10). It was one cubit (1.5 feet) square and two cubits (3 feet) high. It stood in front of the veil leading into the holy of holies.

The veil

There was a veil between the holy place and the holy of holies (Ex. 26:31-33). It was made with fine linen interwoven with blue, purple, and scarlet thread, and the images of the cherubims.

The holy of holies

The holy of holies contained ***the ark of the covenant*** (Heb. 9:1-5). This was a rectangular box 2.5 cubits (3.75 feet) long, 1.5 cubits (2.25 feet) wide, and 1.5 cubits (2.25 feet) high (Ex. 25:10-15). It was made of wood covered with gold inside and out. It contained the ten commandments written on stone called *the testimony* (Ex. 25:16; 31:18; De. 5:5-22). It also contained a gold pot filled with manna and Aaron's rod that budded (Heb. 9:4).

> Exodus 25:10-16 And they shall make an ark *of* shittim wood: two cubits and a half *shall be* the length thereof, and a cubit and a half the breadth thereof, and a cubit and a half the height thereof. 11 And thou shalt overlay it with pure gold, within and without shalt thou overlay it, and shalt make upon it a crown of gold round about. 12 And thou shalt cast four rings of gold for it, and put *them* in the four corners thereof; and two rings *shall be* in the one side of it, and two rings in the other side of it. 13 And thou shalt make staves *of* shittim wood, and overlay them with gold. 14 And thou shalt put the staves into the rings by the sides of the ark, that the ark may be borne with them. 15 The staves shall be in the rings of the ark: they shall not be taken from it. 16 And thou shalt put into the ark the testimony which I shall give thee.

The ark was covered with a lid called ***the mercy seat*** made of solid gold (Ex. 25:17-21). On the mercy seat were carvings of cherubims facing inward with their wings covering the seat (Ex. 25:18-20).

> Exodus 25:17-21 And thou shalt make a mercy seat *of* pure gold: two cubits and a half *shall be* the length thereof, and a cubit and a half the breadth thereof. 18 And thou shalt make two cherubims *of* gold, *of* beaten work shalt thou make them, in the two ends of the mercy seat. 19 And make one cherub on the one end, and the other cherub on the other end: *even* of the mercy seat shall ye make the cherubims on the two ends thereof. 20 And the cherubims shall stretch forth *their* wings on high, covering the mercy seat with their wings, and their faces *shall look* one to another; toward the mercy seat shall the faces of the cherubims be. 21 And thou shalt put the mercy seat above upon the ark; and in the ark thou shalt put the testimony that I shall give thee.

The ark of the covenant was where God's presence dwelt (Ex. 25:22). His glory entered there when the tabernacle was first set up (Ex. 40:33-35).

> Exodus 40:33-35 And he reared up the court round about the tabernacle and the altar, and set up the hanging of the court gate. So Moses finished the work. 34 Then a cloud covered the tent of the congregation, and the glory of the LORD filled the tabernacle. 35 And Moses was not able to enter into the tent of the congregation, because the cloud abode thereon, and the glory of the LORD filled the tabernacle.

No one went into the holy of holies except the high priest once a year to make atonement by sprinkling the blood on the mercy seat (Heb. 9:7; Lev. 16:11-17).

> Hebrews 9:6-7 Now when these things were thus ordained, the priests went always into the first tabernacle, accomplishing the service *of God*. 7 But into the second *went* the high priest alone once every year, not without blood, which he offered for himself, and *for* the errors of the people:

The tabernacle was designed to be portable so that it could be transported during Israel's wanderings in the wilderness. Each major article had rings through which poles were placed so the priests could carry them from place to place (Ex. 25:10-14). The heavier items, such as the boards, the pillars, and the sockets were carried in wagons (Nu. 7:6-8).

The Order of Encampment

The tribes of Israel encamped around the tabernacle.

On the east were the tribes of Issachar, Judah, and Zebulun (Nu. 2:3-9).

On the south were Simeon, Reuben, and Gad (Nu. 2:10-16).

On the west were Ephraim, Manasseh, and Benjamin (Nu. 2:18-24).

On the north were Dan, Asher, and Naphtali (Nu. 2:25-31).

Between the tabernacle and the tribes were the Levites (Nu. 1:52-53).

On the east were Moses, Aaron, and Aaron's sons (Nu. 3:38).

On the west were the Gershonites (Nu. 3:23).

On the south were the Kohathites (Nu. 3:29).

On the north were the Merarites (Nu. 3:35).

The number of men 20 years old and older was 603,550 (Nu. 1:45-46). (This did not include the tribe of Levi.) When women and children and the mixed multitude who left Egypt with them are included, the total number was probably about three million.

"One author estimated that the encampment around the Tabernacle extended approximately 12 square miles. ... If the people traveled 50 abreast, the procession would have stretched for 40 miles" (David Levy).

Interpretation of the Tabernacle

Following are some principles for the right interpretation of Old Testament types:

1. Always see Christ.

As we have seen, the Old Testament is filled with types of Christ.

Jesus said that the entire Old Testament points to Him.

> Luke 24:27 And beginning at Moses and all the prophets, he expounded unto them in all the scriptures the things concerning himself.
>
> Luke 24:44 And he said unto them, These *are* the words which I spake unto you, while I was yet with you, that all things must be fulfilled, which were written in the law of Moses, and *in* the prophets, and *in* the psalms, concerning me.

Though the law of Moses does not provide the perfect righteousness that God demands, it points to the source of this righteousness, which is Christ.

> Romans 3:20-22 Therefore by the deeds of the law there shall no flesh be justified in his sight: for by the law *is* the knowledge of sin. 21 But now the righteousness of God without the law is manifested, BEING WITNESSED BY THE LAW AND THE PROPHETS; 22 Even the righteousness of God *which is* by faith of Jesus Christ unto all and upon all them that believe: for there is no difference:

The law witnesses to salvation by pointing to Christ through its types.

> "As an old writer has well said, contrasting the dispensations, God in the Types of the last dispensation was teaching His children their letters. In this dispensation He is teaching them to put these letters together, and they find that the letters, arrange them as we will, spell CHRIST,

> and nothing but Christ" (Andrew Jukes, *The Law of the Offerings*).

Thus first and foremost the Old Testament types are interpreted by seeing Christ in them.

The tabernacle, priesthood, and offerings are about Christ.

2. Consider the context.

In Bible interpretation, context is the most important principle. I have often said that context is the first, second, and third rule of sound Bible interpretation.

Most of the Bible's types, figures, and parables are interpreted in the immediate context.

Consider the mercy seat (Ex. 25:21-22). The very name and purpose give the meaning. It covered the ark of the covenant containing the Ten Commandments, and it was sprinkled with blood on the Day of Atonement (Lev. 16:14). Thus the mercy seat clearly depicts God's mercy in covering the demands of His holy law by the blood of Christ.

Consider the offerings in Leviticus. The basic meaning is clearly given. They depict the atonement to God for man's sin.

> Leviticus 1:4 And he shall put his hand upon the head of the burnt offering; and it shall be accepted for him to make atonement for him.

The offerings therefore depict in various ways Christ as the sinner's sacrifice.

Consider the Day of Atonement. The overall meaning is plainly given.

> Leviticus 16:30 For on that day shall *the priest* make an atonement for you, to cleanse you, *that* ye may be clean from all your sins before the LORD.

The Day of Atonement depicts the cleansing of the sin of Israel before God. It is therefore a picture of Christ the great High Priest making atonement for man's sin.

The meaning of the two goats of the sin offering of verse 5 is also given.

> Leviticus 16:8 And Aaron shall cast lots upon the two goats; one lot for the LORD, and the other lot for the scapegoat.
>
> Leviticus 16:15-16 Then shall he kill the goat of the sin offering, that *is* for the people, and bring his blood within the vail, and do with that blood as he did with the blood of the bullock, and sprinkle it upon the mercy seat, and before the mercy seat: 16 And he shall make an atonement for the holy *place*, because of the uncleanness of the children of Israel, and because of their transgressions in all their sins: and so shall he do for the tabernacle of the congregation, that remaineth among them in the midst of their uncleanness.
>
> Leviticus 16:21-22 And Aaron shall lay both his hands upon the head of the live goat, and confess over him all the iniquities of the children of Israel, and all their transgressions in all their sins, putting them upon the head of the goat, and shall send *him* away by the hand of a fit man into the wilderness: 22 And the goat shall bear upon him all their iniquities unto a land not inhabited: and he shall let go the goat in the wilderness.

It takes very little Bible knowledge to understand that the two goats represent two aspects of Christ's atonement: the first one signifying *the value* of the atonement as acceptable to God, and the second signifying *the completion* of the atonement in fully taking away our sins.

3. Compare Scripture with Scripture.

When the teaching of the immediate context is exhausted, we then compare Scripture with Scripture by examining interpretations given in other parts of the Bible, such as the following:

> Christ is the lamb of God (Isa. 53:6-7; John 1:29; 1 Cor. 5:7; 1 Pet. 1:19; Rev. 5:6; 7:14; 12:11; 13:8).

Christ is our high priest (Hebrews 3:1; 4:14-15; 7:26; 10:21-22).

The veil into the holiest is Christ (Hebrews 6:18-20; 10:19-20).

The tabernacle is a type of the heavenly tabernacle (Heb. 8:1-2).

The sacrifices were examples of heavenly things (Heb. 8:3-5) .

The tabernacle was a figure of Christ (Heb. 9:1-14).

The shedding of blood is a type of Christ's blood (Heb. 9:19-28).

The tabernacle was a shadow of things to come (Heb. 10:1).

The repetition of the sacrifices signified their imperfection (Heb. 10:1-4).

The sacrifices represent Christ's body which He offered to God (Heb. 10:5-10).

The burning of the sacrifices outside the camp represent Christ (Heb. 13:11-13).

The brass serpent pointed to Christ's cross (John 3:14-15; Nu. 21:5-9).

Christ is the manna (John 6:57-58; Ex. 16:1-24).

Christ is the rock (1 Cor. 10:4; Ex. 17:1-6).

Christ is the firstfruits from the dead (1 Cor. 15:23; Lev. 23:10).

The sweet savour offerings depict Christ offering Himself to God (Eph. 5:2).

The peace offerings depict Christ making peace through the blood of His cross (Col. 1:20).

The dietary laws and the sabbath were shadows of things to come (Col. 2:16-17).

Believers are the firstfruits (Jam. 1:18; Lev. 23:17).

Believers are priests (1 Pet. 2:5).

The silver atoning money point to Christ's blood (1 Pet. 1:18-19).

The lamb without blemish signifies Christ's sinlessness (1 Pet 1:19).

Incense is associated with the prayers of the saints (Rev. 8:3-4).

White raiment represents righteousness (Rev. 19:8).

Hyssop signifies the application of salvation to one's life (Psa. 51:7).

God's people are His jewels, which reminds us of the jewels on the high priest's breastplate (Mal. 3:17).

4. Consider the biblical use of words.

Another way to interpret Old Testament types is by tracing words through the Bible with a concordance.

Consider, for example, the word *salt*. The offerings were to include salt (Lev. 2:13). By examining the biblical use of salt in various passages, we can see what this means.

Following are a couple of examples:

Salt refers to a preservative influence (Mat. 5:13). Salt stops corruption, as when salted meat is preserved by not allowing it to rot. Likewise the Spirit of Christ is a preservative both in the believer and in society, as God's Spirit strived with men before the Flood (Genesis 6).

Salt refers to flavoring (Job 6:6). As a spice, salt increases the pleasure of eating. Christ is the spice of life. Without him everything is bland and ultimately meaningless, but with Him everything is delightful.

Salt refers to wholesome words that edify (Col. 4:6). No one ever spoke such edifying words as Jesus. He is the eternal Word of God, and every word that proceeds from His mouth is perfect.

Salt refers to the surety of God's covenants (2 Ch. 13:5), and in Christ all of the promises of God are yea and amen (2 Cor. 1:20).

5. Consider the law of first mention.

Another way to interpret Old Testament types is the law of first mention. Every part of the Bible was designed and foreplanned by God.

> Psalms 119:89 For ever, O LORD, thy word is settled in heaven.

When the Bible first mentions a word or teaching, it is important and should be examined carefully. Consider the sheep, which was one of the offerings (Ex. 20:24). The first mention of a sheep is in Genesis 4:2. It was a sheep that Abel offered to the Lord as a sacrifice for sin (Ge. 4:4). We learn from this that the sheep represents Christ as an innocent victim who is offered to God in the sinner's place.

Major Lessons of the Tabernacle

Like all of the types in the Old Testament, the tabernacle points to Christ and to salvation in Him, which is made perfectly clear in the Epistle of Hebrews.

> Hebrews 8:1-2 Now of the things which we have spoken *this is* the sum: We have such an high priest, who is set on the right hand of the throne of the Majesty in the heavens; 2 A minister of the sanctuary, and of the true tabernacle, which the Lord pitched, and not man.

> Hebrews 9:6-11 Now when these things were thus ordained, the priests went always into the first tabernacle, accomplishing the service *of God.* 7 But into the second *went* the high priest alone once every year, not without blood, which he offered for himself, and *for* the errors of the people: 8 The Holy Ghost this signifying, that the way into the holiest of all was not yet made manifest, while as the first tabernacle was yet standing: 9 Which *was* a figure for the time then present, in which were offered both gifts and sacrifices, that could not make him that did the service perfect, as pertaining to the conscience; 10 *Which stood* only in meats and drinks, and divers washings, and carnal ordinances, imposed *on them* until the time of reformation. 11 But Christ being come an high priest of good things to come, by a greater and more perfect tabernacle, not made with hands, that is to say, not of this building.

> Hebrews 9:19-24 For when Moses had spoken every precept to all the people according to the law, he took the blood of calves and of goats, with water, and scarlet wool, and hyssop, and sprinkled both the book, and all the people, 20 Saying, This *is* the blood of the testament which God hath enjoined unto you. 21 Moreover he sprinkled with blood both the tabernacle, and all the vessels of the ministry. 22 And almost all things are by the law purged with blood; and without shedding of blood is no remission. 23 *It was* therefore necessary that the patterns of things in

the heavens should be purified with these; but the heavenly things themselves with better sacrifices than these. 24 For Christ is not entered into the holy places made with hands, *which are* the figures of the true; but into heaven itself, now to appear in the presence of God for us.

Hebrews 10:11-12 And every priest standeth daily ministering and offering oftentimes the same sacrifices, which can never take away sins: 12 But this man, after he had offered one sacrifice for sins for ever, sat down on the right hand of God.

The tabernacle deals with all of the glorious truths of the gospel, such as the following:

Christ's Incarnation

The tabernacle points to Christ's incarnation. The eternal creator God was made flesh and dwelt or tabernacled among us.

John 1:1-3, 14 In the beginning was the Word, and the Word was with God, and the Word was God. 2 The same was in the beginning with God. 3 All things were made by him; and without him was not any thing made that was made. ... And the Word was made flesh, and dwelt among us, (and we beheld his glory, the glory as of the only begotten of the Father,) full of grace and truth.

This was God's goal before He made man. In His omniscience and foreknowledge, He knew that the first man would fall. He planned to come into the world, to be born as the sinless God-Man, to make the atonement for man's sins, to rise from the dead, and to take His seat forever at the head of the new creation.

The following verses refer to Christ's incarnation:

"God with us" (Mat. 1:23)

"the word was made flesh" (Jn. 1:14)

> "no man hath seen God at any time; the only begotten Son ... hath declared him" (Jn. 1:18)
>
> "he that hath seen me hath seen the Father" (Jn. 14:9)
>
> "God sending his own Son in the likeness of sinful flesh" (Rom. 8:3)
>
> "and took upon him the form of a servant, and was made in the likeness of men" (Phil. 2:7)
>
> "the image of the invisible God" (Col. 1:16)
>
> "in him dwelleth all the fulness of the Godhead bodily" (Col. 2:9)
>
> "God was manifest in the flesh" (1 Tim. 3:16)
>
> "the express image of his person" (Heb. 1:3)
>
> "For verily he took not on *him the nature of* angels; but he took on *him* the seed of Abraham" (Heb. 2:16).

The incarnation of Christ stands on the virgin birth. Without the virgin birth there is no God manifest in the flesh, no sinless man, no substitute, and no atonement. If Christ had been born by a natural birth, with a human father, he would have inherited sinful flesh from fallen Adam.

> "Wherefore, as by one man sin entered into the world, and death by sin; and so death passed upon all men, for that all have sinned" (Rom. 5:12).

If Jesus had even one sin, if He had committed even one infraction of God's law, he would have died for his own sin, because the wages of sin is death (Rom. 6:23). It was because of the virgin birth that Jesus was called "that holy thing" (Luke 1:35).

> "As we dwell upon the tabernacle, we are anticipating, if we grasp its spiritual truths, that which God desired from the beginning, and for which He has been laboring, and which His adorable Son, our Lord, has made possible through His atoning death. 'He will rejoice over thee with joy; he will

rest in his love, he will joy over thee with singing' (Zeph. 3:17)" (Samuel Ridout, *Lectures on the Tabernacle*).

Christ's atoning sacrifice

The tabernacle teaches Christ's atoning sacrifice. At the heart of the tabernacle was the brazen altar and the blood sacrifices. These point to the price that was paid for man's redemption, which was Christ's blood and death. The tabernacle points to the cross of Christ which is the central act of human history and which will be the central act of eternity. God's people will sing of the power of the blood forever.

The following verses describe Christ's atonement:

> "And the blood shall be to you for a token upon the houses where ye *are*: and when I see the blood, I will pass over you, and the plague shall not be upon you to destroy *you*, when I smite the land of Egypt" (Ex. 12:13).
>
> "But he *was* wounded for our transgressions, *he was* bruised for our iniquities: the chastisement of our peace *was* upon him; and with his stripes we are healed. All we like sheep have gone astray; we have turned every one to his own way; and the LORD hath laid on him the iniquity of us all" (Isaiah 53:5-6).
>
> "For this is my blood of the new testament, which is shed for many for the remission of sins" (Mat. 26:28).
>
> "For even the Son of man came not to be ministered unto, but to minister, and to give his life a ransom for many" (Mk. 10:45).
>
> "The next day John seeth Jesus coming unto him, and saith, Behold the Lamb of God, which taketh away the sin of the world" (John 1:29).
>
> "I am the good shepherd: the good shepherd giveth his life for the sheep" (John 10:11).
>
> "Take heed therefore unto yourselves, and to all the flock, over the which the Holy Ghost hath made you overseers, to

feed the church of God, which he hath purchased with his own blood" (Acts 20:28).

"Being justified freely by his grace through the redemption that is in Christ Jesus: Whom God hath set forth *to be* a propitiation through faith in his blood, to declare his righteousness for the remission of sins that are past, through the forbearance of God" (Rom. 3:24-25).

"Who was delivered for our offences, and was raised again for our justification" (Rom. 4:25).

"Much more then, being now justified by his blood, we shall be saved from wrath through him" (Rom. 5:9).

"Being justified freely by his grace through the redemption that is in Christ Jesus: Whom God hath set forth *to be* a propitiation through faith in his blood, to declare his righteousness for the remission of sins that are past, through the forbearance of God" (Rom. 3:24-25).

"For I delivered unto you first of all that which I also received, how that Christ died for our sins according to the scriptures" (1 Cor. 15:3).

"For he hath made him *to be* sin for us, who knew no sin; that we might be made the righteousness of God in him" (2 Cor. 5:21).

"Who gave himself for our sins, that he might deliver us from this present evil world, according to the will of God and our Father" (Gal. 1:4).

"I am crucified with Christ: nevertheless I live; yet not I, but Christ liveth in me: and the life which I now live in the flesh I live by the faith of the Son of God, who loved me, and gave himself for me" (Gal. 2:20).

"In whom we have redemption through his blood, the forgiveness of sins, according to the riches of his grace" (Eph. 1:7).

"But now in Christ Jesus ye who sometimes were far off are made nigh by the blood of Christ" (Eph. 2:13).

And that he might reconcile both unto God in one body by the cross, having slain the enmity thereby: (Eph. 2:16)

"In whom we have redemption through his blood, the forgiveness of sins, according to the riches of his grace" (Eph. 1:7).

"And walk in love, as Christ also hath loved us, and hath given himself for us an offering and a sacrifice to God for a sweetsmelling savour" (Eph. 5:2).

"And, having made peace through the blood of his cross, by him to reconcile all things unto himself; by him, *I say*, whether *they be* things in earth, or things in heaven. And you, that were sometime alienated and enemies in *your* mind by wicked works, yet now hath he reconciled In the body of his flesh through death, to present you holy and unblameable and unreproveable in his sight" (Col. 1:20-22).

"Who gave himself a ransom for all, to be testified in due time" (1 Tim. 2:6).

"Who gave himself for us, that he might redeem us from all iniquity, and purify unto himself a peculiar people, zealous of good works" (Titus 2:14).

"But Christ being come an high priest of good things to come, by a greater and more perfect tabernacle, not made with hands, that is to say, not of this building; Neither by the blood of goats and calves, but by his own blood he entered in once into the holy place, having obtained eternal redemption *for us*" (Heb. 9:11-12).

"How much more shall the blood of Christ, who through the eternal Spirit offered himself without spot to God, purge your conscience from dead works to serve the living God?" (Heb. 9:14).

"And almost all things are by the law purged with blood; and without shedding of blood is no remission" (Heb. 9:22).

"By the which will we are sanctified through the offering of the body of Jesus Christ once *for all*" (Heb. 10:10).

"But this man, after he had offered one sacrifice for sins for ever, sat down on the right hand of God" (Heb. 10:12).

"For by one offering he hath perfected for ever them that are sanctified" (Heb. 10:14).

"Having therefore, brethren, boldness to enter into the holiest by the blood of Jesus, By a new and living way, which he hath consecrated for us, through the veil, that is to say, his flesh" (Heb. 10:19-20).

"Forasmuch as ye know that ye were not redeemed with corruptible things, *as* silver and gold, from your vain conversation *received* by tradition from your fathers; But with the precious blood of Christ, as of a lamb without blemish and without spot" (1 Pet. 1:18-19).

"Who his own self bare our sins in his own body on the tree, that we, being dead to sins, should live unto righteousness: by whose stripes ye were healed."(1 Pet. 2:24).

"For Christ also hath once suffered for sins, the just for the unjust, that he might bring us to God, being put to death in the flesh, but quickened by the Spirit" (1 Pet. 3:18).

"And he is the propitiation for our sins: and not for ours only, but also for *the sins of* the whole world" (1 Jn. 2:2).

"Hereby perceive we the love *of God*, because he laid down his life for us: and we ought to lay down *our* lives for the brethren" (1 Jn. 3:16).

"And from Jesus Christ, *who is* the faithful witness, *and* the first begotten of the dead, and the prince of the kings of the earth. Unto him that loved us, and washed us from our sins in his own blood" (Rev. 1:5).

"And they sung a new song, saying, Thou art worthy to take the book, and to open the seals thereof: for thou wast slain, and hast redeemed us to God by thy blood out of every kindred, and tongue, and people, and nation" (Rev. 5:9).

My hope is built on nothing less,
Than Jesus' blood and righteousness.
I dare not trust the sweetest frame,
But wholly lean on Jesus' Name.
On Christ the solid rock I stand,
All other ground is sinking sand.

The atonement of Christ on Calvary provided redemption not only for individual sinners, but also for the whole universe.

> "God, through the blood of Christ's cross, has reconciled all things unto Himself, not only things on earth, but things in heaven (Col. 1. 20). Defilement had entered into the heavens above, through the fall of angels, before it had entered into the earth through the fall of man. The work of atonement is not only the ground on which God can forgive sinners, but it lies at the foundation of universal security. The question of sin and creature responsibility has been settled for ever at the cross. He who descended first into the lower parts of the earth has also ascended up far above all heavens, that He might fill all things. His atoning work is not only the basis of stability below, but the keystone of universal security above, throughout all ages. God 'having made known unto us the mystery of His will, according to His good pleasure which He hath purposed in Himself: that in the dispensation of the fulness of times He might gather together in one all things in Christ, both which are in the heavens, and which are on earth; even in Him' (Eph. 1. 9, 10)" (Thomas Newberry, *Types of the Levitical Offerings*).

Man's sinful condition

The tabernacle teaches man's sinful condition in a multitude of ways.

The truth of man's sinful condition is taught by the high white walls of the court which shut men out unless they enter through the one door.

The truth of man's sinful condition is seen in the fact that man must approach God by way of the sacrificial altar. He must lay his hand on the sacrifice, showing that it must die in his place. Only by means of the sacrifice can the individual be accepted by God.

The truth of man's sinful condition is seen in that he must wash in the laver before he can serve God.

The truth of man's sinful condition is seen in that a high priest must enter into the presence of God in his place. This happened once a year on the Day of Atonement when the high priest alone entered the holy of holies to offer the blood atonement for the nation.

Following are some of the verses that describe man's fallen condition:

> "But we are all as an unclean *thing*, and all our righteousnesses *are* as filthy rags; and we all do fade as a leaf; and our iniquities, like the wind, have taken us away" (Isa. 64:6).
>
> "All we like sheep have gone astray; we have turned every one to his own way; and the LORD hath laid on him the iniquity of us all" (Isa. 53:6).
>
> "The heart *is* deceitful above all *things*, and desperately wicked: who can know it? "(Jer. 17:9).
>
> "For *there is* not a just man upon earth, that doeth good, and sinneth not" (Ec. 7:20).
>
> "... in thy sight shall no man living be justified" (Psa. 143:2).
>
> "As it is written, There is none righteous, no, not one" (Rom. 3:10).
>
> "For all have sinned, and come short of the glory of God" (Rom. 3:23).

"If we say that we have no sin, we deceive ourselves, and the truth is not in us" (1 John 1:8).

God's holiness and love

The tabernacle and the offerings are a dramatic picture of God's character both in his holiness and in His love. The tabernacle depicts both the goodness and the severity of the Lord (Rom. 11:22), both His office as Judge and His office as Saviour.

The creator God is so awfully holy that He punishes every sin, and ever sinner who dies without atonement will suffer forever in the lake of fire. That is holiness beyond human comprehension.

At the same time, God is so compassionate that He took the sinner's punishment upon Himself and offers salvation to every rebel. That is love beyond human comprehension.

> "Because God is infinitely holy, He cannot condone the smallest sin (although there are no small sins, for all sins are great sins). To emphasize the awfulness of sin in the sight of a holy God, we have but to go back to the first sin of the human race. Adam and Eve had eaten of the fruit of the tree which God had prohibited. Now that, of course, seems in itself but a little thing. We would call it mere petty larceny, eating one fruit from a forbidden tree. In the estimate of men, and according to our moral standards, that was only a little sin. ... But God did not consider it as such, for God knows nothing about 'little' sins. Listen, friend, so great was that sin in the sight of God that He not only cursed man from the garden, imposed the penalty of death upon him and upon all his offspring, but God even cursed the entire creation, the earth, the birds, the animals, and every creature over which Adam was placed as the federal head. God did not wait until man had committed murder before He cursed him, but this so-called 'LITTLE SIN' was the occasion for God's awful penalty and judgment. ... By the grace of God, we, therefore, shall lift

our voice against sin, not merely as a human weakness, not merely as the mistakes of a race trying to climb upward by evolutionary processes, but as that vicious, selfish, filthy thing which lies at the basis and root of all of man's troubles and trials, and which is a rebellion against a thrice-holy God, which must result in the punishment of the sinner in an eternal hell, unless it is taken care of by the blood atonement of the Son of God" (M.R. DeHaan, M.D., *The Tabernacle*, 1955).

Repentance and faith

The tabernacle teaches that though God has provided salvation, men must receive it. Each individual has to enter the one door of the tabernacle court and bring the correct sacrifice to the brazen altar before God in the prescribed way.

This signifies that each sinner must come to God and acknowledge his sin and put his faith in Jesus Christ as the only Lord and Saviour. When the worshiper put his hands on the sacrifice, he was signifying his need of it and his identification with it and his acceptance of it (Lev. 1:4).

Entering the tabernacle's one door signifies repentance toward God. It signifies "turning to God from idols" (1 Thess. 1:9). Entering the door also signifies faith in Christ as pictured by the sacrifice on the brazen altar.

Reconciliation and Communion

The tabernacle depicts God reconciled with His redeemed people (Ex. 25:8; 29:44-45; Lev. 20:26). God wants to dwell with man. He made man in His image so that He might have fellowship with man. We see this for a brief time in the Garden of Eden when God and Adam communed together.

When the first man fell, man became at enmity with God and the relationship was broken. Man was separated from God by sin.

God initiated the plan that He had made before Creation to enter the world as a perfect man through the virgin birth, to make atonement for man's sin and to redeem the creation.

God does not want merely to be reconciled to man. He wants to fellowship with man. The tabernacle depicts this wonderful truth. God invites sinners to be justified by entering the one door and trusting in the sacrifices of the brazen altar. This is justification. He then invites justified sinners to wash at the laver and to enter into an eternal experience of intimate fellowship with the Almighty. The New Testament believer is invited to walk in fellowship with the Father and the Son.

> 1 John 1:3 That which we have seen and heard declare we unto you, that ye also may have fellowship with us: and truly our fellowship *is* with the Father, and with his Son Jesus Christ.

The tabernacle points ultimately to the New Jerusalem where God will dwell with His people forever in the new heaven and new earth.

> Revelation 21:3 And I heard a great voice out of heaven saying, Behold, the tabernacle of God *is* with men, and he will dwell with them, and they shall be his people, and God himself shall be with them, *and be* their God.

The late I.M. Haldeman, pastor of First Baptist Church of New York City, observed:

> "God created the first man that He might dwell in him. Man failed, he sinned, and God's creation rest was broken up. The purpose of God is unchangeable. It was necessary that sooner or later there should be a man in whom He could dwell, a man who should be His manifestation, His visibility and incarnation. ...
>
> "The tabernacle now ordered of God to be set up in the wilderness, and whose plan of construction was given in minute detail to Moses, was intended to be, not merely the official dwelling place of God in Israel, but a symbol, a

picture and a prophecy of the man in whom God should become incarnate, the man who should be His final and eternal dwelling place. That man exists today as the antitypical fulfillment of God's purposes. The Apostle John testifies concerning Him: 'In the beginning was the Word, and the Word was with God, and the Word was God.' This person called the Word of God, the Almighty maker of heaven and earth, came into the world and 'was made flesh.'

"The verb and tense form, 'was made,' is literally 'became,' and carries the thought, not of passivity, but activity. He became flesh by His own action. This definition of the verb form is corroborated in Hebrews 2:14. 'Forasmuch then as the children are partakers of flesh and blood, he also himself likewise took part of the same.' In becoming flesh He is represented as the sole and responsible actor; He is not the object of some extraneous action that makes Him to become flesh, He is Himself the actor who so definitely and personally acts that He becomes flesh.

"This construction is emphasized in Hebrews 5:16. 'He took not on him the nature of angels; but he took on him the seed of Abraham.' That is, human nature. The Greek verb rendered, 'took on him,' is, *epilambano*, and signifies, 'to lay hold of,' 'to assume.' The verb is the indicative present, the voice the middle or reflexive. ... He who was the eternal Word of God, personally, actively and in individual responsibility assumed for Himself a human nature of flesh and blood.

"John testifies further concerning this incarnation, 'The Word became flesh and dwelt among us.' He not only says the Creator of the universe became flesh and blood, but that He 'dwelt among us.' The word 'dwelt' is, literally, 'tabernacled.' The Word became flesh and tabernacled among us.' .... Thus the purpose of God was achieved. He found His dwelling place and rest in man. ...

"He whom we know as our Lord Jesus Christ is none other than that Son of God and God the Son who created the universe; that creative Word who in Genesis 1:26 breaks the silence of Godhead, saying, 'Let us make man in our image.' ... By the same omnipotence with which He created all things (so that without Him there was not one thing made that was made) He created for Himself a sinless, perfect human nature, took it into union with His infinite person and personally dwelt in it as His Tabernacle--His dwelling place among men. ...

"Wonderful beyond words is the person of Him whom we style as our Lord Jesus Christ. He is 'the man Christ Jesus.' He in whom the fulness of the Being of God now dwells and abidingly rests not only because of the perfection of His humanity, but, also, because of the redemption He achieved by offering that humanity in sacrificial death making an atonement for sin, demonstrating the inexorableness of divine righteousness, satisfying all its claims, justifying God in all his ways and thereby opening up a legal channel through which the love of God might flow righteously and in saving value to all who by faith should offer up His crucified Son as a sacrifice for sin and claim Him as a personal substitute under the judgment due them.

"In Him the rest of God is not creation rest, it is redemption rest. The conscience of God is at rest because of His law justified, His grace proclaimed and His love revealed. Here, indeed, is 'the true tabernacle which God pitched, and not man' (Hebrews 8:1)" (I.M. Haldeman, *The Tabernacle Priesthood and Offerings*, 1925).

Justification and Sanctification

The tabernacle depicts the two aspects of our salvation: justification and sanctification. We are justified once for all by the blood of Christ, but we must be sanctified day by day as we walk through this polluted world.

Christ's high priesthood

The tabernacle points to Christ as the risen High Priest. Having made the acceptable sacrifice for our sins, He has risen from the dead and ever lives to make intercession for us. The risen Christ is typified by the high priest and by the gold-covered articles in the tabernacle. He is the Light of the world, the Mediator and Intercessor, the Bread of life.

Pilgrimage

The portable tabernacle that was carried through the wilderness depicts the believer's pilgrimage as he journeys through this foreign world on the way to his eternal home.

God dwelt among them in the tabernacle.
But now the holy spirit dwells within us.

Construction of the Tabernacle

1. It was built according to God's Word in the smallest detail (Ex. 25:9).

As we have seen, Moses was shown an actual pattern of the tabernacle (Exodus 25:40; 26:30; Acts 7:44).

Six times God instructed Moses to build the tabernacle in the exact manner that he had been shown (Ex. 25:9, 40; 26:30; 29:35; 31:11; 36:1).

And it is repeated 18 times that Moses and Israel did all that the Lord commanded (Ex. 38:21, 22; 39:1, 5, 7, 21, 26, 29, 31, 32, 42, 43; 40:16, 21, 25, 27, 29, 32).

Moses did not change anything, not the type of material or the colors or the size of the objects. He did not omit anything or add anything. He could have said, "The tabernacle needs a floor; let's add a carpet," or, "There should be a roof over the altar of sacrifice so that the rain doesn't quench the fire," or, "We need to add a few more pillars to make the court walls stronger," or, "The tabernacle doesn't need four coverings; let's omit one of them and let's put the nice-looking rams' skins dyed red on the outside."

Moses did not do this. He was a great example for us. He did not serve God according to His own thinking. He was "faithful in all his house" (Heb. 3:5).

The priests were instructed to preserve every part of the tabernacle. For example, the sons of Merari were in charge of the boards, the bars, the pillars, and the sockets, plus the pins and cords and everything associated with the tabernacle structure. They were instructed as follows:

> "... and by name ye shall reckon the instruments of the charge of their burden" (Num. 4:32).

It appears that the priests were literally to have a name for every tiny thing for inventory purposes.

"An inventory was taken of every particular, even to the very pins belonging to each part, that nothing might be wanting when the tabernacle was set up" (*Treasury of Scripture Knowledge*).

This is what God wants from His people today. "It is required in a steward that a man be found faithful" (1 Cor. 4:2).

The church is the house of God today (1 Tim. 3:15), and we are to construct the tabernacle of the New Testament church after the exact pattern that was given by the apostles and prophets at the dawn of the age. We are to fight for the faith once delivered to the saints (Jude 3). We are to follow Paul's policy by teaching the revealed truth to faithful men who can teach the same to others (2 Tim. 2:2).

We do not build churches according to the "church fathers." Many have been led into the arms of Rome by that path, because the "church fathers" so called, who introduced such things as infant baptism, were actually the fathers of the Roman Catholic Church.

We don't build according to an "emerging" plan for a new age. The emerging crowd wants to turn the tabernacle into an art center and replace the teaching priests with mutual sharing.

We don't build according to a seeker-sensitive plan. The seeker-sensitive crowd wants to spice up the old tabernacle, replace the dull badger's skin with something more exciting, exchange the outdated materials with space age plastics, throw open the curtain door to let in more light, teach the priests some new dance moves to make the offerings more interesting, and replace the boring shofar horns with a full-blown rock band.

We don't build according to the modernistic plan. Modernists want to strangle the sacrifices so there isn't such a bloody mess in the court. Everyone knows that all of that blood is disgusting and unnecessary, since we are saved by Christ's life and example and not by the cross.

We don't build according to the great leaders of our denomination, regardless of what the denomination might be. Independent Baptists, for example, pride themselves in being "biblicists," but in many ways they are as tradition bound as Episcopalians. If a Jack Hyles or a Lee Roberson or a Bob Jones did something a certain way, even the wrong way, that becomes set in stone, and it is unacceptable and hurtful to test them and their methods by God's Word. The pattern for the construction of the tabernacle of the New Testament church ceases to be the original divine pattern and is replaced with a man-made one, and because they fear man more than God, the builders are afraid to correct what their forefathers changed.

We also don't build the tabernacle of the New Testament church according to the popular philosophy that there are "non-essentials" which we can ignore for the sake of a broader unity or for the sake of evangelism or social work. Not everything in the tabernacle is of the same importance, but everything was given by God and thus has some importance and not one thing was to be despised.

What is man to decide what is "non-essential" in God's Word? Where did God give us the authority to change anything or downgrade the value of anything? To the contrary, Jesus instructed the churches to teach all things (Mat. 28:20). And Paul held the same "all things" program (Acts 20:27). He taught Timothy to keep the New Testament commandments "without spot" (1 Timothy 6:13-14). That refers to the details, to the "small" things. See also 1 Corinthians 11:2, where Paul praised the church at Corinth for keeping everything he had taught them, even the things pertaining to hair length and the practice of the Lord's Supper as he taught in that particular chapter.

1 Corinthians 11:2 Now I praise you, brethren, that ye remember me in all things, and keep the ordinances, as I delivered *them* to you.

This reminds us of the importance of maintaining the purity of God's Word. We cannot maintain the purity of the New Testament church unless we have the pure Word of God as our pattern. Jesus taught that every jot and tittle of the original Scriptures are from God (Mat. 5:18). Paul taught that all Scripture is given by divine inspiration (2 Tim. 3:16). Peter taught that the prophets who wrote the Scripture were moved by the Holy Spirit (2 Pet. 1:21).

Further, God has promised to preserve the Scriptures. Jesus promised this when He instructed the churches to teach all things that He has commanded to the end of the age (Mat. 28:19-20). This implies that the "all things" that are given by divine inspiration will be available to the end of the age. God accomplishes this preservation by His own power, but He also accomplishes it by the diligence of the churches to keep that which is delivered to them (2 Tim. 2:2).

We believe that the God-given, God-preserved Hebrew and Greek Scriptures are found in the Masoretic Hebrew Old Testament and the Received Greek New Testament. This is the Scripture that was put into print and sent to the ends of the earth during the Reformation and the beginning of the modern missionary era. It wasn't until the late 19th century that this Bible was challenged effectively by a different one created by modern textual critics, most of whom were deeply influenced by theological liberalism that was spreading through the churches in that day. We have documented this in the book *The Modern Bible Version Hall of Shame*, available from www.wayoflife.org.

In Bible translation work we need to strive for a literal and majestic translation of the Masoretic Hebrew and Received Greek. We reject the dynamic equivalency and paraphrase methods of translation which rob the readers of the pure words of God.

The details of the tabernacle also teach that God cares about details and He cares about doing things to perfection. We see this lesson repeated everywhere in Scripture and in nature. We see this in the butterfly, with his perfectly balanced wings and the colorization and intricate patterns. If you take a light microscope and look at a butterfly's wing, you continue to see amazing detail and perfection. If you take an electronic microscope and look even deeper, into the living cell, you see the same beautiful detail and perfection. Nothing is haphazard. Nothing is half done. Nothing is unfinished.

Not only is everything well-designed and constructed, but it is also beautifully designed and constructed. This is how God wants man, who is made in His own image, to live his life. In my stint in the U.S. army, we often jokingly said, "That's good enough for government work." It meant that we didn't have to do everything perfectly. But that is not true in God's work! Let us strive for perfection in everything we do as we live our lives before Him.

> 1 Corinthians 10:31 Whether therefore ye eat, or drink, or whatsoever ye do, do all to the glory of God.

Moses did not borrow anything from the pagan culture of that day. His doctrine was given by divine revelation. It came from heaven, not from Egypt or Babylon. Moses grew up in the court of Egypt and his father-in-law was a Midianite priest. He was therefore familiar with every aspect of pagan thinking and religion, but he brought nothing of that into the Jewish faith.

He did not borrow from the pagan mythologies pertaining to human origin and the flood, nor did he borrow from the pagan law codes such as that of Hammurabi. He did not adapt any features of pagan temples into the tabernacle system.

Theological liberals and evangelicals who make this claim are foolish.

For example, the *Archaeological Bible Study Commentary* says, "Instructions for the Hittite ritual of establishing a new temple for a goddess of the night are similar to those God established concerning the tabernacle's instruction."

The Lion Handbook to the Bible says, "Israel appears to have shared many of the techniques and conceptions of sacrifice of her neighbours, but her own observances were set firmly in the framework of God's revelation at Sinai."

This is an unbelieving, contradictory statement. The Bible says Israel's priestly system came by direct revelation from God and that God forbade them to adapt anything whatsoever from their pagan neighbors. There is no middle ground. By studying the religion of Israel's ancient neighbors we can learn much about paganism and we can learn about what Israel did when she apostatized, but we can learn nothing about Israel's pure religion.

2. The tabernacle was built by the people (Ex. 35-36).

God's work is to be supported by God's people.

They gave because they were willing.

> Exodus 35:21-22 And they came, every one whose heart stirred him up, and every one whom his spirit made willing, *and* they brought the LORD'S offering to the work of the tabernacle of the congregation, and for all his service, and for the holy garments. 22 And they came, both men and women, as many as were willing hearted, *and* brought bracelets, and earrings, and rings, and tablets, all jewels of gold: and every man that offered *offered* an offering of gold unto the LORD.

This is the chief thing that God desires.

2 Corinthians 8:12 For if there be first a willing mind, *it is* accepted according to that a man hath, *and* not according to that he hath not.

2 Corinthians 9:6-7 But this *I say*, He which soweth sparingly shall reap also sparingly; and he which soweth bountifully shall reap also bountifully. 7 Every man according as he purposeth in his heart, *so let him give*; not grudgingly, or of necessity: for God loveth a cheerful giver.

They gave according to what they had.

Exodus 35:23 And every man, with whom was found blue, and purple, and scarlet, and fine linen, and goats' *hair*, and red skins of rams, and badgers' skins, brought *them*.

This has always been God's plan for giving. The tithe is a proportional offering. The more one earns, the more one gives. Everyone should contribute something to the Lord's work, both rich and poor. The rich brought the jewels and the gold (Ex. 35:27). The poor brought what they had. This is how Paul taught the churches to give ("as God hath prospered him," 1 Cor. 16:1-2).

God is not impressed with the amount we give; He is impressed with the sacrifice that we make and the passion by which we give. He praised the widow who gave a mere two mites and said that she gave more than the rich men who contributed large amounts, because she gave to God willingly from her poverty.

Luke 21:1-4 And he looked up, and saw the rich men casting their gifts into the treasury. 2 And he saw also a certain poor widow casting in thither two mites. 3 And he said, Of a truth I say unto you, that this poor widow hath cast in more than they all: 4 For all these have of their abundance cast in unto the offerings of God: but she of her penury hath cast in all the living that she had.

Paul praised the churches of Macedonia for giving liberally out of their poverty because of their love for the Lord.

> 2 Corinthians 8:1-2, 5 Moreover, brethren, we do you to wit of the grace of God bestowed on the churches of Macedonia; 2 How that in a great trial of affliction the abundance of their joy and their deep poverty abounded unto the riches of their liberality. ... And *this they did*, not as we hoped, but first gave their own selves to the Lord, and unto us by the will of God.

They gave more than was needed.

> Exodus 36:5-7 And they spake unto Moses, saying, The people bring much more than enough for the service of the work, which the LORD commanded to make. 6 And Moses gave commandment, and they caused it to be proclaimed throughout the camp, saying, Let neither man nor woman make any more work for the offering of the sanctuary. So the people were restrained from bringing. 7 For the stuff they had was sufficient for all the work to make it, and too much.

This was a rare event in the history both of Israel and of the churches. More typically, a small percentage of God's people get behind the Lord's work while the rest are half-hearted.

They worked according to their ability.

> Exodus 36:1 Then wrought Bezaleel and Aholiab, and every wise hearted man, in whom the LORD put wisdom and understanding to know how to work all manner of work for the service of the sanctuary, according to all that the LORD had commanded.

When God calls men to accomplish an enterprise, He equips them for it. The church is a body, and each member is gifted of God to have a part in the Lord's work (1 Cor. 12:27; Rom. 12:4-8).

One of the tests of a spiritual calling is gifting. If a man is not equipped to do a certain ministry, it is because God has not called him to that ministry. This is true for the pastorate, for evangelism, and for any other calling. To be a pastor, for example, one must be able to teach, to lead, to protect, and to warn. If a man is not able to do that work, he is not called to be a pastor. The same is true for every ministry in the church. The Bible instructs us to know our abilities and calling.

> Romans 12:3 For I say, through the grace given unto me, to every man that is among you, not to think *of himself* more highly than he ought to think; but to think soberly, according as God hath dealt to every man the measure of faith.

They worked under the direction of their leaders.

> Exodus 36:1-3 Then wrought Bezaleel and Aholiab, and every wise hearted man, in whom the LORD put wisdom and understanding to know how to work all manner of work for the service of the sanctuary, according to all that the LORD had commanded. 2 And Moses called Bezaleel and Aholiab, and every wise hearted man, in whose heart the LORD had put wisdom, *even* every one whose heart stirred him up to come unto the work to do it: 3 And they received of Moses all the offering, which the children of Israel had brought for the work of the service of the sanctuary, to make it *withal.* And they brought yet unto him free offerings every morning.

Moses taught Bezaleel and Aholiab, and they instructed and led the people in the work. This is the way of peace and harmony in the church.

> 1 Thessalonians 5:11-12 Wherefore comfort yourselves together, and edify one another, even as also ye do. 12 And we beseech you, brethren, to know them which labour among you, and are over you in the Lord, and admonish you;

The women contributed much to the work.

> Exodus 35:25-26 And all the women that were wise hearted did spin with their hands, and brought that which they had spun, *both* of blue, and of purple, *and* of scarlet, and of fine linen. 26 And all the women whose heart stirred them up in wisdom spun goats' *hair.*

Women are very important in the work of God. They cannot be church leaders (1 Timothy 2:12), but they can do many things. As the late R.G. Lee said,

> "...we gladly make declaration that some of the fairest and most fragrant flowers that grow in the garden of God and some of the sweetest and most luscious fruit that ripens in God's spiritual orchards are there because of woman's faith, woman's love, woman's prayer, woman's virtue, woman's tears, woman's devotion to Christ" ("Payday Someday").

Consider the role of women in Jesus' earthly life. The woman at the well brought her village out to hear Him (John 4:28-30). Many women assisted Jesus during His earthly ministry (Lk. 8:2-3). Women opened their homes to Jesus (Luke 10:38-42). It was a woman who anointed Jesus for His burial prior to His death (Mat. 26:6-13). It was mostly women who stood at the cross (Mat. 27:55-56). Women observed Jesus' burial and came to anoint Him after He was dead (Lk. 23:55-56). Women arrived first to the empty tomb and first believed the resurrection (Mat. 28:1-6). It was women who reported the resurrection to the apostles (Mat. 28:7-8).

Women played a large role in the early churches. They were in the upper room on the day of Pentecost (Acts 1:14). They were full of good works (Acts 9:36). They labored with Paul in the gospel (Phil. 4:3). They trained their children and grandchildren (2 Tim. 1:5). The older women taught the younger women (Titus 2:3-5). They were messengers for the congregations (Rom. 16:1-2). They assisted their husbands in planting churches (Rom. 16:3-5; Acts 18:24-26). Women were the firstfruits of the gospel in some places (Acts 16:14). Women showed hospitality to preachers (Acts 16:14-15).

They also worked in a skillful manner.

> Exodus 35:35 Them hath he filled with wisdom of heart, to work all manner of work, of the engraver, and of the cunning workman, and of the embroiderer, in blue, and in purple, in scarlet, and in fine linen, and of the weaver, *even*

> of them that do any work, and of those that devise cunning work.

God's work should receive our very best. As the hymn says, "Give of your best to the Master."

Everything that we do for the Lord should be done to the best of our ability, and we should continually strive to improve and to do better for the One who owns us both by right of creation and by right of redemption.

It is not uncommon for the work of the Lord to be done with a lack of zeal, skill, and excellence that would be unacceptable in other fields. Song leaders are often untrained and ill-prepared and aren't interested in getting training, though courses are available. Musicians are satisfied with a lack of excellence. Teachers come to class without proper preparation, and they aren't the diligent students they should be throughout the week so that they become better teachers. Ushers are unprepared and unprofessional. Workers miss training meetings, and people are late for the services. God deserves better!

The Jews bringing offerings to build the Tabernacle signify believers offering to God that which Christ works in us. They brought that which had been given to them by God when they left Egypt.

> "It is no material offering now; we are not called upon, in that way, to bring our quota of gold, silver, or precious stones; but our hearts must be stirred up, be made willing to enter into what Christ our Lord is, and thus bring it, as it were, to God, who by His Spirit will reveal and cause us to enjoy the blessed Lord fully. We are thus thrown, we might say, upon our own responsibility. Everything is of perfect grace, but it flows through hearts made willing by that grace. Thus Christ must, in some measure, be to our hearts what the gold, silver, etc., speak of. This is no mere intellectual apprehension, but a laying hold of the very springs of our life, thus enabling us to lay them, as it were,

before our gracious God for His use and acceptance" (Samuel Ridout, *Lectures on the Tabernacle*).

The construction of the tabernacle required more than 29 talents (2,726 pounds) of gold, 100 talents (9,400 pounds) of silver, and 70 talents (6,580 pounds) of brass (Ex. 38:24, 27, 29). This is a dramatic picture of the unspeakable value of Christ's atonement. His blood is called precious, meaning of great value (2 Pet. 1:19). It has the power to save every sinner who believes and to redeem the entire fallen creation.

The Repetition of the Tabernacle

There is repetition permeating the tabernacle and the offerings.

For example, there are three doors -- one into the court, one into the holy place, and one into the holy of holies. All three are made of white linen with blue, purple, and scarlet threads, and all three depict Christ as the one Door, the sinless Saviour, the Lord from heaven, the King of kings.

Another example of the repetition is that Christ's atonement is depicted in a multitude of ways: via the altar of sacrifice, via the scarlet color in the veils, via the goat's hair covering, via the red rams-skin covering, via the silver sockets and the silver hooks, via the various sacrifices, etc.

There are two major reasons for the Bible's repetition.

First, it is for emphasis. For example, the phrase "as the Lord commanded" is repeated 14 times in Exodus in relation to the tabernacle. This reinforces the importance of obeying God's Word in all points.

Second, repetition is for teaching. Within the repetitions are variety. For example, each of the doors into the tabernacle is slightly different and depicts Christ as the one Door in different ways. And the various pictures of Christ's atonement, in their variety, show various aspects of this great truth. Many different types are necessary to illustrate the glory of Christ and the fulness of His sacrifice. This is like the four Gospels, each of which has its own special portrait of Christ. It is like painting portraits of a person from different angles.

Every detail of God's Word is important, including the repetition, and we must be careful that we don't let it become tedious. Studying the Bible and learning of Christ requires careful attention to detail and much patience.

The Court of the Tabernacle

Exodus 27:9-18 And thou shalt make the court of the tabernacle: for the south side southward *there shall be* hangings for the court *of* fine twined linen of an hundred cubits long for one side: 10 And the twenty pillars thereof and their twenty sockets *shall be of* brass; the hooks of the pillars and their fillets *shall be of* silver. 11 And likewise for the north side in length *there shall be* hangings of an hundred *cubits* long, and his twenty pillars and their twenty sockets *of* brass; the hooks of the pillars and their fillets *of* silver. 12 And *for* the breadth of the court on the west side *shall be* hangings of fifty cubits: their pillars ten, and their sockets ten. 13 And the breadth of the court on the east side eastward *shall be* fifty cubits. 14 The hangings of one side *of the gate shall be* fifteen cubits: their pillars three, and their sockets three. 15 And on the other side *shall be* hangings fifteen *cubits*: their pillars three, and their sockets three. 16 And for the gate of the court *shall be* an hanging of twenty cubits, *of* blue, and purple, and scarlet, and fine twined linen, wrought with needlework: *and* their pillars *shall be* four, and their sockets four. 17 All the pillars round about the court *shall be* filleted with silver; their hooks *shall be of* silver, and their sockets *of* brass. 18 The length of the court *shall be* an hundred cubits, and the breadth fifty every where, and the height five cubits *of* fine twined linen, and their sockets *of* brass.

The description of the court

The court area which was surrounded by curtain walls (Ex. 27:8-18). It was 100 cubits (150 feet) long by 50 cubits (75 feet) wide (Ex. 27:11-13).

The curtain walls of the court were five cubits (7.5 feet) high (Ex. 27:18). They were made of fine linen (Ex. 27:9).

The curtains hung on pillars. There were 60 pillars altogether: 20 on the south side (Ex. 27:9-10), 20 on the north side (Ex. 27:11), 10 on the west side (Ex. 27:12), 10 on the east side (three on either side of the gate and four for the gate) (Ex. 27:14-16).

Since there is no mention of the use of gold, silver, or brass covering the pillars (Exodus 38:24-31), we assume they were made of unadorned shittim wood.

The pillars were crowned with silver chapiters (or capitals) (Ex. 38:17) and stood on sockets of brass (Ex. 27:11).

The curtains were held together with silver hooks (Ex. 27:10-11).

The tent walls of the court were fastened to the ground by pins and cords (Ex. 35:18).

Spiritual lessons about the court

1. The walls of the court signify fallen man separated from the holy God because of sin.

The white linen symbolizes righteousness (Rev. 19:8). God is perfectly righteous and holy (Psa. 145:7), and He requires perfect righteousness, but man has fallen from the righteous glory he had in the beginning (Rom. 3:23). Fallen man is unclean before God. He is so holy that even man's supposed righteousness appears as filthy rags (Isa. 64:6). Since all men are unrighteous sinners (Rom. 3:10), they cannot approach God without a Saviour.

The height of the walls (7.5 feet high) signifies man's inability to come to God except through salvation. The walls signify man's inability to rise up to God's holy standard.

2. The pillars of shittim wood signify Christ's incarnation and His perfect humanity, as we will see in the study on the boards of the tabernacle.

3. The view from outside the court depicts the perspective of the unsaved sinner.

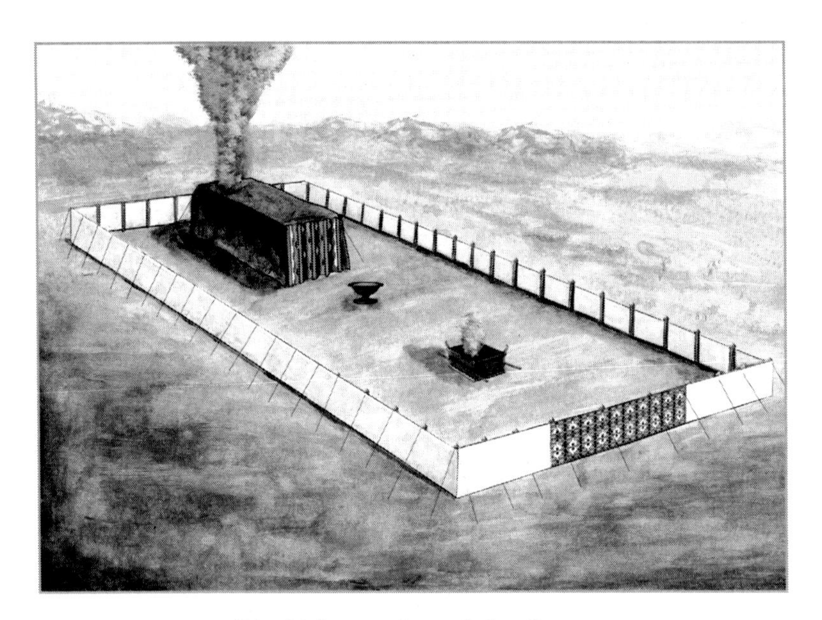

The Tabernacle and the Court

From outside the tabernacle, the only things visible were the white curtains, parts of the wooden pillars, and the dark covering of the tabernacle rising above the height of the walls. (The tabernacle was 15 feet high and therefore could be seen above the 7.5 feet walls.) The sight wasn't particularly inviting.

Likewise the unbeliever sees nothing especially attractive about Christ (Isa. 53:2-3). He is not an exciting sports star or a cool entertainment personality. He is not acclaimed by the world after the fashion of a political hero such as Nelson Mandela or a philosopher-scientist such as Charles Darwin.

Jesus and His cross are not impressive to the "wise" of this world (1 Cor. 1:19-20). In the eyes of unbelievers, Jesus is just a controversial religious man, a noted moral teacher and a man who lived an exemplary life, perhaps, a man from ancient times who died at a young age at the center of a religious controversy.

God has veiled His glory at this present time because He requires that sinners come to Him by faith. Only the Spirit of God can open an individual's eyes so that he can see his need of Christ and thrill at the glories of Christ. This is what God does when the sinner turns in his heart to the truth.

> 2 Corinthians 3:14-16 But their minds were blinded: for until this day remaineth the same vail untaken away in the reading of the old testament; which *vail* is done away in Christ. 15 But even unto this day, when Moses is read, the vail is upon their heart. 16 Nevertheless when it shall turn to the Lord, the vail shall be taken away.

Likewise there is nothing particularly glorious and exciting about the New Testament church in the eyes of unbelievers. Typically, its facilities are ordinary; its ceremonies are boring (for an unbeliever); its beloved book is old and obscure; the preaching is strange; the people are not cool; the sacred music is unexciting to the flesh; the dress is not particularly fashionable.

Only after the sinner repents and trusts Christ and is born again does he see the church in the right light so that it becomes a wonderful thing to attend the house of God and to associate with God's people.

Contemporary churches attempt to remove the natural barrier between the Spirit and the flesh, Christ and the world, by adapting elements from the world that will excite and impress unregenerate people, but by so doing they corrupt the holy things of God and become the enemies of God.

> James 4:4 Ye adulterers and adulteresses, know ye not that the friendship of the world is enmity with God? whosoever therefore will be a friend of the world is the enemy of God.

4. The sockets of brass which formed the foundation of the walls (Ex. 27:10-11, 17) symbolize judgment.

We will see this in the study on the altar of sacrifice. Man is not only shut out from God's presence because of his sin, he is under God's judgment. If he does not receive Christ as Saviour, he will bear his own judgment forever.

5. The pillars crowned with silver capitals depict redemption (Ex. 38:17).

The ransom money was made of silver (Ex. 30:12-13) and pointed to the blood of Christ.

> 1 Peter 1:18-19 Forasmuch as ye know that ye were not redeemed with corruptible things, *as* silver and gold, from your vain conversation *received* by tradition from your fathers; 19 But with the precious blood of Christ, as of a lamb without blemish and without spot:

To ransom means to satisfy a debt with a full payment. It means to appease an offended party (Ex. 21:30). As Joseph was purchased by 20 pieces of silver, so the sinner is purchased from the devil's slave market by Christ's blood (Ge. 37:28).

Thus the walls of the court, even while revealing the sinner's lack of righteousness and his separation from God, spoke of the fact that salvation is available for those who enter by the one Door. The brass sockets threatened judgment but the silver chapiters pointed to salvation.

THE GATE OF THE COURT

> Exodus 27:14-16 The hangings of one side *of the gate shall be* fifteen cubits: their pillars three, and their sockets three. 15 And on the other side *shall be* hangings fifteen *cubits*: their pillars three, and their sockets three. 16 And for the gate of the court *shall be* an hanging of twenty cubits, *of* blue, and purple, and scarlet, and fine twined linen, wrought with needlework: *and* their pillars *shall be* four, and their sockets four.

The description of the gate

The gate on the east side was a cloth curtain 20 cubits (30 feet) long hung on four pillars. The curtain was made of fine linen interwoven with blue, purple, and scarlet thread. It was made of needlework (Ex. 27:16; 38:18). On either side of the gate were curtains of 15 cubits (22.5 feet) hung on three pillars (Ex. 27:14-15).

The spiritual meaning of the gate

1. There was only one gate.

This is a beautiful picture of Christ as the one Saviour, the only way to God.

> John 10:9 I am the door: by me if any man enter in, he shall be saved, and shall go in and out, and find pasture.
>
> John 14:6 Jesus saith unto him, I am the way, the truth, and the life: no man cometh unto the Father, but by me.
>
> Acts 4:12 Neither is there salvation in any other: for there is none other name under heaven given among men, whereby we must be saved.

Any individual who tries to come to God on any other basis is rejected, just as Cain was rejected when he tried to approach God by the works of his hands (Ge. 4:4-5).

The three gates or doors in the tabernacle system (the one into the court, the one into the tabernacle, the one into the holy of holies) depict Christ as the way, the truth, and the life. He is the way of salvation as represented by the door into the court that led to the altar of sacrifice. He is the truth as represented by entrance into the place of the candlestick. He is the life as represented by veil into the holy of holies, which was torn when Christ died.

2. The linen of the door woven with three colors depicts Christ in four ways.

WHITE LINEN, as we have seen, depicts righteousness (Rev. 19:8). In the tabernacle the white linen *depicts Christ's sinless humanity.*

> 1 Peter 2:22 Who did no sin, neither was guile found in his mouth:

Linen was made of flax and could be ordinary or luxurious depending on how it was made. The linen curtains of the tabernacle were "fine linen," meaning the very best quality, pointing to Christ's peerless nature.

The Egyptians were famed for their ability to make fine linen in ancient times, and their tombs preserve many examples such as those we have seen in the Metropolitan Museum of Art in New York City.

> "The linen used by Egyptian royalty was made from thread spun from the fibers of flax straw. Excellent examples of unusually white, tightly woven linen have been found in ancient Egyptian tombs. Some are so finely woven that they cannot be distinguished from silk without the use of a magnifying glass" (*Archaeological Study Bible Notes*, Exodus 25).

I.M. Haldeman observes,

> "Flax is that which comes out of the earth. Considered as to base, the linen represents the humanity of our Lord. Pure white, spotless, these curtains were a fitting symbol of the perfect character of our Lord; as it is written, 'Holy, harmless, undefiled, separate from sinners' (Hebrews 7:26)."

(For more about ancient fine linen see the PowerPoint presentation on Bible Culture in *Bible Times and Ancient Kingdoms*, available from Way of Life Literature)

BLUE, the color of the sky, *signifies Christ as the Lord from Heaven*; it signifies His deity.

> 1 Corinthians 15:47 The first man *is* of the earth, earthy: the second man *is* the Lord from heaven.

PURPLE, the color of royalty (Jud. 8:26), *signifies Christ as King of kings.*

> 1 Timothy 6:14-16 That thou keep *this* commandment without spot, unrebukeable, until the appearing of our Lord Jesus Christ: 15 Which in his times he shall shew, *who is* the blessed and only Potentate, the King of kings, and Lord of lords; 16 Who only hath immortality, dwelling in the light which no man can approach unto; whom no man hath seen, nor can see: to whom *be* honour and power everlasting. Amen.

Today Christ reigns above all in heaven. He will reign over the earth in the Millennium and forever in the new heaven and new earth.

In ancient times in Mesopotamia and the Middle East purple dye was made from a type of snail (*Murex trunculus*). It was called Tyrian purple because the best dye and the best dyed fabrics were made in Tyre and distributed by Phoenician merchants. It was also called royal purple or imperial purple, since it was the clothing of kings. A child born to the imperial family in the Byzantium Empire was said to have been "born in the purple." The price of the dye was often equal to silver and at times reached the price of gold. In some places purple clothing was permitted only to royalty.

SCARLET, the color of blood, *signifies Christ as the Saviour.*

> 1 Timothy 1:15 This *is* a faithful saying, and worthy of all acceptation, that Christ Jesus came into the world to save sinners; of whom I am chief.

Christ's blood can make the sinner's scarlet sins white.

> Isaiah 1:18 Come now, and let us reason together, saith the LORD: though your sins be as scarlet, they shall be as white as snow; though they be red like crimson, they shall be as wool.

We will sing of the cleansing, saving power of Christ's blood forever (Rev. 5:9).

Scarlet also signifies Christ's judgment on those who reject His salvation. He will return clothed in a "vesture dipped in blood" (Rev. 19:13).

Jesus Christ is the Saviour-Lamb for those who accept His blood, and He is the Judge-Lamb for those who reject it.

> Revelation 6:15-16 And the kings of the earth, and the great men, and the rich men, and the chief captains, and the mighty men, and every bondman, and every free man, hid themselves in the dens and in the rocks of the mountains; 16 And said to the mountains and rocks, Fall on us, and hide us from the face of him that sitteth on the throne, and from the wrath of the Lamb:

The scarlet is *always* mentioned last when the colors are listed. See Exodus 25:4; 26:1, 31, 36; 27:16; 28:5, 6, 8, 15, 33; 35:6, 23, 25, 35; 36:8, 35, 37; 38:18, 23; 39:1, 2, 3, 5, 8, 24, 29. Perhaps this teaches that if Jesus were not the sinless Son of God (as signified by the white linen, blue, and purple), He could not have made the acceptable atonement for man's sins (as signified by the scarlet). Only the virgin-born "God manifest in the flesh" could save men from their sins.

The four colors woven together by skillful needlework signify Christ's perfectly balanced life. He is man and God. He is holy and compassionate. He is humble and bold. He is patient and firm. He warns of judgment and offers salvation from judgment. He comforts and He rebukes. He loved and honored his parents but He put God first. He kept every law of God in perfect harmony with the other laws.

In contrast, other men are unbalanced. Noah was strong in faith but weak in regard to wine. David was passionate toward God but weak toward his family. Every man falls short of the glory of God (Rom. 3:23), but Christ is the very glory of God. Every believer partakes of Christ's glory, but Christ is the fullness of God's glory (John 1:14, 16).

> "God's glory was the test, and that was manifested in perfection everywhere. He was not more perfect in rebuking sin and hypocrisy than in pardoning and healing the sin-sick soul. Grace did not eclipse righteousness, nor righteousness grace. Patience was ever coupled with promptness; firmness with gentleness. As the hymn says, 'Thy name encircles every grace, that God as Man could show; there only could He fully trace a life divine below'" (Samuel Ridout, *Lectures on the Tabernacle*).

3. The gate's width (30 feet) signifies the broadness of God's offer of salvation.

God desires that all men be saved (1 Tim. 2:3-4), and He invites all men to come through the preaching of the gospel (Mark 16:15). Rich and poor, educated and uneducated, male and female, elderly and youth, any rank, class, or nationality can come.

4. The absence of cherubims woven into the gate of the court (unlike the veil that divided the holy place from the holy of holies, Ex. 26:31) signifies God's welcome to sinners.

The cherubims guarded the holy presence of God and kept sinners out rather than welcomed them in (Ge. 3:24; Psa. 99:1).

5. The four pillars of the gate signify the Gospels which give a four-fold portrait of Christ.

Matthew presents Jesus as King; Mark presents Jesus as Servant; Luke presents Jesus as perfect Man; John presents Jesus as God.

6. The gate had to be entered.

The sacrifices pointed to the One whose sacrifice was sufficient to save all men, but in practice the sacrifice of Christ saves only those who personally believe (John 3:16).

Looking at the gate, studying the gate, even admiring the gate was not enough to bring the individual into God's covenant. He had to enter the gate and come under the protection of the offerings on the altar of sacrifice.

The tabernacle pictures salvation as both inclusive and exclusive. It is inclusive in that it is available to all, but it is exclusive in that it is given only to those who receive Christ.

The entering of the gate signifies repentance and faith (Acts 20:21). Repentance is pictured by the worshiper turning his back to the sinful world and to all of the false religions of the world in order to enter God's true salvation. Faith is pictured by the worshiper trusting in the one door and the altar of sacrifice, signifying faith in Christ alone as Saviour.

Over the past 2,000 years many have stood without, hearing of and even admiring Christ, but they did not repent and put their faith in Christ. They did not surrender to Christ as Lord and Saviour, and as a result they died and went out into eternity without a Redeemer, bearing their own sins. These will appear at the Great White Throne and be judged by their works before a thrice holy, sin-hating God. As a consequence they will be cast into the lake of fire (Revelation 20:11-15).

Many "evangelicals" today teach that there is a possibility of being saved apart from faith in Christ. Billy Graham, the most influential evangelical of the 20th century, said this multiple times beginning in 1978. In an interview with *McCall's* magazine, Graham said:

> "I used to believe that pagans in far-off countries were lost--were going to hell--if they did not have the Gospel of Jesus Christ preached to them. I no longer believe that. ... I believe that there are other ways of recognizing the existence of God--through nature, for instance--and plenty of other opportunities, therefore, of saying 'yes' to God" (Billy Graham, "I Can't Play God Anymore," *McCall's*, Jan. 1978).

In 1985, when reporter David Colker asked Graham, "What about people of other faiths who live good lives but don't profess a belief in Christ?" Graham replied,

> "I'm going to leave that to the Lord. He'll decide that" (*Los Angeles Herald Examiner*, July 22, 1985).

That might sound God-honoring, but it isn't, because God has already decided this matter and has stated His decision in words that could not be plainer:

> "He that believeth on him is not condemned: but he that believeth not is condemned already, because he hath not believed in the name of the only begotten Son of God. ... He that believeth on the Son hath everlasting life: and he that believeth not the Son shall not see life; but the wrath of God abideth on him" (John 3:18, 36).

That is not man's judgment; it is Christ's judgment; and every preacher is obligated to proclaim God's judgment to this sinful world.

7. Once the sinner entered the court through the one gate he found himself safe within the white walls.

This signifies the believer is eternally safe in Christ. The same walls that keep the sinner from God before he believes, become his protection after He believes. This is the theme of Ephesians 1:3.

> Blessed *be* the God and Father of our Lord Jesus Christ, who hath blessed us with all spiritual blessings in heavenly *places* in Christ:

The key phrase is "in Christ."

The white walls and the brass sockets, signifying God's perfect holiness and judgment of sin, are a fearful sight when viewed from outside of salvation, but once the sinner comes to Christ and is washed in the blood, he is no longer afraid because his judgment fell upon Christ and he is clothed in Christ's very righteousness.

The unsaved sinner will experience the Lamb's eternal wrath, but the believer experiences the Lamb's eternal salvation.

THE ALTAR OF SACRIFICE

> Exodus 27:1-8 And thou shalt make an altar *of* shittim wood, five cubits long, and five cubits broad; the altar shall be foursquare: and the height thereof *shall be* three cubits. 2 And thou shalt make the horns of it upon the four corners thereof: his horns shall be of the same: and thou shalt overlay it with brass. 3 And thou shalt make his pans to receive his ashes, and his shovels, and his basons, and his fleshhooks, and his firepans: all the vessels thereof thou shalt make *of* brass. 4 And thou shalt make for it a grate of network *of* brass; and upon the net shalt thou make four brasen rings in the four corners thereof. 5 And thou shalt put it under the compass of the altar beneath, that the net may be even to the midst of the altar. 6 And thou shalt make staves for the altar, staves *of* shittim wood, and overlay them with brass. 7 And the staves shall be put into the rings, and the staves shall be upon the two sides of the altar, to bear it. 8 Hollow with boards shalt thou make it: as it was shewed thee in the mount, so shall they make *it*.

The description of the altar

The brazen altar or altar of sacrifice was made of wood covered with brass. It was five cubits (7.5 feet) square and three cubits (4.5 feet) high and had horns on the four corners.

There was a network of brass into into which rings were attached to hold the staves when the altar was carried.

It was here that the sacrifices described in Leviticus were offered. The sacrifices were killed on the north side of the altar (Lev. 1:11) and the ashes were placed on the east side toward the gate (Lev. 1:16).

The spiritual meaning of the altar

The brazen altar or altar of sacrifice depicts the cross of Christ, where Jesus shed His blood and died as the "lamb of God" (Jn. 1:29).

As the sinner approached God from outside the tabernacle walls, walking toward the tabernacle where God dwelt, he first came to the altar of sacrifice, thus signifying that there is no salvation apart from Christ's blood and death. Man can only come to God through the atonement that Jesus made on the cross.

1. The altar was made of shittim wood, or acacia wood.

This is a tree that grew in the desert and signifies Christ's virgin-born, sinless humanity, as we will see in the study on the boards of the tabernacle.

2. The wood covered with brass signifies the judgment that fell upon Christ on the cross when He bore our sins.

The brass serpent that Moses made in Numbers 21:5-9 spoke of God's fiery judgment on rebellious Israel. The fetters that bound Samson and Zedekiah as a punishment for their sins were made of brass (Jud. 16:21; 2 Ki. 25:7). Brass is used to signify the hardness and rebellion of sinners' hearts (Isa. 48:4; Jer. 6:28), and it is our rebellion that Christ bore on the cross.

3. The horns of the altar signify power.

> Psalms 75:4-5 I said unto the fools, Deal not foolishly: and to the wicked, Lift not up the horn: 5 Lift not up your horn on high: speak *not with* a stiff neck.
>
> Psalms 89:24 But my faithfulness and my mercy *shall be* with him: and in my name shall his horn be exalted.
>
> Psalms 92:10 But my horn shalt thou exalt like *the horn of* an unicorn: I shall be anointed with fresh oil.

> Psalms 112:9 He hath dispersed, he hath given to the poor; his righteousness endureth for ever; his horn shall be exalted with honour.

The horns on the brazen altar signify Christ's authority as the Son of God, as having all authority in heaven and in earth (Mat. 28:18) and thus signify the power of Christ's sacrifice to save to the uttermost.

4. The size of the altar, as the largest article in the tabernacle, signifies the complete efficacy of Christ's atonement.

His atonement is sufficient to save every sinner and to redeem the entire creation from the fall.

It was twice as large as the ark of the covenant which held the holy law, thus depicting the fact that Jesus' sacrifice is more than sufficient for salvation.

> Romans 5:20 Moreover the law entered, that the offence might abound. But where sin abounded, grace did much more abound.

5. When the tabernacle was first set up, fire came from before the Lord and consumed the burnt offering.

> Leviticus 9:24 And there came a fire out from before the LORD, and consumed upon the altar the burnt offering and the fat: *which* when all the people saw, they shouted, and fell on their faces.

God was dwelling in the tabernacle (Ex. 40:33-34), so the fire came from there.

This showed God's pleasure with the tabernacle system, which had been built exactly according to the divine pattern, and it signified His acceptance of Christ's offering on the cross (Isa. 53:3). The fiery judgment of God fell upon Christ in our place when He bore our sins. He "was made sin for us" (2 Cor. 5:21). This is why He cried out on the cross, "My God, my God, why hast thou forsaken me?" (Mat. 27:46).

The Son had been in the Father's bosom for all eternity, meaning that He was in the most intimate and sweet unity and fellowship with the Father, but now He was forsaken (John 1:18).

We do not read that Jesus ever cried out because of the terrible physical pain that was inflicted upon Him, but He cried out in distress at the separation that He bore from the Father.

6. The fire of the altar was to burn continually.

> Leviticus 6:12-13 And the fire upon the altar shall be burning in it; it shall not be put out: and the priest shall burn wood on it every morning, and lay the burnt offering in order upon it; and he shall burn thereon the fat of the peace offerings. 13 The fire shall ever be burning upon the altar; it shall never go out.

The fire always burning signifies the never ceasing aspect of Christ's salvation. It saves completely. It saves forever. "For by one offering he hath perfected for ever them that are sanctified" (Heb. 10:14).

The fire always burning signifies that the altar is always available for the believing sinner. The throne of grace is always beckoning, where there is plenteous mercy and grace to help in time of need.

> Hebrews 4:16 Let us therefore come boldly unto the throne of grace, that we may obtain mercy, and find grace to help in time of need.

7. The altar was carried by two staves.

> Exodus 27:6-7 And thou shalt make staves for the altar, staves *of* shittim wood, and overlay them with brass. 7 And the staves shall be put into the rings, and the staves shall be upon the two sides of the altar, to bear it.

The altar was portable. It traveled. The staves signify the carrying of the gospel through this world.

Perhaps the two staves remind us that it is necessary to preach both the death and the resurrection of Christ. This is the true gospel (1 Cor. 15:3-4). If Christ had died and not risen from the dead, there would be no gospel.

> "Each of the staves was necessary to the brazen altar. The two staves balanced it. Say all you can say, say all the Scriptures say, about His death; but if He did not rise from the dead, His death was of no more importance than the death of any other man who failed and felt himself forsaken of God. To set aside the death of Christ and speak only of His resurrection, makes His resurrection life of no avail; for if He did not die for our sins, then we are still under the judgment of God and His resurrection is the proof of an infinite and eternal separation between us. Both sides of the Gospel must be preached" (I.M. Haldeman).

8. Two lambs were burned on the altar every day, morning and evening.

> Exodus 29:38-42 Now this *is that* which thou shalt offer upon the altar; two lambs of the first year day by day continually. 39 The one lamb thou shalt offer in the morning; and the other lamb thou shalt offer at even: 40 And with the one lamb a tenth deal of flour mingled with the fourth part of an hin of beaten oil; and the fourth part of an hin of wine *for* a drink offering. 41 And the other lamb thou shalt offer at even, and shalt do thereto according to the meat offering of the morning, and according to the drink offering thereof, for a sweet savour, an offering made by fire unto the LORD. 42 *This shall be* a continual burnt offering throughout your generations *at* the door of the tabernacle of the congregation before the LORD: where I will meet you, to speak there unto thee.

The offering of the lamb signifies Christ's death on the cross (John 1:29). He died in the sinner's place. He was made sin for us (2 Cor. 5:21).

The Altar of Sacrifice - © *GoodSalt*

The offering of a lamb both morning and evening signifies the completeness and fulness of Christ's atonement. He paid the full price for man's sin. He is the perfect Saviour who offers perfect salvation. By His one offering we are perfected forever (Heb. 10:14).

The morning and evening sacrifices point to the time of Christ's suffering. He was crucified at the third hour or 9 a.m. (Mark 15:25), which was the time of the morning sacrifice, and he died at the ninth hour or 3 p.m. (Mark 15:34), which was the time of the evening sacrifice.

The sacrificed lamb also depicts the believer's death in Christ. The fallen man cannot be renewed; he is under God's condemnation and must die. This is what baptism pictures (Rom. 6:3-4). The believer has died with Christ and risen with Christ. This is true spiritually and positionally in this present world, and it will be fulfilled physically when we receive the resurrection body.

The meal and wine offered with the lamb signify Christ as the Bread of Life. Through faith in Christ we not only receive forgiveness of sins and eternal life, we also have a relationship with God as sons, and we fellowship with Him and live by Him. We sup with him (Rev. 3:20). We find pasture in Him (John 10:9).

"They starve their own souls that keep not up a constant attendance on the throne of grace" (Matthew Henry).

THE LAVER

> Exodus 30:17-21 And the LORD spake unto Moses, saying, 18 Thou shalt also make a laver *of* brass, and his foot *also of* brass, to wash *withal*: and thou shalt put it between the tabernacle of the congregation and the altar, and thou shalt put water therein. 19 For Aaron and his sons shall wash their hands and their feet thereat: 20 When they go into the tabernacle of the congregation, they shall wash with water, that they die not; or when they come near to the altar to minister, to burn offering made by fire unto the LORD: 21 So they shall wash their hands and their feet, that they die not: and it shall be a statute for ever to them, *even* to him and to his seed throughout their generations.

The description of the laver

The laver for washing was located in front of the entrance to the tabernacle (Ex. 30:17-21).

It had a foot which was its base.

It was made of women's brass looking glasses (Ex. 38:8).

Its size and capacity is not stated.

The spiritual meaning of the laver

The laver signifies cleansing of sin from the Christian life to maintain fellowship with God.

> Ephesians 5:26 That he might sanctify and cleanse it with the washing of water by the word,

The water of the laver represents the washing of sin through confession.

> 1 John 1:5-9 This then is the message which we have heard of him, and declare unto you, that God is light, and in him is no darkness at all. 6 If we say that we have fellowship with him, and walk in darkness, we lie, and do not the truth: 7 But if we walk in the light, as he is in the light, we have fellowship one with another, and the blood of Jesus Christ his Son cleanseth us from all sin. 8 If we say that we have no sin, we deceive ourselves, and the truth is not in us. 9 If we confess our sins, he is faithful and just to forgive us *our* sins, and to cleanse us from all unrighteousness.

1. The laver depicts both justification and sanctification, salvation and Christian living, relationship and fellowship.

The priest was washed entirely in water when he started his ministry, which depicts regeneration.

> Leviticus 8:6 And Moses brought Aaron and his sons, and washed them with water.

After that the priest was required to wash his hands and feet before he could enter the tabernacle to serve God.

> Exodus 30:19-20 For Aaron and his sons shall wash their hands and their feet thereat: 20 When they go into the tabernacle of the congregation, they shall wash with water, that they die not; or when they come near to the altar to minister, to burn offering made by fire unto the LORD.

There was one bath and many washings. This signifies that sinners must be washed once by the blood of Christ, and they must then be cleansed daily by confession and obedience.

1 Corinthians 6:11 And such were some of you: but ye are washed, but ye are sanctified, but ye are justified in the name of the Lord Jesus, and by the Spirit of our God.

1 John 1:9 If we confess our sins, he is faithful and just to forgive us *our* sins, and to cleanse us from all unrighteousness.

First, there is eternal salvation, then there is sanctification for daily living. First, there is *relationship* wherein the believing sinner becomes a child of God through faith in Christ's blood, then there is *fellowship* with God as the believer walks in obedience to God.

This was what Jesus taught when He washed the disciples' feet.

John 13:8-11 Peter saith unto him, Thou shalt never wash my feet. Jesus answered him, If I wash thee not, thou hast no part with me. 9 Simon Peter saith unto him, Lord, not my feet only, but also *my* hands and *my* head. 10 Jesus saith to him, He that is washed needeth not save to wash *his* feet, but is clean every whit: and ye are clean, but not all. 11 For he knew who should betray him; therefore said he, Ye are not all clean.

When Peter asked Jesus to wash him entirely, Jesus replied that there is one washing of the body and many washings of the feet.

"Jesus saith to him, He that is washed [*louo*] needeth not save to wash his feet [*nipto*], but is clean every whit: and ye are clean, but not all" (John 13:10).

In this verse, the first Greek word for wash is *louo*, meaning to bathe. It refers to the bath of regeneration ("by the washing of regeneration," Titus 3:5).

The second Greek word for wash is *nipto*, which is used for washing one's face and hands and feet (Mat. 6:17; 15:2).

The two-fold truth of the laver is also taught in the book of Ephesians. In chapters 1-3 we see the believer's relationship as a child of God. Having redemption by the blood of Christ, he is blessed with all spiritual blessings in Christ (Eph. 1:3, 7). That is eternal salvation. It is not based on what we do. It is a free gift of God's grace.

Then in Ephesians 4-6 we see the believer's daily walk or fellowship with God. In this present life, we must put off the old man in Adam and put on the new man in Christ (Eph. 4:21-24). We see both aspects in Ephesians 5:8.

> For ye were sometimes darkness, but now *are ye* light in the Lord: walk as children of light:

The believer is now light in the Lord. That is his eternal, unchanging position in Christ. Having this new position before God, we should walk as children of light in this present world. We are exhorted to live up to our position before God. This is the evidence and fruit of salvation.

Unlike the priest in the tabernacle, the believer's contamination comes not by the literal dirt of this world, but by sin, and the cleansing we need is not physical but spiritual. The Pharisees erred in focusing on external cleanliness.

> Mark 7:1-4 Then came together unto him the Pharisees, and certain of the scribes, which came from Jerusalem. 2 And when they saw some of his disciples eat bread with defiled, that is to say, with unwashen, hands, they found fault. 3 For the Pharisees, and all the Jews, except they wash *their* hands oft, eat not, holding the tradition of the elders. 4 And *when they come* from the market, except they wash, they eat not. And many other things there be, which they have received to hold, *as* the washing of cups, and pots, brasen vessels, and of tables.

2. The laver was filled from the water from the smitten Rock.

> Exodus 17:5-6 And the LORD said unto Moses, Go on before the people, and take with thee of the elders of Israel; and thy rod, wherewith thou smotest the river, take in thine hand, and go. 6 Behold, I will stand before thee there

upon the rock in Horeb; and thou shalt smite the rock, and there shall come water out of it, that the people may drink. And Moses did so in the sight of the elders of Israel.

Psalms 78:15-16 He clave the rocks in the wilderness, and gave *them* drink as *out of* the great depths. 16 He brought streams also out of the rock, and caused waters to run down like rivers.

1 Corinthians 10:4 And did all drink the same spiritual drink: for they drank of that spiritual Rock that followed them: and that Rock was Christ.

The Rock signified Christ's cross. The water that flows from this Rock is miraculous, living water. It is capable of cleansing every defilement. It is capable of cleansing Noah's sin of drunkenness and Abraham's sin of lying and David's sin of adultery. The living water flowing from Calvary is capable of cleansing the sins of the whole world.

3. The laver was always available, day or night.

The laver's size is not given, signifying the limitless grace of God. The Lord does not get tired of hearing our confessions. He is faithful and just to forgive our sins (1 Jn. 1:9).

God is *faithful to forgive* because He is merciful. That is God's nature; that is what He delights in. God is love. He is ready to forgive (Psa. 86:5).

God is *just to forgive* because Christ died for our sins, and therefore God can forgive sins and still be the just Judge of the universe.

Romans 3:25-26 Whom God hath set forth *to be* a propitiation through faith in his blood, to declare his righteousness for the remission of sins that are past, through the forbearance of God; 26 To declare, *I say*, at this time his righteousness: that he might be just, and the justifier of him which believeth in Jesus.

Jesus instructed Peter to forgive a brother's sins "seventy times seven" (Mat. 18:21-22). How much more will God forgive His children who confess their sins as they walk through this filthy world!

4. The laver had to be used.

It was not enough for the priests to know that the laver existed or even to appreciate it as they walked by it on the way to and from the tabernacle. They had to stop and wash.

The same is true in the Christian life. How do we wash in the Lord's laver?

We wash in the Lord's holy laver by daily devotions when we spend time privately with the Lord, giving our full attention to hearing His Word and talking to Him in prayer and intercession. In so doing we are cleansed by His Spirit.

We wash in the Lord's holy laver by memorizing Scripture and meditating upon it (Psa. 119:11, 97).

We wash in the Lord's holy laver by coming to the throne of grace in time of need to obtain mercy and find grace to help (Heb. 4:16).

We wash in the Lord's laver by daily confession (1 John 1:9). Confession means to agree with God against our sin. It means that we don't make excuses for our sin and blame our sins on other people or circumstances, as Adam and Eve did (Ge. 3:12-13). It means that we judge ourselves before God (1 Cor. 11:31). We acknowledge our guilt.

We wash in the Lord's laver by faithful attendance to the assembly and by hearing the Word of God preached and by receiving the exhortation of the brethren (Heb. 10:25).

We wash in the Lord's laver by the Lord's Supper whereby we are reminded of the Lord's atonement and of His imminent return (1 Cor. 11:26), and we examine ourselves before Him (1 Cor. 11:27-31).

5. The laver was made of brass looking glasses (Ex. 38:8).

(For photos and descriptions of ancient brass looking glasses from Egypt and elsewhere, see the PowerPoint presentation on Bible Culture in the course *Bible Times and Ancient Kingdoms*, available from Way of Life Literature.)

The brass looking glasses signify that the Bible both reveals sin and cleanses sin.

> James 1:22-25 But be ye doers of the word, and not hearers only, deceiving your own selves. 23 For if any be a hearer of the word, and not a doer, he is like unto a man beholding his natural face in a glass: 24 For he beholdeth himself, and goeth his way, and straightway forgetteth what manner of man he was. 25 But whoso looketh into the perfect law of liberty, and continueth *therein*, he being not a forgetful hearer, but a doer of the work, this man shall be blessed in his deed.

The Word of God searches the deepest thoughts and motives of the heart (Heb. 4:12). We don't like to see ourselves as God sees us. It isn't pleasant to see our sins and failures, but if we are willing to allow the Lord's laver to do its job, it will cleanse us and make us into Christ's image.

When we neglect God's Word, we backslide spiritually. When we love our sin and hold onto it, we don't want the light of God's Word to expose our sin, and we tend to neglect daily Bible reading and the house of God. Even if we don't stop doing these things, we do them with a lack of spiritual enthusiasm and passion. We lose our first love for Christ. We become lukewarm.

The brass looking glasses signify Christ revealed in His Word.

> 2 Corinthians 3:18 But we all, with open face beholding as in a glass the glory of the Lord, are changed into the same image from glory to glory, *even* as by the Spirit of the Lord.

God has ordained that every believer be conformed to Christ's image.

> Romans 8:28 And we know that all things work together for good to them that love God, to them who are the called according to *his* purpose.

That is our destiny, and the work begins in this present life as we are conformed to Christ's image by the power of the Holy Spirit through daily sanctification. As the Spirit of God reveals Christ (the New Man) in the Scriptures, we reject the old man that we inherited from Adam and put on the New Man.

> Ephesians 4:20-24 But ye have not so learned Christ; 21 If so be that ye have heard him, and have been taught by him, as the truth is in Jesus: 22 That ye put off concerning the former conversation the old man, which is corrupt according to the deceitful lusts; 23 And be renewed in the spirit of your mind; 24 And that ye put on the new man, which after God is created in righteousness and true holiness.

The brass looking glasses signify the surrender of human vanity and worldliness. These are things that we must renounce and separate from in order to walk with the Lord.

> 1 John 2:15-17 Love not the world, neither the things *that are* in the world. If any man love the world, the love of the Father is not in him. 16 For all that *is* in the world, the lust of the flesh, and the lust of the eyes, and the pride of life, is not of the Father, but is of the world. 17 And the world passeth away, and the lust thereof: but he that doeth the will of God abideth for ever.

As the Israelite women gave up their beloved Egyptian mirrors, so must we give up our love for the evil ways of this world. I recall how that the Lord dealt with me as a new believer about my love for such things as filthy rock & roll and my long hair and vain worldly appearance. As the weeks and months passed, I surrendered my worldly vanities to the Lord one by one, just as the Israelite women surrendered their Egyptian mirrors.

Forty years later the Lord is still calling me to die to the call of the world. He is still calling me to surrender particular things that creep into my Christian life that are not edifying. In the 1990s, I developed a love for baseball and became captivated with the Seattle Mariners pro baseball team. I was working outside in those days, mowing lawns, cutting and selling firewood, landscaping, applying pesticides to lawns and gardens, and I listened to every game on the radio. I kept up with my favorite players' statistics. I studied baseball and learned how to score it. I took my teenage boys to a major league game in the Seattle Kingdome once a month. It was such an amazing waste of time, at best! I found that I wasn't spending as much time studying the Bible and writing and teaching as I had before. And the pro baseball atmosphere was worldly, filled with pride and vanity and rock & roll and immodesty and worldly commercialism. It is no secret that professional sports are all about money. I thank the Lord that He dealt with me about the fact that my infatuation with baseball was hindering my Christian life and was a poor example to my boys. I gave it up and returned to my first love for the Lord, and I have never regretted it.

When we look into the Lord's laver, we see ourselves as we really are and we see what the Lord wants us to be.

6. The laver had to be used continually.

The priests had to wash every time they approached the tabernacle and every time they made offerings.

> Exodus 30:20 When they go into the tabernacle of the congregation, they shall wash with water, that they die not; or when they come near to the altar to minister, to burn offering made by fire unto the LORD:

They had to wash whenever they touched something unclean.

> Leviticus 22:1-6 And the LORD spake unto Moses, saying, 2 Speak unto Aaron and to his sons, that they separate themselves from the holy things of the children of Israel,

> and that they profane not my holy name *in those things* which they hallow unto me: I *am* the LORD. 3 Say unto them, Whosoever *he be* of all your seed among your generations, that goeth unto the holy things, which the children of Israel hallow unto the LORD, having his uncleanness upon him, that soul shall be cut off from my presence: I *am* the LORD. 4 What man soever of the seed of Aaron *is* a leper, or hath a running issue; he shall not eat of the holy things, until he be clean. And whoso toucheth any thing *that is* unclean *by* the dead, or a man whose seed goeth from him; 5 Or whosoever toucheth any creeping thing, whereby he may be made unclean, or a man of whom he may take uncleanness, whatsoever uncleanness he hath; 6 The soul which hath touched any such shall be unclean until even, and shall not eat of the holy things, unless he wash his flesh with water.

The laver instructs us not to grow weary at the presence and reality of sin in this life, not to grow weary of judging ourselves and confessing our sins. The Psalmist expressed this as follows:

> Psalms 73:12-14 Behold, these *are* the ungodly, who prosper in the world; they increase *in* riches. 13 Verily I have cleansed my heart *in* vain, and washed my hands in innocency. 14 For all the day long have I been plagued, and chastened every morning.

We see unbelievers who are "free" to enjoy life apart from being concerned about pleasing God, and we are tempted to throw off Christ's yoke and live like that. The laver speaks to this issue. The washing in the laver was a continual and tedious process. The floor of the court and the tabernacle was the ground itself, and the priests were barefoot, so they were contaminated with every step they took. Their hands were contaminated by the handling of the offerings, the blackened altar, the ashes. There was no end to the need of washing. Likewise in this present life the believer lives in a world of sin and has the enemy of sin still living within him, so he is continually in need of cleansing in order to remain in fellowship with his holy Lord and Saviour.

> 1 John 1:8-9 If we say that we have no sin, we deceive ourselves, and the truth is not in us. 9 If we confess our sins, he is faithful and just to forgive us *our* sins, and to cleanse us from all unrighteousness.

The laver refutes the error of any doctrine of a sinless perfection experience. We want to have perfect victory and some theological systems offer it, but this is not our experience in this present life. God has ordained that we live by faith.

> Hebrews 11:6 But without faith *it is* impossible to please *him*: for he that cometh to God must believe that he is, and *that* he is a rewarder of them that diligently seek him.

> Romans 8:24 For we are saved by hope: but hope that is seen is not hope: for what a man seeth, why doth he yet hope for?

In order to live by faith we must be compassed about with sin, weakness, lack, trouble, and testing.

Thus instead of a redemption body, we presently live in a "body of this death" (Rom. 7:24). Instead of a glorious renewed world, we live in a world of corruption (Rom. 8:22-23). Instead of perfect joy, we have groaning (Rom. 8:23). Instead of sight, we have hope (Rom. 8:24). Instead of liberty, we are subject to the bondage of corruption (Rom. 8:21). This is why God does not take away the "old man." John said that if we say we have no sin we deceive ourselves (1 John 1:8). It is God's will that we not sin (1 John 2:1), and one glorious day we will be delivered from the very presence of sin and from the "body of this death." But in this present life, we do sin and God has made full and perfect provision for it in Christ.

> 1 John 2:1-2 My little children, these things write I unto you, that ye sin not. And if any man sin, we have an

> advocate with the Father, Jesus Christ the righteous: 2 And he is the propitiation for our sins: and not for ours only, but also for *the sins of* the whole world.

The laver refutes emerging church false teachers (e.g., Brennan Manning, Charles Swindoll, John Eldridge, David Miller) who promote the lie that being washed by Christ means the believer does not have to walk in strict obedience and repentance and confession, that he is free simply to enjoy life, to be "wild at heart" and to follow "the renegade path of Christianity." They call strict Christian living "Phariseeism."

But the liberty they promise is not what the Bible promises for this present life. We will enjoy that type of life one day, and we look forward to it with great anticipation. We will be delivered from the present bondage into the glorious liberty of the sons of God at Christ's return (Romans 8:19-25). But in this present life we still live in a body of death (Rom. 7:24), and we don't yet have our glorified body. We must therefore chasten and judge ourselves lest we be judged of the Lord (1 Cor. 11:28-31). We must bring the body into subjection lest we be castaways (1 Cor. 9:27). We must walk in fear and trembling (Phil. 2:12) and prepare for the judgment seat of Christ (2 Cor. 5:10). We must subject ourselves to the chastening hand of God (Hebrews 12:4-13).

In this present life we have many enemies, and we must walk in soberness and watchfulness (1 Pet. 5:8). We must beware lest we be spoiled by false teachers (Col. 2:8) or led away with the error of the wicked (2 Pet. 3:17) or lose our full reward (2 John 8).

We are to walk so carefully that we are to avoid even the very *appearance* of evil (1 Th. 5:22). We are to have *no* fellowship with the works of darkness (Eph. 5:11) and are not to touch even the garment spotted by sin (Jude 23).

The washing at the laver points to this type of biblical strictness in the Christian life.

The Tabernacle Itself

Exodus 26:1-37 Moreover thou shalt make the tabernacle *with* ten curtains *of* fine twined linen, and blue, and purple, and scarlet: *with* cherubims of cunning work shalt thou make them. 2 The length of one curtain *shall be* eight and twenty cubits, and the breadth of one curtain four cubits: and every one of the curtains shall have one measure. 3 The five curtains shall be coupled together one to another; and *other* five curtains *shall be* coupled one to another. 4 And thou shalt make loops of blue upon the edge of the one curtain from the selvedge in the coupling; and likewise shalt thou make in the uttermost edge of *another* curtain, in the coupling of the second. 5 Fifty loops shalt thou make in the one curtain, and fifty loops shalt thou make in the edge of the curtain that *is* in the coupling of the second; that the loops may take hold one of another. 6 And thou shalt make fifty taches of gold, and couple the curtains together with the taches: and it shall be one tabernacle. 7 And thou shalt make curtains *of* goats' *hair* to be a covering upon the tabernacle: eleven curtains shalt thou make. 8 The length of one curtain *shall be* thirty cubits, and the breadth of one curtain four cubits: and the eleven curtains *shall be all* of one measure. 9 And thou shalt couple five curtains by themselves, and six curtains by themselves, and shalt double the sixth curtain in the forefront of the tabernacle. 10 And thou shalt make fifty loops on the edge of the one curtain *that is* outmost in the coupling, and fifty loops in the edge of the curtain which coupleth the second. 11 And thou shalt make fifty taches of brass, and put the taches into the loops, and couple the tent together, that it may be one. 12 And the remnant that remaineth of the curtains of the tent, the half curtain that remaineth, shall hang over the backside of the tabernacle. 13 And a cubit on the one side, and a cubit on the other side of that which remaineth in the length of the curtains of the tent, it shall hang over the sides of the tabernacle on this side and on that side, to cover it. 14 And thou shalt make a covering for the tent *of* rams' skins dyed red, and a covering above *of* badgers' skins. 15 And thou shalt make boards for the tabernacle *of* shittim wood standing up. 16 Ten cubits *shall be* the length of a board, and a cubit and a half *shall be* the breadth of one board. 17 Two tenons *shall there be* in one board, set in order one against another: thus shalt thou make for all the boards of the tabernacle. 18 And thou shalt make the boards for the tabernacle, twenty boards on the south side southward. 19 And thou shalt make forty sockets of silver under the twenty boards; two sockets under one board for his two tenons, and two sockets under another board for his two tenons. 20 And for the second side of the tabernacle on the north side *there shall be* twenty boards: 21 And their forty sockets *of* silver; two sockets under one board, and two sockets under another board. 22 And for the sides of the tabernacle westward thou shalt make six boards. 23 And two boards shalt thou make for the corners of the tabernacle in the two sides. 24 And they shall be coupled together beneath, and they shall be coupled together above the head of it unto one ring: thus shall it be for them both; they shall be for the two corners. 25 And they shall be eight boards, and their sockets *of* silver, sixteen sockets; two sockets under one board, and two sockets under another board. 26 And thou shalt make bars *of* shittim wood; five for the boards of the one side of the tabernacle, 27 And five bars for the boards of the other side of the tabernacle, and five bars for the boards of the side of the tabernacle, for the two sides westward. 28 And the middle bar in the midst of the boards shall reach from end to end. 29 And thou shalt overlay the boards with gold, and make their rings *of* gold *for* places for the bars: and thou shalt overlay the bars with gold. 30 And thou shalt rear up the tabernacle according to the fashion thereof which was shewed thee in the mount. 31 And thou shalt make a vail *of* blue, and purple, and scarlet, and fine twined linen of cunning work: with cherubims shall it be made: 32 And thou shalt hang it upon four pillars of shittim *wood* overlaid with gold: their hooks *shall be of* gold, upon the four sockets of silver. 33 And thou shalt hang up the vail under the taches, that thou mayest bring in thither within the vail the ark of the testimony: and the vail shall divide unto you between the holy *place* and the most holy. 34 And thou shalt put the mercy seat upon the ark of the testimony in the most holy *place.* 35 And thou shalt set the table without the vail, and the candlestick over against the table on the side of the tabernacle toward the south: and thou shalt put the table on the north side. 36 And thou shalt make an hanging for the door of the tent, *of* blue, and purple, and scarlet, and fine twined linen, wrought with needlework. 37 And thou shalt make for the hanging five pillars *of* shittim *wood*, and overlay them with gold, *and* their hooks *shall be of* gold: and thou shalt cast five sockets of brass for them.

The description of the tabernacle

The tabernacle was a rectangular tent that sat inside the court area. It was 30 cubits (45 feet or 13.7 meters) long, 10 cubits (15 feet or 4.5 meters) wide, and 10 cubits (15 feet or 4.5 meters) high.

The tabernacle was divided into two compartments: The holy place and the most holy or holy of holies. *The holy place* was 20 cubits (30 feet) long and 10 cubits (15 feet) wide and 10 cubits (15 feet) high. It is also called the sanctuary (Heb. 9:2). The **holy of holies** was a perfect cube 10 cubits (15 feet) long and wide and high. Sometimes the holy of holies is called the holy place (Heb. 9:25).

The side and rear walls were made with **boards covered with gold** (Ex 26:15-30). The boards were 10 cubits (15 feet) high and 1.5 cubits (2.25 feet) wide (Ex. 26:16). There were a total of 48 boards: 20 on the south side and 20 on the north (Ex. 26:18, 20), six on the west or rear side (Ex. 26:22). There was also one board at each rear corner to anchor the sections together (Ex. 26:23-24). The boards stood upright and gold-plated wooden bars tied them together (Ex. 26:27-28).

Tabernacle: The Holy Place and the Holy of Holies - © SermonView

The bottom of each board fit into two **sockets of silver** (Ex. 26:19). Each socket weighed one talent (94 pounds) Ex. 38:27). Thus the entire tabernacle rested on a strong silver foundation.

The tabernacle was roofed with **four cloth and skin coverings**. First was a covering of linen entwined with blue, purple, and scarlet, and engraved with images of the cherubims (Ex. 26:1-6). The covering was made of 11 curtains hooked together with gold hooks inserted into blue loops. This was the covering that could be seen by the priests from inside the tabernacle. Next was a covering made of goats' hair (Ex. 26:7-13). Over this was a covering made of rams' skins dyed red (Ex. 26:14). Finally, there was a covering made of badgers' skins (Ex. 26:14). This was the covering that was seen from outside the tabernacle.

The walls and roof of the tabernacle were fastened to the ground by **pins and cords** (Ex. 35:18).

The spiritual meaning of the tabernacle and its articles

The priest approached the tabernacle through the one gate and the altar of sacrifice and laver. Being cleansed positionally and practically, he could enter the tabernacle and behold the glories of the resurrected Christ by means of the light and find spiritual food and communion with God.

This is a picture of the Christian life. After we are born again through faith in Christ's cross and after we are washed from our daily sin by confession, we can enjoy fellowship with Christ. It is a choice that each believer makes. I can spend as much time in the holy place and in the very holy of holies as I want. I can come before the throne of grace as often as I wish. I can set my affection on things above as much as I want (Col. 3:1-2). I can be like Joshua who "departed not out of the tabernacle" (Ex. 33:11). What a great privilege and blessing! What a definite test of wisdom!

The closer the priest came to the holy of holies, the more he saw of Christ's glory. From outside he could only see the unattractive covering of badgers' skins and part of the door with its white linen intermixed with blue, purple, and scarlet. When he entered the holy place, he saw the golden walls and the colorful ceiling with the cherubim and the beautiful golden lampstand, the incense altar, and the table of shewbread. The holy of holies could not be entered except by the high priest on the Day of Atonement, but it is open now to the believer, and we can enter into the very presence of God.

We will never cease learning about the infinite Christ, as His wisdom and character are infinite.

THE BOARDS

1. The boards of shittim wood covered with gold signify Christ as the divine man.

The shittim wood was a common tree that grew in the desert. It signifies Christ's perfect humanity as we see in Isaiah 53:2.

First, the shittim wood depicts Christ as "a root out of a dry ground." The shittim or acacia tree grew in the desert where other trees could not grow. This signifies Christ's supernatural birth. Just as it is unnatural for a root to grow out of dry ground, so Christ's birth was not natural. He is the virgin-born, sinless Man. He was born of a woman, but He is not of this world.

Further, the shittim tree depicts Christ's lack of comeliness. The shittim tree is an ordinary tree. It doesn't have the glory and stature of the cedar or fir or the value and multipurpose of the olive tree, which provides a variety of food and oil as well as wood for construction. Cedar, fir, and olive were used in Solomon's Temple (1 Ki. 6:15, 31-33), which points to Christ in His millennial glory. But for the tabernacle, ordinary shittim wood was used, because it well signifies Christ's first coming in the form of a servant to die for man's sin.

> Philippians 2:6-8 Who, being in the form of God, thought it not robbery to be equal with God: 7 But made himself of no reputation, and took upon him the form of a servant, and was made in the likeness of men: 8 And being found in fashion as a man, he humbled himself, and became obedient unto death, even the death of the cross.

In appearance, Jesus was an ordinary Jewish man. He wasn't from some exotic, influential place like Tyre or Babylon. He was born in a stable in the lowly town of Bethlehem in the tiny country of Israel. He wasn't a wealthy man, a great property owner, or a captain of industry. He wasn't a famous author or poet or scholar or entertainer. He wasn't a graduate of a famous school. He was merely the son of a common carpenter. How true is Isaiah's prophecy that, in the eyes of the world, "he hath no form nor comeliness; and when we shall see him, there is no beauty that we should desire him" (Isa. 53:2).

In the tabernacle the wood is covered with costly, beautiful gold, which represents Christ's divinity.

The gold covered boards and the gold objects in the tabernacle depict Christ in His resurrection glory. He is no longer a babe in a manger or a lowly carpenter's son or a crucified man. Having suffered these things, He has entered into His glory (Luke 24:26).

The Catholic Church most often depicts Christ as a babe or as a man hanging on a cross or as a dead man in Mary's arms. But He is not any of that today. He rose from the dead in resurrection glory and ascended up on high to sit at the right hand of God. He is the High Priest in glory today, and that is what we see in the interior of the tabernacle.

The boards teach us that the humanity of Christ and the deity of Christ are formed into one Man, the Second Man (1 Cor. 15:47). He is not part man and part God. He is wholly man and wholly God. He is the God man. He is God manifest in the flesh (1 Tim. 3:16), God made flesh (John 1:1, 14), the Lord from heaven (1 Cor. 15:47), the image of the invisible God (Col. 1:15; 2 Cor. 4:4), the one in whom dwells the fullness of the Godhead bodily (Col. 2:9), the express image of God's person (Heb. 1:3).

Jesus was not man for His brief earthly sojourn only; He is a man forever. He sits enthroned in heaven as "the man Christ Jesus" (1 Tim. 2:5).

The person of Christ is the most amazing, mysterious, fascinating, important fact of human history. The Bible does not say that Jesus Christ was merely a good man or a renowned religious leader or a great prophet or a guru or an angel or an avatar (a divine being descended to earth). It does not say that God dwelt for a while in a human body. It says that Jesus was Almighty God made man.

He is God, the creator of all things, the Son of God who was forever with the Father (John 1:1-3).

He was made flesh (John 1:14). This was by means of the virgin birth. He was born of the virgin as a holy man, but He was still the Son of God (Luke 1:35). God prepared a body for Him (Heb. 10:5).

He took part of the same flesh and blood as man (Heb. 2:14) but without sin (Heb. 4:15). He was not of the nature of angels but of the nature of Abraham (Heb. 2:16).

All of this was depicted by the tabernacle and its articles that were made of acacia wood covered with gold.

2. The corner boards which bound the structure together signify Jesus as the chief cornerstone of the temple of God.

> Isaiah 28:16 Therefore thus saith the Lord GOD, Behold, I lay in Zion for a foundation a stone, a tried stone, a precious corner *stone*, a sure foundation: he that believeth shall not make haste.

THE SILVER SOCKETS

> Exodus 26:19-21 And thou shalt make forty sockets of silver under the twenty boards; two sockets under one board for his two tenons, and two sockets under another board for his two tenons. 20 And for the second side of the tabernacle on the north side *there shall be* twenty boards: 21 And their forty sockets *of* silver; two sockets under one board, and two sockets under another board.

1. The silver sockets formed the foundation for the boards and depict redemption, which is the foundation of the Christian life and the foundation for God's eternal kingdom.

The sockets were made from the silver shekels that were given as ransom money.

> Exodus 30:13-16 This they shall give, every one that passeth among them that are numbered, half a shekel after the shekel of the sanctuary: (a shekel *is* twenty gerahs:) an

> half shekel *shall be* the offering of the LORD. 14 Every one that passeth among them that are numbered, from twenty years old and above, shall give an offering unto the LORD. 15 The rich shall not give more, and the poor shall not give less than half a shekel, when *they* give an offering unto the LORD, to make an atonement for your souls. 16 And thou shalt take the atonement money of the children of Israel, and shalt appoint it for the service of the tabernacle of the congregation; that it may be a memorial unto the children of Israel before the LORD, to make an atonement for your souls.

As the tabernacle was upheld by the silver sockets, so our eternal salvation is founded upon the redemption price that Christ paid on the cross (1 Pet. 1:18-19).

2. The foundation speaks of the great value of Christ's blood as unspeakably "precious."

> 1 Peter 1:18-19 Forasmuch as ye know that ye were not redeemed with corruptible things, *as* silver and gold, from your vain conversation *received* by tradition from your fathers; 19 But with the precious blood of Christ, as of a lamb without blemish and without spot:

Each socket weighed a talent or about 94 pounds (Ex. 38:27). The total amount of silver in the tabernacle's foundation was about 9,400 pounds (4,263 kilograms or 4.2 metric tons). What a solid foundation! Christ's blood is able save as many as come to Him and is able to redeem the entire creation unto God.

3. The silver foundation speaks of the vastness of Christ's redemption.

The talent in each socket represented 3,000 shekels of the silver ransom money which was the amount given by 6,000 men (each giving one-half shekel). (There were 603,550 men who gave one-half shekel each for a total of 301,775 shekels, Ex. 28:26. 300,000 shekels represented 100 talents, Ex. 38:27.) Since there were two silver sockets under each board, this represented the ransom money for 12,000 men. This points to the multitudes without number who will be redeemed from every nation (Rev. 7:9).

4. The silver sockets speak of separation.

Just as the tabernacle was separated from the ground by the silver sockets, the believer is forever separated from the world and the old creation by the blood of Christ.

> Romans 6:6 Knowing this, that our old man is crucified with *him*, that the body of sin might be destroyed, that henceforth we should not serve sin.
>
> 2 Corinthians 5:17 Therefore if any man *be* in Christ, *he is* a new creature: old things are passed away; behold, all things are become new.
>
> Galatians 6:14 But God forbid that I should glory, save in the cross of our Lord Jesus Christ, by whom the world is crucified unto me, and I unto the world.

THE ROOF OF FOUR COVERINGS

> Exodus 26:1-14 Moreover thou shalt make the tabernacle *with* ten curtains *of* fine twined linen, and blue, and purple, and scarlet: *with* cherubims of cunning work shalt thou make them. 2 The length of one curtain *shall be* eight and twenty cubits, and the breadth of one curtain four cubits: and every one of the curtains shall have one measure. 3 The five curtains shall be coupled together one to another; and *other* five curtains *shall be* coupled one to another. 4 And thou shalt make loops of blue upon the edge of the one curtain from the selvedge in the coupling; and likewise shalt thou make in the uttermost edge of *another* curtain, in the coupling of the second. 5 Fifty loops shalt thou make in the one curtain, and fifty loops shalt thou make in the edge of the curtain that *is* in the coupling of the second; that the loops may take hold one of another. 6 And thou shalt make fifty taches of gold, and couple the curtains together with the taches: and it shall be one tabernacle. 7 And thou shalt make curtains *of* goats' *hair* to be a

covering upon the tabernacle: eleven curtains shalt thou make. 8 The length of one curtain *shall be* thirty cubits, and the breadth of one curtain four cubits: and the eleven curtains *shall be all* of one measure. 9 And thou shalt couple five curtains by themselves, and six curtains by themselves, and shalt double the sixth curtain in the forefront of the tabernacle. 10 And thou shalt make fifty loops on the edge of the one curtain *that is* outmost in the coupling, and fifty loops in the edge of the curtain which coupleth the second. 11 And thou shalt make fifty taches of brass, and put the taches into the loops, and couple the tent together, that it may be one. 12 And the remnant that remaineth of the curtains of the tent, the half curtain that remaineth, shall hang over the backside of the tabernacle. 13 And a cubit on the one side, and a cubit on the other side of that which remaineth in the length of the curtains of the tent, it shall hang over the sides of the tabernacle on this side and on that side, to cover it. 14 And thou shalt make a covering for the tent *of* rams' skins dyed red, and a covering above *of* badgers' skins.

1. The coverings depict how the glory of Christ (signified by the linen intertwined with blue, purple, and scarlet) was veiled when He was on earth.

> Isaiah 53:2 For he shall grow up before him as a tender plant, and as a root out of a dry ground: he hath no form nor comeliness; and when we shall see him, *there is* no beauty that we should desire him.

> Philippians 2:7-8 But made himself of no reputation, and took upon him the form of a servant, and was made in the likeness of men: 8 And being found in fashion as a man, he humbled himself, and became obedient unto death, even the death of the cross.

To look at Christ in the flesh during His first coming, one saw nothing extraordinary, just a Jewish carpenter and religious teacher. Only those who walked with Him and saw Him through the eye of faith could see His glory.

John 1:14 And the Word was made flesh, and dwelt among us, (and we beheld his glory, the glory as of the only begotten of the Father,) full of grace and truth.

Likewise those standing outside looking toward the tabernacle could see only an ordinary covering of black skins, but those who entered by means of the altar of sacrifice and the laver of washing enjoyed the beauty of the interior: the gold-covered boards, and the lovely ceiling of woven linen curtains held together by taches of pure gold, the gold covered objects, all illuminated by the seven lamps of the candlestick.

2. The curtains of fine-twined linen, blue, purple, and scarlet depict Christ as the righteous Man, the God man, the King of kings, and the Saviour, as we have seen.

This is what the priest saw from inside the tabernacle. He was surrounded with images of Christ in His glory.

3. The number of curtains was 10 (Ex. 26:1), reminding us of the Ten Commandments, which Christ kept in perfection.

He had no other gods before God the Father, never bowed before an idol (he told Satan, "Get thee hence," when invited to worship him), never used God's name in vain, never desecrated the sabbath. Instead, He loved God with all His being and came to this world to do His Father's will. He loved obeying the Father more than His daily food (John 4:34). As for the other commandments, He honored His mother and father, did not kill, commit adultery, steal, bear false witness against his neighbor, or covet his neighbor's goods. Instead He loved even His enemies and made Himself poor that His neighbors might be made rich (2 Cor. 8:9).

4. The goat's hair curtain and ram's skin curtain signify Christ's atonement.

The goat was a sin offering (Lev. 4:24; 9:15; 16:9; Nu. 15:27; 28:22; 29:22; Eze. 43:25). Likewise the rams' skins dyed red point to the ram as a sin offering (Lev. 5:15). The color red points to the blood of Christ which was the basis of all of the offerings. It was a ram that God supplied as a sacrifice in the place of Isaac (Ge. 22:11-13). Thus the curtain of goat's hair and the curtain of rams' skins were yet another picture of Christ's atonement and the fact that sinners have no acceptance before God apart from this. These depict the believer priest inside the tabernacle wrapped safely in Christ's salvation.

> "The whole building was enveloped in this fabric; as if to enunciate the great truth, that God could have no tabernacle amongst men, and could not display His glory and beauty in the midst of them, unless His dwelling-place proclaimed, in every part, the fact that sin and infirmity had been fully met by a perfect sacrifice" (Henry Soltau, *The Tabernacle*).

5. The final cover of badgers' skins was practical as well as symbolic.

We don't know exactly what the badger was, but we know that its skin was used for shoes (Ezek. 16:10). Therefore, it was a tough, weather-resistant covering to protect the tabernacle.

6. The pins and cords that fastened the tabernacle to the ground (Ex. 35:18) signify the security of Christ's salvation.

Christ is the nail that is fastened in a sure place.

> Isaiah 22:23 And I will fasten him *as* a nail in a sure place; and he shall be for a glorious throne to his father's house.

Because of the nails that pierced Christ's hands and feet and the blood that was thus shed, He laid the foundation for the salvation of individual sinners and ultimately for the salvation of the creation itself.

He will bring God's kingdom to this world and eventually create the new heaven and the new earth, and nothing can stop this. Of the increase of his government and peace there shall be no end.

> Isaiah 9:7 Of the increase of *his* government and peace *there shall be* no end, upon the throne of David, and upon his kingdom, to order it, and to establish it with judgment and with justice from henceforth even for ever. The zeal of the LORD of hosts will perform this.

The hope He gives to His saints is "an anchor of the soul, both sure and stedfast" (Heb. 6:19).

Every promise of God in Him is yea and amen (2 Cor. 1:20).

> "The nail driven down into the place of death, there bruised and made nought him that had the power of death; and having this secure foundation, the nail has become the strength of all God's building. All rests on Him. All hangs for support and sustainment on Him. And He is the beginning of that new and glorious creation, which shall endure for ever" (Henry Soltau, *The Tabernacle*).

The Holy Place

The first compartment in the tabernacle, the holy place depicts the believer fellowshipping with God in Christ. He has entered the door of the tabernacle and put his faith in Christ's sacrifice as depicted by the brazen altar. He has been bathed in the laver and is now entered into the service of God.

The candlestick, incense alter, and table of shewbread

The three articles in the room--the candlestick, the table of shewbread, and the incense altar--signify Christ as Light, Bread, and Intercessor. Jesus Christ is everything to the believer.

> 1 Corinthians 1:30-31 But of him are ye in Christ Jesus, who of God is made unto us wisdom, and righteousness, and sanctification, and redemption: 31 That, according as it is written, He that glorieth, let him glory in the Lord.

Ephesians 1:3 Blessed *be* the God and Father of our Lord Jesus Christ, who hath blessed us with all spiritual blessings in heavenly *places* in Christ:

Colossians 2:9-10 For in him dwelleth all the fulness of the Godhead bodily. 10 And ye are complete in him, which is the head of all principality and power:

The essence of the Christian life is to walk with and serve and learn of Christ.

Matthew 11:28-30 Come unto me, all *ye* that labour and are heavy laden, and I will give you rest. 29 Take my yoke upon you, and learn of me; for I am meek and lowly in heart: and ye shall find rest unto your souls. 30 For my yoke *is* easy, and my burden is light.

The Israelites were exhorted not only to obey and serve God but also to *cleave unto* Him (De. 13:4).

We can walk with God like Enoch. We can seek God passionately like David. We can sit at His feet and learn of Him like Mary.

Genesis 5:24 And Enoch walked with God: and he *was* not; for God took him.

Psalms 27:8 *When thou saidst*, Seek ye my face; my heart said unto thee, Thy face, LORD, will I seek.

Psalms 42:1 As the hart panteth after the water brooks, so panteth my soul after thee, O God.

Psalms 63:1 O God, thou *art* my God; early will I seek thee: my soul thirsteth for thee, my flesh longeth for thee in a dry and thirsty land, where no water is;

Psalms 84:2 My soul longeth, yea, even fainteth for the courts of the LORD: my heart and my flesh crieth out for the living God.

Luke 10:39 And she had a sister called Mary, which also sat at Jesus' feet, and heard his word.

THE DOOR INTO THE HOLY PLACE

> Exodus 26:36-37 And thou shalt make an hanging for the door of the tent, *of* blue, and purple, and scarlet, and fine twined linen, wrought with needlework. 37 And thou shalt make for the hanging five pillars *of* shittim *wood*, and overlay them with gold, *and* their hooks *shall be of* gold: and thou shalt cast five sockets of brass for them.

The tabernacle had one entrance on the east side called the door. It was made of a curtain of fine linen interwoven with blue, purple, and scarlet thread made of needlework. It hung on five pillars of wood covered with gold. These were topped with gold capitals and rested in brass sockets (Ex. 36:38). The curtain hung on hooks of gold.

1. The door pictures Christ as the sinless Son of God, the Saviour, the King of kings, the Lord from heaven, as depicted by the various colors.

2. The pillars of wood covered with gold picture Christ as perfect Man and God in one Person.

3. The chapiters which crowned the pillars depict Christ crowned and seated at the right hand of God (Psa. 110:1). He is "crowned with glory and honour" (Heb. 2:9). He has been exalted above all and been given a name which is above every name (Eph. 1:21; Phil. 2:9).

4. The pillars rested in brass sockets, signifying judgment, picture Christ's suffering on the cross as the foundation of His work as High Priest.

> Revelation 1:15 And his feet like unto fine brass, as if they burned in a furnace; and his voice as the sound of many waters.

THE LAMPSTAND

> Exodus 25:31-39 And thou shalt make a candlestick *of* pure gold: *of* beaten work shall the candlestick be made: his shaft, and his branches, his bowls, his knops, and his

flowers, shall be of the same. 32 And six branches shall come out of the sides of it; three branches of the candlestick out of the one side, and three branches of the candlestick out of the other side: 33 Three bowls made like unto almonds, *with* a knop and a flower in one branch; and three bowls made like almonds in the other branch, *with* a knop and a flower: so in the six branches that come out of the candlestick. 34 And in the candlestick *shall be* four bowls made like unto almonds, *with* their knops and their flowers. 35 And *there shall be* a knop under two branches of the same, and a knop under two branches of the same, and a knop under two branches of the same, according to the six branches that proceed out of the candlestick. 36 Their knops and their branches shall be of the same: all it *shall be* one beaten work *of* pure gold. 37 And thou shalt make the seven lamps thereof: and they shall light the lamps thereof, that they may give light over against it. 38 And the tongs thereof, and the snuffdishes thereof, *shall be of* pure gold. 39 *Of* a talent of pure gold shall he make it, with all these vessels.

The Hebrew word translated candlestick in the KJV is *menorah*.

The golden lampstand had seven lamps. It was made of solid gold and was located on the south side of the room (Ex. 26:35). This was on the left side as the priest entered the holy place from the court. There was a central shaft with three branches coming out of each side with a lamp on the top of each. On each branch were three bowls made like almond leaves and flowers, and on the main shaft there were four of these bowls (Ex. 25:33-34).

Its dimensions are not given, but it was constructed with a talent of gold (about 125 troy pounds or 94 regular pounds, a troy pound having 12 ounces rather than 16 ounces) (Ex. 25:39).

The Golden Lampstand - © *SermonView*

The seven lamps were fueled by pure olive oil and were to be kept lit at all times.

> Exodus 27:20-21 And thou shalt command the children of Israel, that they bring thee pure oil olive beaten for the light, to cause the lamp to burn always. 21 In the tabernacle of the congregation without the vail, which *is* before the testimony, Aaron and his sons shall order it from evening to morning before the LORD: *it shall be* a statute for ever unto their generations on the behalf of the children of Israel.

> Leviticus 24:2-4 Command the children of Israel, that they bring unto thee pure oil olive beaten for the light, to cause the lamps to burn continually. 3 Without the vail of the testimony, in the tabernacle of the congregation, shall Aaron order it from the evening unto the morning before the LORD continually: *it shall be* a statute for ever in your

generations. 4 He shall order the lamps upon the pure candlestick before the LORD continually.

For a demonstration of an ancient olive oil lamp see the PowerPoint presentation "Bible Culture" in the *Bible Times and Ancient Kingdoms* course, which is available from Way of Life Literature.

1. The lampstand signifies Christ as the light of the world.

> John 8:12 Then spake Jesus again unto them, saying, I am the light of the world: he that followeth me shall not walk in darkness, but shall have the light of life.

Light signifies spiritual wisdom and understanding.

> Daniel 5:14 I have even heard of thee, that the spirit of the gods *is* in thee, and *that* light and understanding and excellent wisdom is found in thee.

The lampstand depicts Christ giving spiritual understanding to men through His Spirit and His Word.

> Psalms 119:105 Thy word *is* a lamp unto my feet, and a light unto my path.

> Psalms 119:130 The entrance of thy words giveth light; it giveth understanding unto the simple.

The lampstand's solid gold construction signifies Christ as the eternal Son of God.

There was no wood beneath the gold, because the Son of God has always been the Light of men even before His incarnation as a man. We see Him personified as Wisdom in Proverbs 8. He is the source of all wisdom.

> Proverbs 8:14-16 Counsel *is* mine, and sound wisdom: I *am* understanding; I have strength. 15 By me kings reign, and princes decree justice. 16 By me princes rule, and nobles, *even* all the judges of the earth.

It is God who gives wisdom unto the wise, and knowledge to them that know understanding (Dan. 2:20-21). Man's skill in designing and making things is from God (Ex. 31:3, 6).

The lampstand's gold also signifies the value of God's light and wisdom.

It is better than anything else in this life.

> Proverbs 8:11, 18-19 For wisdom *is* better than rubies; and all the things that may be desired are not to be compared to it. ... Riches and honour *are* with me; *yea*, durable riches and righteousness. 19 My fruit *is* better than gold, yea, than fine gold; and my revenue than choice silver.

The wisdom of God shows us where we came from and why we are here and where we are going. It explains salvation. It explains every mystery that needs to be explained. It is worth more than all of the world's gold and jewels.

I recall how I stumbled through this world in darkness before I was converted. I didn't know where I came from or where I was going. I didn't know who God was or what He was like. I read history books, but I didn't understand history. I saw the creation, but I didn't understand what I was seeing.

But in God's light, we see light (Psa. 36:9). Everything becomes clear as we walk in the light of Christ and His Word. We can rightly understand the light of creation and the light of conscience as we interpret these through the light of Scripture. We can rightly interpret the things we see in creation, and we can rightly weigh those things that are in our hearts.

We can see everything the unbeliever sees, but we can see so much more. I can visit a beautiful garden, for example, and enjoy the flowers and shrubs and trees as the unbeliever does, but I can enjoy so much more because I know the One who created these things. I understand that the very design of the creation testifies of Him, and I learn spiritual lessons from the creation to which the unbeliever is blind. In the creation, I see the very glory of God (Psa. 19:1).

What great light we have in the Scripture when it is opened to our understanding by the indwelling Christ! We have the light of origins in Genesis, the light of the mystery of suffering in Job, the light of practical living in Proverbs, the light of true philosophy in Ecclesiastes, the light of world history in Daniel, the light of the peerless Person of Christ in the Gospels, the light of the blessed gospel in Romans, the light of true Christian living in the Epistles, and the light of the future in Revelation. Every book of the Biblical Canon has its own particular light to shine into this dark world for those who have eyes to see.

The lampstand's sevenfold nature signifies the perfection of Christ's light.

There are no mistakes, no lies. God's Word is only truth and all truth.

> Proverbs 8:6-8 Hear; for I will speak of excellent things; and the opening of my lips *shall be* right things. 7 For my mouth shall speak truth; and wickedness *is* an abomination to my lips. 8 All the words of my mouth *are* in righteousness; *there is* nothing froward or perverse in them.

The bowls of flowering almonds represent Christ's resurrection glory (Ex. 25:33-35)

We see this in the almond branch of Numbers.

> Numbers 17:8 And it came to pass, that on the morrow Moses went into the tabernacle of witness; and, behold, the rod of Aaron for the house of Levi was budded, and brought forth buds, and bloomed blossoms, and yielded almonds.

Aaron's cut off branch lived and flowered and brought forth fruit. This depicts Christ's death and resurrection. Just as the flowering almond branch of Numbers 17 proved that Aaron was the divinely-chosen high priest, so Christ's resurrection marks Him as the Son of God.

> Romans 1:3-4 Concerning his Son Jesus Christ our Lord, which was made of the seed of David according to the

> flesh; 4 And declared *to be* the Son of God with power, according to the spirit of holiness, by the resurrection from the dead:

He shines His glorious resurrection light into the heart of every believer.

The lampstand's lights were intended to shine light first on the lampstand itself.

> Numbers 8:2 Speak unto Aaron, and say unto him, When thou lightest the lamps, the seven lamps shall give light over against the candlestick.

This teaches us that the main thing we need to see when we walk in God's light is Christ Himself. This is the chief objective of the Holy Spirit, signified by the oil.

> John 16:13-14 Howbeit when he, the Spirit of truth, is come, he will guide you into all truth: for he shall not speak of himself; but whatsoever he shall hear, *that* shall he speak: and he will shew you things to come. 14 He shall glorify me: for he shall receive of mine, and shall shew *it* unto you.

When we read the Bible, the main thing we should see is Christ. When we teach and preach the Bible, the main thing we should show the people is Christ.

The presence of the lampstand in the holy place and therefore only available for the priests, reminds us that the unbeliever does not have the light of life and thus does not understand the mysteries of life.

The unbeliever is spiritually blind.

> 1 Corinthians 2:14 But the natural man receiveth not the things of the Spirit of God: for they are foolishness unto him: neither can he know *them*, because they are spiritually discerned.

> 2 Corinthians 4:3-4 But if our gospel be hid, it is hid to them that are lost: 4 In whom the god of this world hath blinded the minds of them which believe not, lest the light

> of the glorious gospel of Christ, who is the image of God, should shine unto them.

Spiritual light comes only by Jesus Christ.

M.R. DeHaan, who was a medical doctor, said,

> "This explains why the Bible remains to a great degree a closed book to the most educated but unconverted man, while it is an open book to the most ignorant believers. This explains why a man may be educated and trained and hold all the theological degrees that all of the theological seminaries in the world can bestow upon him, and yet be utterly blind to the great spiritual revelations of the Word of God, while a poor, uneducated believer will see truths and revelations of infinite depth and glory in this Book of books."

I experienced this in my own life. Though I grew up in church and learned of the things of Christ from an early age, and though I won Sword Drills and Bible knowledge contests, and though I went through the motions of "believing in Christ" and being baptized at about age 11, I didn't understand the Bible until I was converted at age 23. Before that, it was merely an ancient, puzzling book containing strange stories that seemingly had nothing to do with my daily life.

I have witnessed this in our decades of missionary work in Nepal. I have taught the Bible and preached the gospel at the main university campus in Kathmandu, and the students and professors, though puffed up in their education, do not understand even the ABCs of God's Word until they believe, whereas, there are many humble believers in our churches who are illiterate but who understand the great mysteries of life and can receive spiritual truth from the Bible because of the light they have from the indwelling Holy Spirit.

The priest had to trim the wicks of the lamps each evening and morning with the golden tongs and snuffdishes.

> Exodus 25:38 And the tongs thereof, and the snuffdishes thereof, *shall be of* pure gold.

> Exodus 27:21 In the tabernacle of the congregation without the vail, which *is* before the testimony, Aaron and his sons shall order it from evening to morning before the LORD: *it shall be* a statute for ever unto their generations on the behalf of the children of Israel.

Likewise the believer must keep the light burning brightly in his life by such things as a daily time in God's Word and meditating in God's Word (Psa. 1:3), by faithfulness to a biblically-sound assembly to hear the preaching and teaching (Heb. 10:25), by crying out for wisdom (Prov. 2:3-5), by not trusting his own understanding but rather by seeking God's will in everything (Prov. 3:5-6), by asking for wisdom without doubting (Jam. 1:5-7), by not walking in sin and thereby grieving the Holy Spirit who is our Teacher (Eph. 4:30), and by not despising God's Word and thus quenching the Spirit (1 Th. 5:19-20).

The light of Christ grows dim when the believer backslides and his attention is turned toward himself and toward the world instead of toward Christ. This is what happened in Eli's day. The lamps were to be kept burning at all times, but Eli didn't keep them burning.

> 1 Samuel 3:3 And ere the lamp of God went out in the temple of the LORD, where the ark of God *was*, and Samuel was laid down *to sleep*;

Eli the high priest was backslidden and as a result the entire country was backslidden.

> 1 Samuel 3:1 And the child Samuel ministered unto the LORD before Eli. And the word of the LORD was precious in those days; *there was* no open vision.

> Judges 21:25 In those days *there was* no king in Israel: every man did *that which was* right in his own eyes.

If the lamp wicks in the tabernacle were not well maintained, the light would become dim. Even so, the careless believer can become backslidden and hardened so that he does not hear the Spirit's voice and his testimony becomes ruined. Peter warns that if the believer does not grow, he can become "blind, and cannot see afar off" and can even forget that he was purged from his old sins (2 Pet. 1:9). This does not mean he can lose his salvation. It means he becomes spiritually weak; he remains a spiritual baby.

If not properly maintained, the lamp wicks in the tabernacle would give off smoke and thus irritate the eyes of the priest. Likewise the believer who is backslidden can actually become discouraged with and offended at God's Word. Instead of a blessing, the Word of God can become an irritant. The backslidden believer can become frustrated with preachers and with the brethren who try to exhort him.

> Judges 21:25 In those days *there was* no king in Israel: every man did *that which was* right in his own eyes.

2. The lampstand also signifies believers today as the light of God to the nations.

> Matthew 5:14-16 Ye are the light of the world. A city that is set on an hill cannot be hid. 15 Neither do men light a candle, and put it under a bushel, but on a candlestick; and it giveth light unto all that are in the house. 16 Let your light so shine before men, that they may see your good works, and glorify your Father which is in heaven.

> Philippians 2:14-16 Do all things without murmurings and disputings: 15 That ye may be blameless and harmless, the sons of God, without rebuke, in the midst of a crooked and perverse nation, among whom ye shine as lights in the world; 16 Holding forth the word of life; that I may rejoice in the day of Christ, that I have not run in vain, neither laboured in vain.

These passages teach that to be effectual witnesses to the unsaved we must maintain a good testimony.

The testimony of Christians is often the opposite of "blameless and harmless." Consider the Catholic Church with its thieving, fornicating, murderous history. Closer to home, there are not a few Baptist churches whose pastors have stolen money or borrowed money and not paid it back or committed adultery with church members, etc., and thus brought reproach upon the name of Christ in the community.

We once had a church member who was evicted from her rented room because she didn't pay her bills, and as she was being thrown out she threatened the Hindu landlord with God's judgment because she was "mistreating one of the Lord's saints." The fact is that it was this backslidden professing Christian who was mistreating the unbelieving landlord by her wretched testimony, because she was a stumbling block to that landlord's salvation.

There have been times when I have gotten disgusted with the crazy drivers in Kathmandu and yelled at them for their mindless, reckless driving, but each time I have done that I realized that I am hurting my Christian testimony and that I can't yell at a driver and then try to witness to him for Christ!

One of the first jobs I got after I was converted was working at a printing company. There were two presses, one that I operated and one that was operated by another man. He claimed to be a Christian, but he put pictures of immodestly-clothed women in his work area. When I replaced his pictures with Bible verses, he got upset and removed the verses. His testimony was zero. If a believer has a poor testimony at work, he can't effectively witness to his boss or fellow workers, because they won't see past his hypocrisy. The same is true for one's family members. In order to witness effectively, we must maintain a blameless and harmless testimony before the world.

> Be a light for Jesus, brightly shine each day;"
> Radiate the Saviour, in the home, at play.

Others soon will see it, as you onward go;
Keep on burning brightly, with a steady glow.

Never let it flicker, never let it dim;
Trim your lamp for Jesus, let it shine for Him.
Shine on thru the darkness, precious in God's sight
Are His own dear children, walking in His light.

See Revelation 1 where the individual churches are depicted as golden candlesticks.

> Revelation 1:12-13, 20 And I turned to see the voice that spake with me. And being turned, I saw seven golden candlesticks; 13 And in the midst of the seven candlesticks one like unto the Son of man, clothed with a garment down to the foot, and girt about the paps with a golden girdle. ... The mystery of the seven stars which thou sawest in my right hand, and the seven golden candlesticks. The seven stars are the angels of the seven churches: and the seven candlesticks which thou sawest are the seven churches.

The churches are depicted as golden because the regenerated members are in Christ. They reflect Christ's own value before God. He is the gold, and we are in Him!

The churches are the Lord's witnesses in this dark world. Each church is the pillar and ground of the truth (1 Tim. 3:15). A pillar is a support. It holds something up. Likewise the churches are to lift up Christ before this fallen world. Every believer is an ambassador for Christ (2 Cor. 5:20).

We must preach the pure light and reject the corrupt light of false teaching and human philosophy.

The pure light is the inerrant, infallible, divinely-preserved Scripture.

The pure light is the true Jesus Christ as revealed in Scripture as opposed to "another christ." The biblical Christ is the eternal Son of God, the Creator of all things, the virgin born "God manifest in the flesh." He is sinless. He is the One who died to make atonement for man's sin, the One who rose from the dead and is seated at the right hand of God, the One who is coming again to judge the world and to rule and reign for ever. He is the sole mediator between God and man, the One who desires that all men be saved.

The pure light is the pure gospel (Gal. 1:6-8). The gospel that Paul preached is summarized in 1 Corinthians 15.

> 1 Corinthians 15:3-4 For I delivered unto you first of all that which I also received, how that Christ died for our sins according to the scriptures; 4 And that he was buried, and that he rose again the third day according to the scriptures:

It is a gospel of pure grace without admixture of works. It does not include baptism or sacraments or church membership. It is a gospel that promises eternal security because it is a gospel that was purchased entirely by Christ and offered to the sinner as a free gift. Thus the recipient of the true gospel can know that he has eternal life (1 John 5:11-13).

The pure light is uncorrupted doctrine (Titus 2:7).

> "As the light of the Candlestick was not the light of nature, but a light specially provided of God; as the light was fed and made possible only by the oil, and the oil is a symbol of the Holy Spirit, then the Church is not in the world to give the light of nature to men, but the light and truth that comes through the energy and revelation of the Spirit. The Church is not here to give instruction in the things of nature. The Church is not here to become a school, an academy, a college or a university of human knowledge. It is not the function of the Church to educate in the sciences, to deal in the philosophy and speculations of men; the Church is not called on to educate or culture the nature man in any direction. These things lie in the realm of human research and the light of applied reason. Just as the light of the Candlestick revealed what was hidden from the light of nature, even the wonders of the sanctuary, the symbols of redemption and glory, so the Church is to set

before men what the light of nature cannot reveal concerning these things.

"The Church is to set before men the things that are supremely worth knowing, and the knowledge of which makes for life eternal: The fact of God, His being and relationship to man, man's fall, his sin, the full meaning of death, the way of redemption through sacrificial death and blood, eternal life and immortality, the glorious ultimate of the earth when it shall be delivered from sin, sickness, sorrow and death, warning men that apart from the crucified, risen and ascended Son of God eternity holds neither life nor the hope of it, but only death and endless loss.

"The Church is to preach all this by and through the Holy Scriptures as the inspired, inerrant, infallible Word of God, and to preach it, proclaim it in the energy and demonstration of the Spirit. In short the Church is to give the light of God's revealed truth to the world" (I.M. Haldeman).

THE OIL

Exodus 27:20-21 And thou shalt command the children of Israel, that they bring thee pure oil olive beaten for the light, to cause the lamp to burn always. 21 In the tabernacle of the congregation without the vail, which *is* before the testimony, Aaron and his sons shall order it from evening to morning before the LORD: *it shall be* a statute for ever unto their generations on the behalf of the children of Israel.

The lamps were fueled by pure olive oil.

The oil represents the Holy Spirit (1 Sam. 16:13). It is the Holy Spirit who enables us to see Christ and to understand the Scripture. He is the "unction" and divine Teacher (1 John 2:20, 27). The indwelling Spirit is the difference between the saved man and the natural man (1 Cor. 2:12-16). The Holy Spirit shows the believer the mind of Christ in God's Word.

1. In the tabernacle the oil had to be replenished each day.

Likewise the believer must daily seek the Spirit's help and yield to His control. The believer receives the Holy Spirit when he trusts Christ as Lord and Saviour (Eph. 1:12-14), but the believer must walk in the Spirit (Eph. 5:16) and be filled with or controlled by the Spirit (Eph. 5:18).

The believer is sealed with the indwelling Spirit of God and is in no danger of losing the Spirit. He is sealed even if he sins and grieves the Spirit (Eph. 4:30). The believer never needs more of the Holy Spirit; he needs to surrender more to the Spirit's control.

When Mom was a girl, her family didn't have electricity so they used kerosene lamps. She loved to read and would often read late at night in the room she shared with her younger sister, Esther. If she was engrossed and read too long, the oil would run out and she would wake Esther up to go with her to the barn out back of the house to replenish the kerosene bowl, since she was afraid to go alone.

Thank the Lord that the oil supply in the Christian life is inexhaustible.

2. The five unwise virgins in Jesus' parable in Matthew 25:1-13 signify nominal Christians who are not born again and do not have the Holy Spirit. Paul said, "if any man have not the Spirit of Christ, he is none of his" (Rom. 8:9).

3. The oil was made by beating pure olive oil (Ex. 27:20).

This signifies the perfections of the Holy Spirit as God the Spirit. It also perhaps signifies the Holy Spirit's suffering, in that He is grieved with sin (Eph. 4:3; Isa. 63:10).

TABLE OF SHEWBREAD

Exodus 25:23-30 Thou shalt also make a table *of* shittim wood: two cubits *shall be* the length thereof, and a cubit the breadth thereof, and a cubit and a half the height thereof. 24 And thou shalt overlay it with pure gold, and make thereto a crown of gold round about. 25 And thou shalt make unto it a border of an hand breadth round about, and thou shalt make a golden crown to the border thereof round about. 26 And thou shalt make for it four rings of gold, and put the rings in the four corners that *are* on the four feet thereof. 27 Over against the border shall the rings be for places of the staves to bear the table. 28 And thou shalt make the staves *of* shittim wood, and overlay them with gold, that the table may be borne with them. 29 And thou shalt make the dishes thereof, and spoons thereof, and covers thereof, and bowls thereof, to cover withal: *of* pure gold shalt thou make them. 30 And thou shalt set upon the table shewbread before me alway.

Exodus 26:35 And thou shalt set the table without the vail, and the candlestick over against the table on the side of the tabernacle toward the south: and thou shalt put the table on the north side.

The table of shewbread was located on the north side of the room, which was on the right as the priest entered the holy place.

The table was made of wood covered with gold. It was two cubits (3 feet) long, a cubit (1.5 feet) wide, and a cubit and a half (2.25 feet) high. It had a double crown around the top (Ex. 25:24-25).

On the table were placed 12 loaves or cakes of bread in two rows of six each (Lev. 24:5-6). The Hebrew word "maharawkaw," translated "row," means "an arrangement; concretely, a pile." It could refer either to a row or a stack. Jewish tradition says that the loaves were stacked on each other, six to a stack. This is probable since the table was only 1.5 wide x 3 feet long and since each loaf was large. Each was made with two tenth deals or one-fifth of an ephah of flour (Lev. 24:5); since an ephah was 4.8 US gallons, one-fifth was about 3.8 quarts.

The Table of Shewbread - © GoodSalt

Frankincense was placed upon the bread for a memorial unto the Lord (Lev. 24:7).

The bread was replaced each sabbath (Lev. 24:8).

The priests ate the bread when they ministered in the holy place (Lev. 24:9).

The table of shewbread pictures Christ as the bread of life and the believer's communion with Him (Jn. 6:48, 58).

1. The gold-covered wooden table depicts Christ as the divine man who made the acceptable sacrifice so that He could become the mediator between God and man and so that man could fellowship with God.

2. The crown around the table depicts Christ as risen from the dead and seated in heaven at the right hand of God as King of kings.

3. The double crown (Ex. 25:24-25) depicts double authority and double safety. The crown kept the bread from falling off the table. Likewise the believer is perfectly safe in

Christ. We are in the hands of the Son and of the Father (John 10:28-29).

This is the only item in the tabernacle that is not measured in cubits. It is measured by the "hand breadth," which certainly reminds us of Christ's nail-scarred hand!

4. The bread depicts Christ as the Bread of Life.

The fine flour depicts Christ's holy life and "the consistency and uniformity of His character."

The flour was repeatedly sifted and blended together so there were no lumps or imperfections. Christ is perfect in every aspect of His character. As we see the Gospels, there are no flaws, no weaknesses, no imbalances. Christ is the New Man to whose image the believer is ordained to be conformed (Rom. 8:29).

The baking of the bread depicts Christ's suffering for us. He endured the fire of the cross.

The constant display of the bread in the tabernacle before the holy of holies signifies God the Father's continual pleasure with the Son.

The frankincense depicts that which is set apart exclusively to God (Lev. 24:7; 2:16). Only the Father knows the Son perfectly, and only the Father gets perfect pleasure from the Son (Mat. 11:27). Consider how Jesus faced the terrible cup of the wrath of God and was willing to drink it.

> Matthew 26:36-42 Then cometh Jesus with them unto a place called Gethsemane, and saith unto the disciples, Sit ye here, while I go and pray yonder. 37 And he took with him Peter and the two sons of Zebedee, and began to be sorrowful and very heavy. 38 Then saith he unto them, My soul is exceeding sorrowful, even unto death: tarry ye here, and watch with me. 39 And he went a little further, and fell on his face, and prayed, saying, O my Father, if it be possible, let this cup pass from me: nevertheless not as I will, but as thou *wilt*. 40 And he cometh unto the disciples,

and findeth them asleep, and saith unto Peter, What, could ye not watch with me one hour? 41 Watch and pray, that ye enter not into temptation: the spirit indeed *is* willing, but the flesh *is* weak. 42 He went away again the second time, and prayed, saying, O my Father, if this cup may not pass away from me, except I drink it, thy will be done.

I.M. Haldeman observes,

"Frankincense was a sweet gum. When fire was applied it gave forth a fragrance that pleased. That represents the attitude of the Son of God to the Father (John 4:34; 8:29). ... The more He was tried the more it was manifest that He sought to please the Father and fulfill His will. Behold Him there in the garden. ... 'If it be possible let this cup pass from me.' ... He sees the cup; He sees the dregs. He sees the bottom of it, the unspeakable horror and woe and hell and wordless anguish of the cross--all in that cup. And all His soul, and all the fire of the perfectness of hate against sin and shame in His soul cry out and throb in Him, till every essence of His perfect humanity revolts; and all He is of God and all the claims He has on the Father, and the assurance that should He press for it the Father who has always answered Him will answer Him now--all this drives in a sharp, stinging torment of justified pain--innocence, purity, holiness, sinlessness, flow upward like a tidal wave of demand to the very throne of God. If He let it roll on in prayer it must be answered and He must be delivered--the cup will be put aside. But listen to the most wonderful, 'nevertheless' that ever came from human lips. 'Nevertheless, not as I will, but as thou wilt.' Surely, there is frankincense in that!" (I.M. Haldeman)

The bread depicts the believer accepted by God in Christ.

1 Corinthians 10:16-17 The cup of blessing which we bless, is it not the communion of the blood of Christ? The bread which we break, is it not the communion of the body of Christ? 17 For we *being* many are one bread, *and* one body: for we are all partakers of that one bread.

> Ephesians 1:6 To the praise of the glory of his grace, wherein he hath made us accepted in the beloved.

The reason that the believer can be a sweet fragrance unto God is because he is clothed in Christ.

> "The shewbread sets forth Christ in the perfection of His person, and the frankincense upon them tells of His fragrance and sweet savor to God; but they also show Christ's people in Him, ever before God according to the value and fragrance of what the Lord is. They are not seen in what they are in themselves, which could not be a sweet savor to God, but as in Christ, and thus acceptable according to what He is before God. Thus in the twelve loaves we see not only the perfections of Christ, but of His people in Him" (Samuel Ridout, *Lectures on the Tabernacle*).

The eating of the bread by the priests depicts the saint becoming one with Christ by believing on Him (John 6:57-58) and then growing spiritually by walking in fellowship with Him (Mat. 11:29).

He invites every sinner to sup with Him (Rev. 3:20). We do this spiritually in this present life. Eating the bread means to abide in Christ through His Word.

> John 15:3-4 Now ye are clean through the word which I have spoken unto you. 4 Abide in me, and I in you. As the branch cannot bear fruit of itself, except it abide in the vine; no more can ye, except ye abide in me.

Jesus taught that man does not live by physical bread alone but by every word of God (Mat. 4:4). Eating the bread is Mary sitting at Jesus' feet to hear His Word (Lk.10:39). It is Paul counting his past life as garbage compared to the knowledge of Christ (Phil. 3:7-8).

We will sup with Christ literally in His kingdom (Mat. 26:29; Luke 22:29-30) and sup with Him forever in the New Jerusalem.

The bread had to be eaten regularly, meaning the believer cannot take his relationship with Christ for granted but must actively commune with him in prayer and Bible study and service.

The bread was always available and fresh.

> Leviticus 24:5-8 And thou shalt take fine flour, and bake twelve cakes thereof: two tenth deals shall be in one cake. 6 And thou shalt set them in two rows, six on a row, upon the pure table before the LORD. 7 And thou shalt put pure frankincense upon each row, that it may be on the bread for a memorial, even an offering made by fire unto the LORD. 8 Every sabbath he shall set it in order before the LORD continually, being taken from the children of Israel by an everlasting covenant.

The believer can be spiritually fed and refreshed at all times through Christ.

The bread was large, each loaf being made of about 3.8 quarts. This signifies the sufficiency of Christ to meet every need. He is the infinite, eternal Son of God, and He can feed every person who has ever lived. He is an inexhaustible supply of life.

The bread was of the highest quality ("fine flour," Lev. 24:5). This signifies that Christ is pure, and every Word of God that reveals Christ is pure (Prov. 30:5).

What a waste it is for a believer to spend his time feeding on the husks of this world--on vain novels and Hollywood and Nashville and human philosophy and psychology and success principles--when he could be feeding on the pure, unadulterated Bread of Christ!

INCENSE ALTAR

> Exodus 30:1-10 And thou shalt make an altar to burn incense upon: *of* shittim wood shalt thou make it. 2 A cubit *shall be* the length thereof, and a cubit the breadth thereof;

foursquare shall it be: and two cubits *shall be* the height thereof: the horns thereof *shall be* of the same. 3 And thou shalt overlay it with pure gold, the top thereof, and the sides thereof round about, and the horns thereof; and thou shalt make unto it a crown of gold round about. 4 And two golden rings shalt thou make to it under the crown of it, by the two corners thereof, upon the two sides of it shalt thou make *it*; and they shall be for places for the staves to bear it withal. 5 And thou shalt make the staves *of* shittim wood, and overlay them with gold. 6 And thou shalt put it before the vail that *is* by the ark of the testimony, before the mercy seat that *is* over the testimony, where I will meet with thee. 7 And Aaron shall burn thereon sweet incense every morning: when he dresseth the lamps, he shall burn incense upon it. 8 And when Aaron lighteth the lamps at even, he shall burn incense upon it, a perpetual incense before the LORD throughout your generations. 9 Ye shall offer no strange incense thereon, nor burnt sacrifice, nor meat offering; neither shall ye pour drink offering thereon. 10 And Aaron shall make an atonement upon the horns of it once in a year with the blood of the sin offering of atonements: once in the year shall he make atonement upon it throughout your generations: it *is* most holy unto the LORD.

Exodus 30:34-38 And the LORD said unto Moses, Take unto thee sweet spices, stacte, and onycha, and galbanum; *these* sweet spices with pure frankincense: of each shall there be a like *weight*: 35 And thou shalt make it a perfume, a confection after the art of the apothecary, tempered together, pure *and* holy: 36 And thou shalt beat *some* of it very small, and put of it before the testimony in the tabernacle of the congregation, where I will meet with thee: it shall be unto you most holy. 37 And *as for* the perfume which thou shalt make, ye shall not make to yourselves according to the composition thereof: it shall be unto thee holy for the LORD. 38 Whosoever shall make like unto that, to smell thereto, shall even be cut off from his people.

The High Priest and the Incense Altar - © GoodSalt

Leviticus 16:12 And he shall take a censer full of burning coals of fire from off the altar before the LORD, and his hands full of sweet incense beaten small, and bring *it* within the vail.

The incense altar stood in front of the veil leading into the holy of holies. Made of wood covered with gold, it was one cubit (1.5 feet) square and two cubits (3 feet) high. It had a crown around the top and horns at the corners.

The high priest burned incense on it every morning and evening (Ex. 30:7-8).

A special incense was burned on the altar which was not to be used for any other purpose (Ex. 30:34-38).

The incense was burned upon coals taken from the altar of sacrifice (Lev. 16:12).

Blood was applied to the altar once a year on the Day of Atonement (Ex. 30:10).

The incense altar pictures Christ's intercessory prayer for the believer.

1. The wood and gold of the altar depict Christ as the sinless, divine Man.

2. The horns of the incense altar represent Christ as having all authority in heaven and in earth (Mat. 28:18). As we saw on the study of the brazen altar, horns represent power (Psa. 75:4-5; 89:24; 91:10; 112:9). When Christ prays for His people, His prayers are have divine authority! Every word that Christ speaks is infallible and unbreakable.

3. The blood applied on the incense altar teaches that Christ is our intercessor on the basis of His blood atonement on the cross (Ex. 30:10).

The same teaching is seen in the fact that the coals on which the incense was burned came from the altar of sacrifice (Lev. 16:12). Christ had to suffer for our sins before He could intercede for us. He must be my Saviour before He can be my Intercessor.

> "The incessant service of intercession is the result of, and is grounded upon, the shedding of Christ's blood. It is

perpetuating the voice of that precious blood in God's presence, and it shelters those who have been atoned for by that blood under the full fragrance of Him that shed it. As the incense altar was established on the ground of the sprinkled blood on the Day of Atonement, so the Lord Jesus takes His place as the interceding High Priest, because He has fully answered for sin by the sacrifice of Himself. His death has met the wrath of God, and saved His people from all condemnation. ... His intercession covers every failure of which they may be guilty as the children of God, and continues on their great salvation in all its completeness until the very end--the day of their redemption; when they will stand in resurrection glory around the Lamb, and when their salvation in the fullest sense of the word will be perfected" (Henry Soltau, *The Tabernacle*).

4. The cloud of incense wafting up before the ark of the covenant depicts the fragrance of Christ before the Father.

The incense altar was "most holy unto the LORD" (Ex. 30:10). It depicts the acceptance of Christ by the Father. The Father is well pleased with and satisfied with Christ in His earthly life, in His death, and in His resurrection glory.

5. The incense was offered on the altar morning and evening as a perpetual thing (Ex. 30:7-8).

This signifies that Christ is always praying for His people. He is always available to hear our prayers and to help us. He is always available to forgive us when we sin. When we call heaven's throne room, we will never get a busy signal.

6. The meaning of Christ's intercession is explained in the following major Bible passages:

Christ's intercession means that He appears in the presence of God "for us," making us acceptable to God because of His one sacrifice.

Hebrews 9:24-26 For Christ is not entered into the holy places made with hands, *which are* the figures of the true;

but into heaven itself, now to appear in the presence of God for us: 25 Nor yet that he should offer himself often, as the high priest entereth into the holy place every year with blood of others; 26 For then must he often have suffered since the foundation of the world: but now once in the end of the world hath he appeared to put away sin by the sacrifice of himself.

Christ's intercession means that He continues the work of our salvation so that we will be saved to the uttermost.

Hebrews 7:25 Wherefore he is able also to save them to the uttermost that come unto God by him, seeing he ever liveth to make intercession for them.

We are saved by Christ's death, and we are saved by His resurrection life (Rom. 5:10). His intercession is a guarantee of eternal security.

Christ's intercession means that He is an advocate when we sin.

1 John 2:1-2 My little children, these things write I unto you, that ye sin not. And if any man sin, we have an advocate with the Father, Jesus Christ the righteous: 2 And he is the propitiation for our sins: and not for ours only, but also for *the sins of* the whole world.

Christ made the propitiation for our sins, and He is righteous in our place. The reason that we can confess our sins and be forgiven is Christ's intercessory work. Our confessions are acceptable only because Christ was punished for our sins. Thus God is just to forgive our sins.

Christ's intercession means that He does not allow Satan's charges against us to condemn us.

Romans 8:34-35 Who *is* he that condemneth? *It is* Christ that died, yea rather, that is risen again, who is even at the right hand of God, who also maketh intercession for us. 35 Who shall separate us from the love of Christ? *shall* tribulation, or distress, or persecution, or famine, or nakedness, or peril, or sword?

The accuser of the brethren is Satan (Rev. 12:10). But the only thing that Jesus need do to destroy the effect of his accusations is to raise His nail-pierced hand as a testimony to the fact that He died for those sins.

Christ's intercession means that He is working all things together for good according to His plan.

> Romans 8:28, 34 And we know that all things work together for good to them that love God, to them who are the called according to *his* purpose. ... Who *is* he that condemneth? *It is* Christ that died, yea rather, that is risen again, who is even at the right hand of God, who also maketh intercession for us.

Observe that Romans 8:28 is directly connected with Romans 8:34. All things work together in the believer's life for good because Christ is alive and is interceding for him. Every event of life is under His almighty control. There is no "happenstance," no "luck" in the believer's life.

> Proverbs 16:33 The lot is cast into the lap; but the whole disposing thereof *is* of the LORD.

When Ruth's "hap was to light on a part of the field belonging unto Boaz" (Ruth 2:3), that was only a "hap" from Ruth's perspective. She searched for a field in which to gather the "handfuls on purpose" that the reapers left behind according to God's law (Lev. 19:9-10), and she "happened" to choose the field of Boaz, and it "happened" to work out wonderfully well. But from God's perspective it was an eternal plan that He was working out in her life. Ruth had put her faith in Jehovah God, and He was working all things for good in her life according to His eternal purpose in Christ. Ruth became the wife of the wealthy, kind Boaz and became a great-grandmother of Jesus! In her wildest dreams, she could not have planned and secured such a thing.

Christ's intercession means that He is always available to provide mercy and grace to help.

> Hebrews 4:14-16 Seeing then that we have a great high priest, that is passed into the heavens, Jesus the Son of God, let us hold fast *our* profession. 15 For we have not an high priest which cannot be touched with the feeling of our infirmities; but was in all points tempted like as *we are, yet* without sin. 16 Let us therefore come boldly unto the throne of grace, that we may obtain mercy, and find grace to help in time of need.

He is the compassionate high priest who is touched with the feelings of our infirmities. He knows our frame and remembers that we are dust.

7. We have an example of Christ's intercession in Peter's life.

> Luke 22:31-32 And the Lord said, Simon, Simon, behold, Satan hath desired *to have* you, that he may sift *you* as wheat: 32 But I have prayed for thee, that thy faith fail not: and when thou art converted, strengthen thy brethren.

Christ did not keep Peter from the trial; He gave the devil permission to sift him. But He kept Peter in the trial and kept his faith intact and used the trial to strengthen him.

We see again that it is the devil who is the accuser of the brethren and against whom the Lord intercedes (Revelation 12:9-10).

Consider the case of Job.

> Job 1:6-11 Now there was a day when the sons of God came to present themselves before the LORD, and Satan came also among them. 7 And the LORD said unto Satan, Whence comest thou? Then Satan answered the LORD, and said, From going to and fro in the earth, and from walking up and down in it. 8 And the LORD said unto Satan, Hast thou considered my servant Job, that *there is* none like him in the earth, a perfect and an upright man, one that feareth God, and escheweth evil? 9 Then Satan answered the LORD, and said, Doth Job fear God for nought? 10 Hast not thou made an hedge about him, and

about his house, and about all that he hath on every side? thou hast blessed the work of his hands, and his substance is increased in the land. 11 But put forth thine hand now, and touch all that he hath, and he will curse thee to thy face.

Satan accused Job of serving God only because of God's blessings and predicted that if God removed the blessings, Job would curse God. The devil was allowed to sift Job in a terrible way by killing his children, destroying his riches, taking away his health, and turning his own wife and friends against him. Through this trial Job kept his faith and grew greatly in his understanding of and relationship with God, and at the end God blessed him with twice as much as he had before (Job 42:12). This is how God deals with His own and it shows the effectualness of Christ's intercession.

Those who draw back are those who do not believe to the saving of the soul.

Hebrews 10:38-39 Now the just shall live by faith: but if any man draw back, my soul shall have no pleasure in him. But we are not of them who draw back unto perdition; but of them that believe to the saving of the soul

They have "faith," but it is not saving faith. It is the "faith" of those described in John 2, which was faith in something other than Christ as only Lord and Saviour.

John 2:23-24 Now when he was in Jerusalem at the passover, in the feast *day*, many believed in his name, when they saw the miracles which he did. 24 But Jesus did not commit himself unto them, because he knew all *men*,

The main thing for which Christ intercedes is that the believer will keep his faith and that he will grow through every trial. This is why the true believer cannot lose his faith. It is impossible. He is upheld in Christ's almighty prayers. The believer's faith is attached to the one who has risen from the dead and is seated in heaven at the right hand of God. The believer's hope is called "an anchor of the soul, both sure and stedfast" (Heb. 6:19). This is not because his faith is almighty; it is because his faith is kept by Christ's almighty intercession, so the cord of faith is unbreakable! We are "kept by the power of God through faith" (1 Pet. 1:5).

The late Baptist pastor I.M. Haldeman comments as follows:

> "Again and again when the believer is on the edge where it seems the next step would make him slip, plunge and fall into the black abyss of unbelief, there comes as directly out of Heaven itself a touch of power that repudiates even the thought of doubt or question and gives him a vigor of faith such as he never dreamed ever could be his. Yonder at the throne He has seen our special need and prayed for us.
>
> "What an amazing fact it is, that He who is the Master of Heaven and earth prays for us--and prays in Heaven on the throne of the Highest. It may not be that He is praying for just the things we wish, nor even such we dream we need, but the fact that He is praying for us is beyond definition of all it demonstrates of interest in, of grace and care for us.
>
> "Believe He is praying for us, and what matter the cloud-covered sky, the tempest swirling and uprooting all things we hold dear, leaving us neither root nor branch in those things; what matter though we stand with hands folded, hands of helplessness, and the fragments of shattered plans scattered at our feet; what matter though our soul be filled with darkness and our lips be dumb and faith shivers and begins to grope and at times stops and listens to subtle questions filled with a hiss, the hiss of the serpent; what matter that at its worst if, through it all and at the last, we can believe, and will believe in spite of every increeping fear, that He is yonder back of storm or woe praying for us, interceding for us? To believe that, gives assurance He will meet us in the blessing such as never could have come had the answer been in response to our own poor, blind, unthinking and wholly selfish prayer.

"How often we escape sickness, disease, the assault of circumstance and sudden death because He has prayed, has interceded on our behalf and caused the special providences to be swung over us and along our path, we shall never know till the record of it is read to us when we stand face to face with Him in the glory hour.

"If there are times when faith would sink and sink as in the anguish of a drowning soul and then suddenly rises as on a swelling tide which lifts us out of the deeps of dark distress till we find firm footing on the shore of peace and rest again in His Word and truth, it is because He prays for us, because He neither slumbers nor sleeps nor closes His eyelids, but open-eyed and watchful bears us on His heart and lifts us in unfailing petition before the Father's throne" (I.M. Haldeman).

The incense altar also pictures the believer's prayers to God as accepted in Christ.

Psalms 141:2 Let my prayer be set forth before thee *as* incense; *and* the lifting up of my hands *as* the evening sacrifice.

Revelation 5:8 And when he had taken the book, the four beasts and four *and* twenty elders fell down before the Lamb, having every one of them harps, and golden vials full of odours, which are the prayers of saints.

1. The believer's prayers are a sweet savor unto God because we offer them in Christ's name.

In ourselves our prayers are not acceptable to God, but in Christ they are perfectly acceptable. We can only come to the Father through Christ (John 14:6). When we come in Christ, our prayers are accepted and are effectual to change things in this world (Rev. 8:3-5). We don't understand prayer, but we know that God wants His people to pray without ceasing, and in the incense altar we see that God accepts our prayers in Christ, that He is pleased with our prayers, and that He acts through them.

"William W. Walford was a blind English preacher of lowly birth. Although he did not possess a formal education, people called him 'the walking Bible' because of his ability to quote Scripture with great preciseness. Although he was unable to see the beauty of this world, the glories of heaven were opened to him through the privilege of prayer. Spending many sweet hours in the throne room of intercessory prayer, he was moved to pen these words in 1842:

Sweet hour of prayer, sweet hour of prayer
That calls me from a world of care,
And bids me at my Father's throne
Make all my wants and wishes known.

In seasons of distress and grief,
My soul has often found relief,
And oft escaped the tempter's snare,
By thy return, sweet hour of prayer" (David Levy, *The Tabernacle*).

2. The blood sprinkled on the incense altar reminds us that we cannot pray acceptably except through the blood of Christ.

Speaking the words "in Jesus' name" at the end of a prayer is not a mere religious ritual. It is an acknowledgement of the fact that sinners can only approach God acceptably through Jesus Christ and on the basis of His cross work.

I.M. Haldeman observed,

"Our Lord as High priest, not only lifts up His prayers in our behalf, but takes our own prayers and presents them like incense before the Father's throne. Scripture gives us a very dramatic illustration how He does this. As it is written: 'And another angel came and stood at the altar, (the altar of incense shown in heaven) having a golden censer; and there was given unto him much incense, that he should offer it with the prayers of all saints upon the golden altar which was before the throne' (Revelation 8:3). What a picture that is. Like that angel the Lord takes the prayers of the believer and presents them before God in the fragrance of His high priestly character and on the basis of His perfect sacrifice. Without His intercession not a single petition of ours would ever ascend to the Court of Heaven. No prayer of ours would ever reach the Father. He says so, 'No man cometh unto the Father, but by me' (John 14:6)."

3. The incense burning morning and evening (Ex. 30:7-8) reminds us that the believer-priest should pray without ceasing.

Persistence is an essential aspect of effectual prayer.

> Luke 18:1 And he spake a parable unto them *to this end*, that men ought always to pray, and not to faint;
>
> Romans 12:12 Rejoicing in hope; patient in tribulation; continuing instant in prayer;
>
> Ephesians 6:18 Praying always with all prayer and supplication in the Spirit, and watching thereunto with all perseverance and supplication for all saints;
>
> 1 Thessalonians 5:17 Pray without ceasing.
>
> Colossians 4:2 Continue in prayer, and watch in the same with thanksgiving.
>
> 1 Peter 4:7 But the end of all things is at hand: be ye therefore sober, and watch unto prayer.

4. The incense altar was the central object in the tabernacle, signifying that prayer is the central act of worship.

This is particularly true of thanksgiving prayer and intercessory prayer. Why is offering praise called a sacrifice in Hebrews 13:15? It is because praise is contrary to our old, selfish, unthankful nature.

According to Romans 1:21, unthankfulness was a characteristic of human nature from the beginning of the fall, and 2 Timothy 3:1-2 says that unthankfulness is a major characteristic of end-time apostasy.

When the believer offers praise to God, he is denying his old nature and his old ways and is walking in the way of Christ, the New Man.

> Matthew 11:25 At that time Jesus answered and said, I thank thee, O Father, Lord of heaven and earth, because thou hast hid these things from the wise and prudent, and hast revealed them unto babes.
>
> Matthew 15:36 And he took the seven loaves and the fishes, and gave thanks, and brake *them*, and gave to his disciples, and the disciples to the multitude.
>
> Matthew 26:27 And he took the cup, and gave thanks, and gave *it* to them, saying, Drink ye all of it;
>
> John 11:41 Then they took away the stone *from the place* where the dead was laid. And Jesus lifted up *his* eyes, and said, Father, I thank thee that thou hast heard me.

To pray for others (1 Tim. 2:1) is to forget about one's selfish interests. To pray for others is to die to self, which is a fundamental part of fruitful, God-pleasing Christian living.

5. The incense burned on the altar was to be holy according to the recipe given by God (Ex. 30:8-9, 37-38).

Likewise our worship of God must be pure according to His Word. We cannot offer to God any worship that is mixed with the things of the world. There must be no strange incense, no strange oil (Ex. 30:31-32), no strange fire (Lev. 10:1-2).

God requires worship in truth (John 4:24). There must be no intermingling of error. This condemns every form of apostate Christianity such as Roman Catholicism, which is a mixture of truth and error. It condemns the papacy, a special priesthood, infant baptism, the mass, prayers to the dead, the intercession of Mary, the veneration of relics. It condemns contemporary worship, which is an unholy mixture of Christ and the world. It condemns contemplative prayer with its roots in pagan mysticism and Roman Catholic monasticism.

The Holy of Holies

The holy of holies was a perfect cube 10 cubits (15 feet) long and wide and high. Sometimes the holy of holies is called the holy place (Heb. 9:25). It was here that the presence of God dwelt (Ex. 25:21-22; Lev. 16:2).

THE VEIL INTO THE HOLY OF HOLIES

> Exodus 26:31-33 And thou shalt make a vail *of* blue, and purple, and scarlet, and fine twined linen of cunning work: with cherubims shall it be made: 32 And thou shalt hang it upon four pillars of shittim *wood* overlaid with gold: their hooks *shall be of* gold, upon the four sockets of silver. 33 And thou shalt hang up the vail under the taches, that thou mayest bring in thither within the vail the ark of the testimony: and the vail shall divide unto you between the holy *place* and the most holy.

The veil between the holy place and the holy of holies was made with fine linen interwoven with blue, purple, and scarlet thread, and engraved with the images of the cherubims.

The veil was held up by four pillars of wood overlaid with gold and fitted into silver sockets, and it hung from silver hooks. There were no chapiters or capitals on the pillars as there were with the pillars surrounding the court (which had silver chapiters, Ex. 38:17) or the pillars that upheld the curtain into the holy place (which had golden chapiters, Ex. 36:38).

1. The veil's composition of fine linen interwoven with blue, purple, and scarlet thread (Ex. 26:31-33) depicts Christ as the sinless God-Man, the Lord from heaven, the King of kings, and the Saviour, as we have seen.

2. This veil signified that the way into the presence of God was not yet open because Christ had not yet died.

The cherubims that were woven into the veil portray the cherubims that guard the holy presence of God.

> Genesis 3:24 So he drove out the man; and he placed at the east of the garden of Eden Cherubims, and a flaming sword which turned every way, to keep the way of the tree of life.

When Christ died, the veil in the temple was torn into two parts. Matthew emphasizes the fact of this event by saying, "BEHOLD, the veil of the temple was rent in twain from the top to the bottom" (Mat. 27:51)

The Rent Veil of the TEMPLE - *© GoodSalt*

He draws the reader's attention to the event. He wants us to meditate on this.

Jewish tradition says that the veil in Herod's Temple was as thick as a man's hand when measured across the palm.

By the tearing of the veil, God was saying that the way into His very presence was open for those who put their faith in Christ.

> Hebrews 10:19-20 Having therefore, brethren, boldness to enter into the holiest by the blood of Jesus, 20 By a new and living way, which he hath consecrated for us, through the veil, that is to say, his flesh;

3. The pillars on which the veil hung, made of wood covered with gold, depict Christ's humanity and deity as revealed in the Four Gospels.

They rested in silver sockets, depicting Christ's atonement.

The pillars had no capitals, perhaps depicting Christ being "cut off but not for himself" as described in Daniel 9:26. Compared with the other pillars of the tabernacle, these alone do not have capitals. Something seems to be missing. There appears to be a blemish in the design, but it is not a blemish. The missing capitals point to Christ's wounds which are a permanent reminder of His death on the cross (John 20:2). Just as the seemingly blemished pillars could be observed in the holy place, so Christ's wounds can be seen today in the holy place in heaven.

THE ARK OF THE COVENANT

> Exodus 25:10-16 And they shall make an ark *of* shittim wood: two cubits and a half *shall be* the length thereof, and a cubit and a half the breadth thereof, and a cubit and a half the height thereof. 11 And thou shalt overlay it with pure gold, within and without shalt thou overlay it, and shalt make upon it a crown of gold round about. 12 And thou shalt cast four rings of gold for it, and put *them* in the four corners thereof; and two rings *shall be* in the one side of it, and two rings in the other side of it. 13 And thou shalt make staves *of* shittim wood, and overlay them with gold. 14 And thou shalt put the staves into the rings by the sides of the ark, that the ark may be borne with them. 15 The staves shall be in the rings of the ark: they shall not be taken from it. 16 And thou shalt put into the ark the testimony which I shall give thee.

> Hebrews 9:3-4 And after the second veil, the tabernacle which is called the Holiest of all; 4 Which had the golden censer, and the ark of the covenant overlaid round about with gold, wherein *was* the golden pot that had manna, and Aaron's rod that budded, and the tables of the covenant;

The holy of holies contained the ark of the covenant. This was a rectangular box 2.5 cubits (3.75 feet) long, 1.5 cubits (2.25 feet) wide, and 1.5 cubits (2.25 feet) high (Ex. 25:10-15). It was made of wood covered with gold inside and out, and it had a crown of gold around the top.

It contained the Ten Commandments written on stone called the testimony (Ex. 25:16, 21; 31:18; 34:29; De. 5:5-22).

It also contained a gold pot filled with manna and Aaron's rod that budded (Heb. 9:4). By the time that the ark was placed in Solomon's Temple, these items had disappeared (1 Ki. 8:9).

The Ark of the Covenant

1. The ark containing the Ten Commandments represents Christ bearing the law of God in His heart and in His very being as the holy, sinless Son of God.

> Psalms 40:6-8 Sacrifice and offering thou didst not desire; mine ears hast thou opened: burnt offering and sin offering hast thou not required. 7 Then said I, Lo, I come: in the volume of the book *it is* written of me, 8 I delight to do thy will, O my God: yea, thy law *is* within my heart.

"He was born under the law, circumcised the eighth day according to the law. He kept the law perfectly, perfectly toward God and perfectly toward man. He loved God with all His mind and heart and soul and strength. He was full of the atmosphere of God. Every deed He did He did to glorify Him. Every word He spoke He uttered that He might exalt Him. His very breath distilled the idea of God, and the particular idea and concept of Him as the Father. ... If He loved God with all His being, He loved His neighbor as Himself. ... He was perfect in all the requirements of the law.

In keeping the law He proved He was sinless" (I.M. Haldeman).

2. The crown around the ark depicts Christ as King (Ex. 25:11).

He was born as a king (Mat. 2:2), rode into Jerusalem as a king (John 12:13-15), was crucified as a king (John 19:19), rose as King of kings (1 Tim. 6:15), and will return as King of kings and Lord of lords (Rev. 19:16).

3. Inside the ark with the tables of the ten commandments were the gold pot of manna and Aaron's rod that budded (Heb. 9:4).

The manna pictures Christ as the bread of life which provides eternal life to those who eat it.

Aaron's rod that budded and flowered pictures Christ becoming man, dying, rising from the dead, and being the source of eternal blessing and glory to His people.

THE MERCY SEAT

> Exodus 25:17-22 And thou shalt make a mercy seat *of* pure gold: two cubits and a half *shall be* the length thereof, and a cubit and a half the breadth thereof. 18 And thou shalt make two cherubims *of* gold, *of* beaten work shalt thou make them, in the two ends of the mercy seat. 19 And make one cherub on the one end, and the other cherub on the other end: *even* of the mercy seat shall ye make the cherubims on the two ends thereof. 20 And the cherubims shall stretch forth *their* wings on high, covering the mercy seat with their wings, and their faces *shall look* one to another; toward the mercy seat shall the faces of the cherubims be. 21 And thou shalt put the mercy seat above upon the ark; and in the ark thou shalt put the testimony that I shall give thee. 22 And there I will meet with thee, and I will commune with thee from above the mercy seat, from between the two cherubims which *are* upon the ark

of the testimony, of all *things* which I will give thee in commandment unto the children of Israel.

The ark was covered with a lid called the mercy seat made of solid gold. This is where God's presence dwelt. His glory entered there when the tabernacle was first set up (Ex. 40:33-35). No one went into the holy of holies except the high priest once a year to make atonement by sprinkling the blood on the mercy seat.

Hebrews 9:7 But into the second *went* the high priest alone once every year, not without blood, which he offered for himself, and *for* the errors of the people:

Leviticus 16:11-17 And Aaron shall bring the bullock of the sin offering, which *is* for himself, and shall make an atonement for himself, and for his house, and shall kill the bullock of the sin offering which *is* for himself: 12 And he shall take a censer full of burning coals of fire from off the altar before the LORD, and his hands full of sweet incense beaten small, and bring *it* within the vail: 13 And he shall put the incense upon the fire before the LORD, that the cloud of the incense may cover the mercy seat that *is* upon the testimony, that he die not: 14 And he shall take of the blood of the bullock, and sprinkle *it* with his finger upon the mercy seat eastward; and before the mercy seat shall he sprinkle of the blood with his finger seven times. 15 Then shall he kill the goat of the sin offering, that *is* for the people, and bring his blood within the vail, and do with that blood as he did with the blood of the bullock, and sprinkle it upon the mercy seat, and before the mercy seat: 16 And he shall make an atonement for the holy *place*, because of the uncleanness of the children of Israel, and because of their transgressions in all their sins: and so shall he do for the tabernacle of the congregation, that remaineth among them in the midst of their uncleanness. 17 And there shall be no man in the tabernacle of the congregation when he goeth in to make an atonement in the holy *place*, until he come out, and have made an atonement for himself, and for his household, and for all the congregation of Israel.

1. The fact that the mercy seat perfectly fit the ark and fully covered the law contained therein depicts the completeness of Christ's atonement.

Hebrews 10:10 By the which will we are sanctified through the offering of the body of Jesus Christ once *for all.*

Hebrews 10:14 For by one offering he hath perfected for ever them that are sanctified.

In every generation since the days of the apostles, false teachers have been troubling the churches with the idea that to be right with God one must have faith in Christ PLUS obedience, sacraments, ordinances, etc. The wonderful presence of the mercy seat covering the ark of testimony reminds us that the grace of Christ ALONE and faith in His blood ALONE is sufficient for salvation. Obedience is important, but obedience *follows* salvation and is not mixed up together with salvation.

Ephesians 2:8-10 For by grace are ye saved through faith; and that not of yourselves: *it is* the gift of God: 9 Not of works, lest any man should boast. 10 For we are his workmanship, created in Christ Jesus unto good works, which God hath before ordained that we should walk in them.

The believer's good works add nothing to his eternal salvation. Good works are the fruit of and evidence of salvation. To mix any works with grace destroys grace so that it is no longer grace.

Romans 11:6 And if by grace, then *is it* no more of works: otherwise grace is no more grace. But if *it be* of works, then is it no more grace: otherwise work is no more work.

If I purchase a gift for someone and offer it to him and he pays anything at all in exchange for it, it is no longer a gift.

2. The mercy seat was sprinkled with blood on the Day of Atonement (Heb. 9:7; Lev. 16:11-16), signifying that the cross-work of Christ satisfies the demands of God's holy law and reconciles sinners to God.

> Hebrews 9:7 But into the second *went* the high priest alone once every year, not without blood, which he offered for himself, and *for* the errors of the people:

The Greek word translated "mercy seat" in Hebrews 9:5 is translated "propitiation" in Romans 3:25. It means a covering or a satisfaction of a debt. Jesus Christ wholly satisfied the demands of God's law.

THE CHERUBIMS

> Exodus 25:18-20 And thou shalt make two cherubims *of* gold, *of* beaten work shalt thou make them, in the two ends of the mercy seat. 19 And make one cherub on the one end, and the other cherub on the other end: *even* of the mercy seat shall ye make the cherubims on the two ends thereof. 20 And the cherubims shall stretch forth *their* wings on high, covering the mercy seat with their wings, and their faces *shall look* one to another; toward the mercy seat shall the faces of the cherubims be.

On the mercy seat were carvings of cherubims facing inward with their wings covering the seat.

1. The cherubims are highly placed angelic or living creatures who are associated with God's throne.

Cherubims have the general appearance of a man but have four faces: that of a lion, an ox, an eagle, and a man.

> Ezekiel 1:10 As for the likeness of their faces, they four had the face of a man, and the face of a lion, on the right side: and they four had the face of an ox on the left side; they four also had the face of an eagle.

We don't know if all four faces were depicted in the tabernacle. In the millennial temple, the image of the cherubims will appear between the image of palm trees and only two faces are mentioned: that of a man and a lion.

> Ezekiel 41:18-19 And *it was* made with cherubims and palm trees, so that a palm tree *was* between a cherub and a cherub; and *every* cherub had two faces; 19 So that the face of a man *was* toward the palm tree on the one side, and the face of a young lion toward the palm tree on the other side: *it was* made through all the house round about.

Cherubs have four wings joined to one another and by which they fly in a straight line (Eze. 1:6, 9, 12; 10:11). Their wings make a great noise, like the noise of great waters or a great host.

> Ezekiel 1:6, 9, 12 And every one had four faces, and every one had four wings. ... 9 Their wings *were* joined one to another; they turned not when they went; they went every one straight forward. ... 12 And they went every one straight forward: whither the spirit was to go, they went; *and* they turned not when they went.

> Ezekiel 10:11 When they went, they went upon their four sides; they turned not as they went, but to the place whither the head looked they followed it; they turned not as they went.

> Ezekiel 1:24 And when they went, I heard the noise of their wings, like the noise of great waters, as the voice of the Almighty, the voice of speech, as the noise of an host: when they stood, they let down their wings.

Their appearance is like burning coals of bright fire, with lightning emitting from the fire.

> Ezekiel 1:13 As for the likeness of the living creatures, their appearance *was* like burning coals of fire, *and* like the appearance of lamps: it went up and down among the living creatures; and the fire was bright, and out of the fire went forth lightning.

They move quickly like a flash of lightning.

> Ezekiel 1:14 And the living creatures ran and returned as the appearance of a flash of lightning.

It appears that the throne of God is transported by the cherubims.

> Ezekiel 1:22, 25-28 And the likeness of the firmament upon the heads of the living creature *was* as the colour of the terrible crystal, stretched forth over their heads above. ... 25 And there was a voice from the firmament that *was* over their heads, when they stood, *and* had let down their wings. And above the firmament that was over their heads was the likeness of a throne, as the appearance of a sapphire stone: and upon the likeness of the throne was the likeness as the appearance of a man above upon it. And I saw as the colour of amber, as the appearance of fire round about within it, from the appearance of his loins even upward, and from the appearance of his loins even downward, I saw as it were the appearance of fire, and it had brightness round about. As the appearance of the bow that is in the cloud in the day of rain, so was the appearance of the brightness round about This was the appearance of the likeness of the glory of the LORD...

> Ezekiel 10:18-19 Then the glory of the LORD departed from off the threshold of the house, and stood over the cherubims. 19 And the cherubims lifted up their wings, and mounted up from the earth in my sight: when they went out, the wheels also *were* beside them, and *every one* stood at the door of the east gate of the LORD'S house; and the glory of the God of Israel *was* over them above.

David was instructed to make "the chariot of the cherubims" for Solomon's Temple (1 Ch. 28:18). Psalm 18:10 says Jehovah rides upon a cherubim.

2. In the tabernacle, the cherubims' wings covered the ark (Ex. 25:18-20), signifying that they cover or perhaps guard the holy presence of God.

3. The cherubims looked toward the mercy seat ("their faces shall look one to another, toward the mercy seat," Ex. 25:20).

Thus they were looking at the blood that was applied there by the high priest on the Day of Atonement (Lev. 16:15).

After Adam's fall the cherubims guarded the way to the tree of life and kept sinners out of God's presence (Ge. 3:24). Now the cherubims know that God's holy law is propitiated by Christ's blood and sinners are welcome to come to God through repentance and faith. As they adore the Almighty Creator, they doubtless meditate on these amazing truths which reveal His character. The incarnation, atonement, and resurrection have revealed God in a way that the angels could not have dreamed before the world began. They desire to look into these things.

> 1 Peter 1:12 Unto whom it was revealed, that not unto themselves, but unto us they did minister the things, which are now reported unto you by them that have preached the gospel unto you with the Holy Ghost sent down from heaven; which things the angels desire to look into.

Samuel Ridout comments:

> "They had been associated with the promulgation of the law amid the thick darkness, lightnings and thunderings of Sinai, ready to take vengeance for 'every transgression and disobedience.' But it is the blood upon the mercy seat that fixes the gaze of these ministers of justice and judgment--the blood of the sacrifice sprinkled there on the great Day of Atonement (Lev. 16:14). The blood speaks of judgment already visited upon the Substitute, and it arrests the adoring gaze of these holy servants of God. Instead of flying with the speed of the wind or like the lightning flash upon the enemies of God, they bend with adoring worship upon that which speaks of 'righteousness and peace having kissed each other' (Psa. 85: 10). And well may the angels gaze upon that Sacrifice! There every attribute of God's character shines forth: His righteousness, for He has meted

> out the full penalty for man's sin; His love, for here is His gift to a lost world; His wisdom, for none but God could have devised the wondrous plan" (Samuel Ridout, *Lectures on the Tabernacle*).

4. Satan apparently was the head cherubim. In Ezekiel 28:12-16 Satan is described as the power behind the ancient king of Tyre, and he is called the "anointed cherub" and the "covering cherub" (verses 14, 16). He was "perfect in beauty."

What Was Not in the Tabernacle

It is instructive to think about what *wasn't* in the tabernacle.

No Chair

This reminds us that the work of the Levitical priests was never finished. Those sacrifices could not bring salvation; they only pointed to the salvation that would come by Christ. Salvation wasn't complete until Jesus cried from the cross, "It is finished" just before He surrendered His spirit in death (John 19:30).

> Hebrews 10:11-12 And every priest standeth daily ministering and offering oftentimes the same sacrifices, which can never take away sins: 12 But this man, after he had offered one sacrifice for sins for ever, sat down on the right hand of God.

The fact that there was no chair in the tabernacle also reminds us that the believer-priest should always be busy in the service of the Lord.

> 1 Corinthians 15:58 Therefore, my beloved brethren, be ye stedfast, unmoveable, always abounding in the work of the Lord, forasmuch as ye know that your labour is not in vain in the Lord.

Life is too short to be lazy or to retire from the Lord's business. Slumber produces both physical and spiritual poverty.

> Proverbs 24:33-34 *Yet* a little sleep, a little slumber, a little folding of the hands to sleep: 34 So shall thy poverty come *as* one that travelleth; and thy want as an armed man.

> 1 Thessalonians 5:6-8 Therefore let us not sleep, as *do* others; but let us watch and be sober. 7 For they that sleep sleep in the night; and they that be drunken are drunken in the night. 8 But let us, who are of the day, be sober, putting

on the breastplate of faith and love; and for an helmet, the hope of salvation.

The fact that there was no chair in the tabernacle also reminds us that the believer needs to be always ready for the Lord's return.

The priests had to be ready at a moment's notice to pack up the tabernacle and to take their journey at the trumpet sound.

The imminent return of Christ is a major teaching of the New Testament. True Christianity is to turn to Christ from idols (repentance and faith) to serve Christ in this present world, ever watching for His return.

> 1 Thessalonians 1:9-10 For they themselves shew of us what manner of entering in we had unto you, and how ye turned to God from idols to serve the living and true God; 10 And to wait for his Son from heaven, whom he raised from the dead, *even* Jesus, which delivered us from the wrath to come.

No floor

The floor of the tabernacle was the dirt of the bare ground.

> Numbers 5:17 And the priest shall take holy water in an earthen vessel; and of the dust that is in the floor of the tabernacle the priest shall take, and put *it* into the water:

The priests in the holy place were surrounded by symbols of the resurrection glory of Christ, but their feet were still in this world.

This is a picture of the Christian life. The believer is seated in heavenly places with Christ (Eph. 2:6), but he is still in this fallen world. The believer has put off the old man and put on the new man positionally (Col. 3:9-10), but the old man is still present and must be put off in practice each day (Eph. 4:22-24). The believer has been delivered from Satan's power and translated into Christ's kingdom (Col. 1:13), but he still lives in the world over which Satan is the prince (Eph. 2:2) and he must still put on the whole armor of God to stand against the devil (Eph. 6:11). The believer has eternal redemption, but he presently lives in a fallen world and groans to be delivered from corruption (Rom. 8:22-23). The believer is not in the flesh but in the Spirit (Rom. 8:9), but the flesh is still present and if we do not walk in the Spirit we fulfill the lusts of the flesh (Gal. 5:16-17). For the believer, the body is dead and the Spirit is life (Rom. 8:10), but the body is also still alive and is called "the body of this death" (Rom. 7:14). The believer has eternal rest (Heb. 4:10), but he is also in the most severe spiritual warfare (Eph. 6:10-18).

> "The heavens have been opened over our head. We worship and hold converse with God in the highest glory. And yet our members are here upon this earth; and we walk in the midst of a groaning creation, in a world defaced by sin; marred by the presence and power of death; still lying under the curse, and traversed as to its whole length and breadth, by the serpent's path. ... No wonder the Lord's people have such strange and mingled experiences. In one sense, they are already raised with Christ: in another, they yet expect the resurrection. ... Such are the experiences of the people of God, during the present dispensation, whilst the tabernacle of glory is connected with the wilderness path" (Henry Soltau, *The Tabernacle the Priesthood and the Offerings*).

The fact that there was no floor in the tabernacle exposes the error of monasticism. God has not instructed His people to hide from the world or isolate themselves from the world. It is tempting to buy a farm somewhere and to avoid most contact with the world, but this is exactly the opposite of what Christ has commanded (Matthew 28:19-20; Mark 16:15).

We are to follow Jesus' example. He mingled with the sinners of this world in order to save them. He was called a friend of sinners, but He didn't sin with sinners. Paul taught that we are not to go out of the world by breaking off all association with sinners.

> 1 Corinthians 5:9-10 I wrote unto you in an epistle not to company with fornicators: 10 Yet not altogether with the fornicators of this world, or with the covetous, or extortioners, or with idolaters; for then must ye needs go out of the world.

In contrast to the tabernacle, Solomon's Temple had a floor of gold (1 Ki. 6:30). This points to the eternal reign of Christ. Then His people will dwell in immortal bodies, with no indwelling sin and no possibility of contamination. There will be glory within and glory without! The very streets of the New Jerusalem are paved with gold (Rev. 21:21).

No window

There was no natural light in the tabernacle. Once the priest entered the holy place to worship and to perform his service to the Lord, the curtain of the door fell back into place and he was dependent on the lampstand for light.

Likewise in the service of Christ, the believer is dependent on the Holy Spirit and God's Word and is not allowed to mingle therein the philosophy of this world. We are to delight in the law of the Lord and reject the counsel of the ungodly (Psa. 1:1-2). We are to beware of the philosophy and tradition of men (Col. 2:8).

Theological liberals and the evangelicals who are influenced by them, for example, commit a great error when they try to interpret Genesis 1-3 by the principles of Darwinian evolution, Genesis 6-8 by ancient Babylonian fables, the Mosaic worship system by ancient paganism, and the New Testament by Gnosticism.

Just as the priest was dependent on the oil in the lamps to produce light, the believer is dependent on the Holy Spirit for enlightenment. Only by the Spirit can we rightly interpret the

Bible. We must cast ourselves upon Him for help. He has promised to help and has promised to lead us into truth if we have obedient hearts and continue in God's Word.

> John 7:17 If any man will do his will, he shall know of the doctrine, whether it be of God, or *whether* I speak of myself.

> John 8:31-32 Then said Jesus to those Jews which believed on him, If ye continue in my word, *then* are ye my disciples indeed; 32 And ye shall know the truth, and the truth shall make you free.

Knowing that we are dependent on the Holy Spirit, we must lean not to our own understanding (Prov. 3:5-6). Rather, we must seek wisdom as men seek after silver and cry out for wisdom, which refers to a single-minded passion for truth. Then we will find wisdom.

> Proverbs 2:1-9 My son, if thou wilt receive my words, and hide my commandments with thee; 2 So that thou incline thine ear unto wisdom, *and* apply thine heart to understanding; 3 Yea, if thou criest after knowledge, *and* liftest up thy voice for understanding; 4 If thou seekest her as silver, and searchest for her as *for* hid treasures; 5 Then shalt thou understand the fear of the LORD, and find the knowledge of God. 6 For the LORD giveth wisdom: out of his mouth *cometh* knowledge and understanding. 7 He layeth up sound wisdom for the righteous: *he is* a buckler to them that walk uprightly. 8 He keepeth the paths of judgment, and preserveth the way of his saints. 9 Then shalt thou understand righteousness, and judgment, and equity; *yea*, every good path.

No party band, no comedians, no leeks and melons

The worship of the Lord as presented in Scripture is noted by simplicity and solemnity and holiness and complete separation from the world. There is nothing to please unregenerate man, nothing that appeals to the flesh, nothing patterned after the world.

How different this is from contemporary worship with its party atmosphere and its many elements borrowed directly from the filthy world of secular rock to make it "seeker friendly."

I think of the National Pastors' Conference in San Diego, California, I attended with media credentials in 2009. Sponsored by Zondervan and InterVarsity Press, two of the largest and most influential "evangelical" Christian publishers, and featuring some of the most popular evangelical leaders, it featured ear-splitting rock & roll "worship" complete with smoke and lights and stand-up comedy routines. (See the free eBook *The Emerging Church Is Coming* for a report on this conference, available from www.wayoflife.org.)

The mixed multitude in contemporary churches, which are composed of true saints, "nominal" unregenerate Christians, and out-and-out unbelievers, despise God's simple manna and long for the melons, leeks, and onions of Egypt after the fashion of the mixed multitude that followed ancient Israel out of Egypt (Nu. 11:5).

Many "fundamentalist" Bible-believing churches are only a step behind the out-and-out contemporary ones, having corrupted the Lord's house with their gimmicks and promotions and joking and undue exaltation of big-name preachers and body-swaying soft rock which they have borrowed from the one-world church.

In the 1950s, Dr. M.R. DeHaan issued the following warning about what was happening in his day, at the dawn of the neo-evangelical contemporary movement:

> "Remember also that the bread on the table with the frankincense was the only thing placed upon the table as the food of the priests. There were no sauces and spices and pickles and olives and fancy salads or pie à la mode; just bread. We have drifted far, far away from this simple formula today. Instead of believers coming together to

fellowship around the Lord Jesus Christ, the Bread of Life, without all the extraneous paraphernalia, and just to feed on His Word, we have too often turned our services into a carnival. ... And then we wonder at the worldliness and the shallowness of Christians today. We have added pickles, olives, radishes, and highly seasoned extras, and have relegated the Word of Life to a side dish, which few will touch" (DeHaan, *The Tabernacle*, 1955).

Transportation of the Tabernacle

> And the LORD spake unto Moses, saying, 2 Make thee two trumpets of silver; of a whole piece shalt thou make them: that thou mayest use them for the calling of the assembly, and for the journeying of the camps. 3 And when they shall blow with them, all the assembly shall assemble themselves to thee at the door of the tabernacle of the congregation. 4 And if they blow *but* with one *trumpet*, then the princes, *which are* heads of the thousands of Israel, shall gather themselves unto thee. 5 When ye blow an alarm, then the camps that lie on the east parts shall go forward. 6 When ye blow an alarm the second time, then the camps that lie on the south side shall take their journey: they shall blow an alarm for their journeys. 7 But when the congregation is to be gathered together, ye shall blow, but ye shall not sound an alarm. 8 And the sons of Aaron, the priests, shall blow with the trumpets; and they shall be to you for an ordinance for ever throughout your generations. 9 And if ye go to war in your land against the enemy that oppresseth you, then ye shall blow an alarm with the trumpets; and ye shall be remembered before the LORD your God, and ye shall be saved from your enemies. 10 Also in the day of your gladness, and in your solemn days, and in the beginnings of your months, ye shall blow with the trumpets over your burnt offerings, and over the sacrifices of your peace offerings; that they may be to you for a memorial before your God: I *am* the LORD your God.

The tabernacle was designed to be transported during Israel's wanderings in the wilderness. Each major article had rings through which poles were placed so the priests could carry them from place to place (Ex. 25:10-14). The heavier items such as the boards, pillars, and sockets were carried in wagons.

The Order of March

In Numbers 10:11-36 we see how the tabernacle was dismantled and carried by the priests when Israel moved. First Aaron and his sons covered all of the sacred articles and prepared them for travel. Then the Levites dismantled the tabernacle and transported it.

In the first order marched the tribes of Issachar, Judah, and Zebulun (Nu. 10:13-16).

> Numbers 10:13-16 And they first took their journey according to the commandment of the LORD by the hand of Moses. 14 In the first *place* went the standard of the camp of the children of Judah according to their armies: and over his host *was* Nahshon the son of Amminadab. 15 And over the host of the tribe of the children of Issachar *was* Nethaneel the son of Zuar. 16 And over the host of the tribe of the children of Zebulun *was* Eliab the son of Helon.

After this the court and the tabernacle were carried by the sons of Gershon and Merari.

> Numbers 10:17 And the tabernacle was taken down; and the sons of Gershon and the sons of Merari set forward, bearing the tabernacle.

Gershon carried the curtains, the veils, the coverings, and the hangings (Nu. 4:22-26). Merari carried the boards, bars, pillars, and sockets (Nu. 4:29-32).

> Numbers 4:22-26 Take also the sum of the sons of Gershon, throughout the houses of their fathers, by their families; 23 From thirty years old and upward until fifty years old shalt thou number them; all that enter in to perform the service, to do the work in the tabernacle of the congregation. 24 This *is* the service of the families of the Gershonites, to serve, and for burdens: 25 And they shall bear the curtains of the tabernacle, and the tabernacle of the congregation, his covering, and the covering of the badgers' skins that *is* above upon it, and the hanging for

the door of the tabernacle of the congregation, 26 And the hangings of the court, and the hanging for the door of the gate of the court, which *is* by the tabernacle and by the altar round about, and their cords, and all the instruments of their service, and all that is made for them: so shall they serve.

Numbers 4:29-32 As for the sons of Merari, thou shalt number them after their families, by the house of their fathers; 30 From thirty years old and upward even unto fifty years old shalt thou number them, every one that entereth into the service, to do the work of the tabernacle of the congregation. 31 And this *is* the charge of their burden, according to all their service in the tabernacle of the congregation; the boards of the tabernacle, and the bars thereof, and the pillars thereof, and sockets thereof, 32 And the pillars of the court round about, and their sockets, and their pins, and their cords, with all their instruments, and with all their service: and by name ye shall reckon the instruments of the charge of their burden.

In the second order marched the tribes of Reuben, Simeon, and Gad.

Numbers 10:18-20 And the standard of the camp of Reuben set forward according to their armies: and over his host *was* Elizur the son of Shedeur. 19 And over the host of the tribe of the children of Simeon *was* Shelumiel the son of Zurishaddai. 20 And over the host of the tribe of the children of Gad *was* Eliasaph the son of Deuel.

They were followed by the sons of Kohath carrying the holy articles of the tabernacle: the ark of the covenant, the lampstand, the incense altar, the table of shewbread, the laver, the brazen altar.

Numbers 10:21 And the Kohathites set forward, bearing the sanctuary: and *the other* did set up the tabernacle against they came.

Numbers 4:5-15 And when the camp setteth forward, Aaron shall come, and his sons, and they shall take down the covering vail, and cover the ark of testimony with it: 6 And shall put thereon the covering of badgers' skins, and shall spread over *it* a cloth wholly of blue, and shall put in the staves thereof. 7 And upon the table of shewbread they shall spread a cloth of blue, and put thereon the dishes, and the spoons, and the bowls, and covers to cover withal: and the continual bread shall be thereon: 8 And they shall spread upon them a cloth of scarlet, and cover the same with a covering of badgers' skins, and shall put in the staves thereof. 9 And they shall take a cloth of blue, and cover the candlestick of the light, and his lamps, and his tongs, and his snuffdishes, and all the oil vessels thereof, wherewith they minister unto it: 10 And they shall put it and all the vessels thereof within a covering of badgers' skins, and shall put *it* upon a bar. 11 And upon the golden altar they shall spread a cloth of blue, and cover it with a covering of badgers' skins, and shall put to the staves thereof: 12 And they shall take all the instruments of ministry, wherewith they minister in the sanctuary, and put *them* in a cloth of blue, and cover them with a covering of badgers' skins, and shall put *them* on a bar: 13 And they shall take away the ashes from the altar, and spread a purple cloth thereon: 14 And they shall put upon it all the vessels thereof, wherewith they minister about it, *even* the censers, the fleshhooks, and the shovels, and the basons, all the vessels of the altar; and they shall spread upon it a covering of badgers' skins, and put to the staves of it. 15 And when Aaron and his sons have made an end of covering the sanctuary, and all the vessels of the sanctuary, as the camp is to set forward; after that, the sons of Kohath shall come to bear *it*: but they shall not touch *any* holy thing, lest they die. These *things are* the burden of the sons of Kohath in the tabernacle of the congregation.

In the third order marched the tribes of Ephraim, Manasseh, and Benjamin.

Numbers 10:22-24 And the standard of the camp of the children of Ephraim set forward according to their armies: and over his host *was* Elishama the son of Ammihud. 23

> And over the host of the tribe of the children of Manasseh *was* Gamaliel the son of Pedahzur. 24 And over the host of the tribe of the children of Benjamin *was* Abidan the son of Gideoni.

In the fourth order marched the tribes of Dan, Asher, and Naphtali.

> Numbers 10:25-28 And the standard of the camp of the children of Dan set forward, *which was* the rereward of all the camps throughout their hosts: and over his host *was* Ahiezer the son of Ammishaddai. 26 And over the host of the tribe of the children of Asher *was* Pagiel the son of Ocran. 27 And over the host of the tribe of the children of Naphtali *was* Ahira the son of Enan. 28 Thus *were* the journeyings of the children of Israel according to their armies, when they set forward.

The ark was out in front of the armies of Israel.

> Numbers 10:33 And they departed from the mount of the LORD three days' journey: and the ark of the covenant of the LORD went before them in the three days' journey, to search out a resting place for them.

Spiritual Lessons

The nation of Israel carrying the tabernacle through the wilderness signifies believer-priests carrying Christ through this world.

1. Christ is always with us.

Just as God never left Israel alone in the wilderness, even when He had to chasten them for their sin, so He has promised, "I will never leave thee, nor forsake thee" (Heb. 13:5).

2. We are led by Christ.

God led His people by the ark of the covenant out in front, by the pillar of fire at night and the pillar of smoke by day, by Moses, and by the sounding of the silver trumpets.

Even so, Christ leads His people today by the indwelling Spirit and by the Scriptures and by the ministry of church leaders. Jesus said that He goes before His sheep (John 10:4).

As the trumpets called the Israelites together for solemn assemblies and sacrifices (Nu. 10:10), so the Spirit of God calls believers together to assembly and instructs us about Christ and His atonement (Heb. 10:19-25).

As the trumpets awakened the Israelites and guided them (Nu. 10:2), so the Spirit of God exhorts and leads believers by the preaching of the Word (2 Tim. 4:2).

As the trumpets alerted the Israelites to danger and called them to war (Nu. 10:9), so the Spirit of God exhorts and warns us to be alert against our spiritual enemies and instructs us about how to have victory (Eph. 6:10-19; 1 Pet. 5:8).

3. We are ordered by Christ (Nu. 10:14-27).

Just as the Lord instructed the Israelites to assemble and march in an orderly manner according to the teaching of His Word, so He orders His people today (1 Cor. 11:2; 14:40; 11:2).

As the Israelites were led by men appointed by the Lord, so the assemblies today are to be led by God-called, God-gifted men (Eph. 4:11-14). The church is not a mob or a democracy. It is not operated by people's rights. It is a theocracy that is ordered by God's laws and is under the oversight of God-ordained leaders (Heb. 13:17).

4. We are assigned our places by Christ (Nu. 10:14-27).

Each of the tribes and each of Levi's sons were assigned their marching orders by God. Their leaders led the way (Nu. 10:4).

The sons of Gershon camped on the west and carried the curtains, hangings, and coverings (Nu. 3:23-26). The sons of Kohath camped on the south and carried the holy vessels

(Nu. 3:29-31). These objects were carried on their shoulders by the staves (Nu. 7:9). The sons of Merari camped on the north and carried the framework of the tabernacle and the pillars of the tabernacle and court (Nu. 3:35-37).

Likewise each believer is given gifts and ministries according to God's will.

> Romans 12:3-8 For I say, through the grace given unto me, to every man that is among you, not to think *of himself* more highly than he ought to think; but to think soberly, according as God hath dealt to every man the measure of faith. 4 For as we have many members in one body, and all members have not the same office: 5 So we, *being* many, are one body in Christ, and every one members one of another. 6 Having then gifts differing according to the grace that is given to us, whether prophecy, *let us prophesy* according to the proportion of faith; 7 Or ministry, *let us wait* on *our* ministering: or he that teacheth, on teaching; 8 Or he that exhorteth, on exhortation: he that giveth, *let him do it* with simplicity; he that ruleth, with diligence; he that sheweth mercy, with cheerfulness.

We don't choose our place in God's work, and we don't force our way into any certain position. There is blessing in the church when the members seek their proper place in the body and submit to God-given leaders. This is the way of peace rather than confusion.

5. We lift up Christ before the world.

As the tabernacle was transported and set up before the eyes of the pagan nations, even so believers are ambassadors for Christ to proclaim the gospel to all nations. We are to shine as lights in the world and to hold forth the word of life.

> Philippians 2:15-16 That ye may be blameless and harmless, the sons of God, without rebuke, in the midst of a crooked and perverse nation, among whom ye shine as lights in the world; 16 Holding forth the word of life; that I

may rejoice in the day of Christ, that I have not run in vain, neither laboured in vain.

Romans 10:14-15 How then shall they call on him in whom they have not believed? and how shall they believe in him of whom they have not heard? and how shall they hear without a preacher? 15 And how shall they preach, except they be sent? as it is written, How beautiful are the feet of them that preach the gospel of peace, and bring glad tidings of good things!

6. We are given work to do.

Everything about the tabernacle system was work. It was work to build it, work to take it down, work to transport it, work to set it up, work to maintain it, work to offer the sacrifices and wash at the laver, work to fill the laver and to keep the lamps lit and the incense burning and the bread fresh.

Likewise God has given us real work in this world. Preaching the gospel to the ends of the earth and building Bible-believing churches and teaching the Lord's people to observe all things that Christ has taught us.

Matthew 28:19-20 Go ye therefore, and teach all nations, baptizing them in the name of the Father, and of the Son, and of the Holy Ghost: 20 Teaching them to observe all things whatsoever I have commanded you: and, lo, I am with you alway, *even* unto the end of the world. Amen.

This is real work, and we are to be found faithful in the work when Christ returns. There will be no reward for lazy saints who neglect the work of Christ in this present world. We are exhorted to be always abounding in the work of the Lord (1 Cor. 15:58). Every individual will receive his own reward according to his own LABOUR (1 Cor. 3:8).

Preachers who are worthy of double reward are those who LABOUR in the word and doctrine (1 Tim. 5:17).

Jesus commended the church at Ephesus for its work and labour (Rev. 2:2).

The book of Proverbs, the book of practical godly wisdom, reproves the sluggard repeatedly and in no uncertain terms (Prov. 6:9; 10:26; 12:24; 13:4; 18:9; 19:24; 20:4; 21:25; 24:30-34; 26:16).

Latter History of the Tabernacle

After Israel entered the land and conquered the pagan nations, the tabernacle was first set up at Shiloh in about 1445 BC (Josh. 18:1). It remained there through the days of the judges until the time of Eli, about 320 years. It is called "the tabernacle of Shiloh" in Psalm 78:60.

In 1122 BC, the ark of the covenant was removed from the tabernacle by Eli's wicked sons and brought to Israel's army camp as an aid against the Philistines, but Israel was defeated because of her sin and the ark was captured by the Philistines (1 Sam. 4:1-11). It never returned to Shiloh. It appears that Shiloh was destroyed at that time (Jer. 7:12-14).

After enduring much trouble because of the ark, the Philistines returned it to Israel, and it was kept at Kirjathjearim for 20 years (1 Sam 6:21 - 7:2).

After this, it is possible that the tabernacle was kept at different places. In David's day we read about priests and the shewbread being at Nob (1 Sam. 21:1-6). This doesn't mean that the tabernacle was there, but it is probable. We know for sure that the tabernacle was at Gibeon (1 Ch. 16:39; 21:29).

In 1047 BC, David brought the ark of the covenant from Gibeon to Jerusalem and set it in a "tabernacle" (2 Sam. 6:1-17; 1 Ch. 15).

> 2 Samuel 6:1-17 Again, David gathered together all *the* chosen *men* of Israel, thirty thousand. 2 And David arose, and went with all the people that *were* with him from Baale of Judah, to bring up from thence the ark of God, whose name is called by the name of the LORD of hosts that dwelleth *between* the cherubims. 3 And they set the ark of God upon a new cart, and brought it out of the house of Abinadab that *was* in Gibeah: and Uzzah and Ahio, the sons of Abinadab, drave the new cart. 4 And they brought it out of the house of Abinadab which *was* at Gibeah, accompanying the ark of God: and Ahio went before the

ark. 5 And David and all the house of Israel played before the LORD on all manner of *instruments made of* fir wood, even on harps, and on psalteries, and on timbrels, and on cornets, and on cymbals. 6 And when they came to Nachon's threshingfloor, Uzzah put forth *his hand* to the ark of God, and took hold of it; for the oxen shook *it*. 7 And the anger of the LORD was kindled against Uzzah; and God smote him there for *his* error; and there he died by the ark of God. 8 And David was displeased, because the LORD had made a breach upon Uzzah: and he called the name of the place Perezuzzah to this day. 9 And David was afraid of the LORD that day, and said, How shall the ark of the LORD come to me? 10 So David would not remove the ark of the LORD unto him into the city of David: but David carried it aside into the house of Obededom the Gittite. 11 And the ark of the LORD continued in the house of Obededom the Gittite three months: and the LORD blessed Obededom, and all his household. 12 And it was told king David, saying, The LORD hath blessed the house of Obededom, and all that *pertaineth* unto him, because of the ark of God. So David went and brought up the ark of God from the house of Obededom into the city of David with gladness. 13 And it was *so*, that when they that bare the ark of the LORD had gone six paces, he sacrificed oxen and fatlings. 14 And David danced before the LORD with all *his* might; and David *was* girded with a linen ephod. 15 So David and all the house of Israel brought up the ark of the LORD with shouting, and with the sound of the trumpet. 16 And as the ark of the LORD came into the city of David, Michal Saul's daughter looked through a window, and saw king David leaping and dancing before the LORD; and she despised him in her heart. 17 And they brought in the ark of the LORD, and set it in his place, in the midst of the tabernacle that David had pitched for it: and David offered burnt offerings and peace offerings before the LORD.

This was some sort of tent, but the original tabernacle appears to have stayed in Gibeon, with its brazen altar, and sacrifices continued to be offered there until Solomon finished the temple (2 Ch. 1:3-6).

When Solomon's temple was finished in 1004 BC, the tabernacle and its furniture were kept in the temple storerooms.

> 2 Chronicles 5:1-5 Thus all the work that Solomon made for the house of the LORD was finished: and Solomon brought in *all* the things that David his father had dedicated; and the silver, and the gold, and all the instruments, put he among the treasures of the house of God. 2 Then Solomon assembled the elders of Israel, and all the heads of the tribes, the chief of the fathers of the children of Israel, unto Jerusalem, to bring up the ark of the covenant of the LORD out of the city of David, which *is* Zion. 3 Wherefore all the men of Israel assembled themselves unto the king in the feast which *was* in the seventh month. 4 And all the elders of Israel came; and the Levites took up the ark. 5 And they brought up the ark, and the tabernacle of the congregation, and all the holy vessels that *were* in the tabernacle, these did the priests *and* the Levites bring up.

The ark of the covenant was the only thing from the tabernacle that remained on active duty in the temple.

> 2 Chronicles 5:7-10 And the priests brought in the ark of the covenant of the LORD unto his place, to the oracle of the house, into the most holy *place, even* under the wings of the cherubims: 8 For the cherubims spread forth *their* wings over the place of the ark, and the cherubims covered the ark and the staves thereof above. 9 And they drew out the staves *of the ark*, that the ends of the staves were seen from the ark before the oracle; but they were not seen without. And there it is unto this day. 10 *There was* nothing in the ark save the two tables which Moses put *therein* at Horeb, when the LORD made *a covenant* with the children of Israel, when they came out of Egypt.

On either side of the ark were added newly made cherubims.

> 2 Chronicles 3:10-13 And in the most holy house he made two cherubims of image work, and overlaid them with gold. 11 And the wings of the cherubims *were* twenty cubits long: one wing *of the one cherub was* five cubits, reaching to the wall of the house: and the other wing *was likewise* five cubits, reaching to the wing of the other cherub. 12 And *one* wing of the other cherub *was* five cubits, reaching to the wall of the house: and the other wing *was* five cubits *also*, joining to the wing of the other cherub. 13 The wings of these cherubims spread themselves forth twenty cubits: and they stood on their feet, and their faces *were* inward.

The tabernacle's one candlestick was replaced with 10 candlesticks (2 Ch. 4:7). The tabernacle's laver was replaced with one large "sea" that was 10 cubits (15 feet) in diameter and five cubits (7.5 feet) high, plus 10 smaller lavers (2 Ch. 4:2-6). The tabernacle's one table of shewbread was replaced with 10 tables (2 Ch. 4:8). The tabernacle's brazen altar (which was five cubits square and three cubits high) was replaced with a much larger one 20 cubits (30 feet) long, wide, and high (2 Ch. 4:1). The tabernacle's veil dividing the holy place from the most holy place was replaced with a new one (2 Ch. 3:14).

Pillar of Cloud and Pillar of Fire

> Exodus 13:21-22 And the LORD went before them by day in a pillar of a cloud, to lead them the way; and by night in a pillar of fire, to give them light; to go by day and night: 22 He took not away the pillar of the cloud by day, nor the pillar of fire by night, *from* before the people.

The pillar of cloud and the pillar of fire are mentioned eight times in Scripture. These guided Israel in her wilderness journeys, depicting Christ's guidance of believers through this pilgrim life.

1. The pillar of cloud and fire were never taken away, even when Israel sinned ("it was alway," Nu. 9:16), signifying that Christ will never leave His people. He chastens us but He does not forsake us.

> Hebrews 13:5 *Let your* conversation *be* without covetousness; *and be* content with such things as ye have: for he hath said, I will never leave thee, nor forsake thee.

2. Israel had to be ready to follow the pillar of cloud whenever it moved.

> Numbers 9:18, 20, 21, 23 At the commandment of the LORD the children of Israel journeyed, and at the commandment of the LORD they pitched: as long as the cloud abode upon the tabernacle they rested in their tents. ... 20 And *so* it was, when the cloud was a few days upon the tabernacle; according to the commandment of the LORD they abode in their tents, and according to the commandment of the LORD they journeyed. 21 And *so* it was, when the cloud abode from even unto the morning, and *that* the cloud was taken up in the morning, then they journeyed: whether *it was* by day or by night that the cloud was taken up, they journeyed. ... 23 At the commandment of the LORD they rested in the tents, and at the commandment of the LORD they journeyed: they kept the charge of the LORD, at the commandment of the LORD by the hand of Moses.

Observe the repetition, which is given for emphasis. Following God's guidance is one of the most important things in the Christian life. Every major decision--such as church membership, employment, education, close friendships, relocations, and marriage--must be made in God's perfect will.

To make a major decision outside of God's will can have terrible consequences, as we see in Lot's life when he decided to pitch his tent toward Sodom (Ge. 13:11-12).

Generally God speaks in a still, small voice and He speaks to those who are listening. He wants to guide with His eye rather than with force.

> 1 Kings 19:12-13 And after the earthquake a fire; *but* the LORD *was* not in the fire: and after the fire a still small voice. 13 And it was *so*, when Elijah heard *it*, that he wrapped his face in his mantle, and went out, and stood in the entering in of the cave. And, behold, *there came* a voice unto him, and said, What doest thou here, Elijah?

> Psalms 32:8-9 I will instruct thee and teach thee in the way which thou shalt go: I will guide thee with mine eye. 9 Be ye not as the horse, *or* as the mule, *which* have no understanding: whose mouth must be held in with bit and bridle, lest they come near unto thee.

3. Israel was led to difficult places (such as the wilderness of Sin where there was no water).

Likewise we must be content to follow the Lord wherever He leads and to patiently accept the trials that He sends into our lives. It has been wisely said, "Don't doubt in the dark that which God has shown you in the light." Trials always come; faith is always tested; and we must be careful not to make unwise decisions in the midst of a trial.

4. They were required to stay in one place for extended periods (they were at Sinai for nearly a year).

Numbers 9:19, 22 And when the cloud tarried long upon the tabernacle many days, then the children of Israel kept the charge of the LORD, and journeyed not. ... Or *whether it were* two days, or a month, or a year, that the cloud tarried upon the tabernacle, remaining thereon, the children of Israel abode in their tents, and journeyed not: but when it was taken up, they journeyed.

Likewise we must be patient. We must be "ready to go, ready to stay."

5. God's guidance was clear to Israel each step of their journey.

Likewise He will make His guidance clear today for those who seek Him and wait for Him. He knows how to make things clear. He knows how to speak to us, and we should wait until we are sure of His leading. Many times we are tempted to quit a situation without the clear leadership of God, but we should wait until His will is perfectly clear before making a move, and then we should not make another move until the guidance is equally clear.

One way that I personally test God's will is to wait to see if a certain impression of leading gets clearer rather than less clear. I have told many preachers, "If God wants you to leave this place, He will make it as clear as He made it when you came here, and you should wait until that is the case."

God is not the author of confusion but of peace (1 Cor. 14:33). If God is in a decision, the confusion will dissipate and we should wait for that.

6. God's guidance was clear, first to the leaders and then to the entire camp.

Numbers 10:11-13 And it came to pass on the twentieth *day* of the second month, in the second year, that the cloud was taken up from off the tabernacle of the testimony. 12 And the children of Israel took their journeys out of the wilderness of Sinai; and the cloud rested in the wilderness of Paran. 13 And they first took their journey according to the commandment of the LORD by the hand of Moses.

Likewise today He makes His guidance clear to the church leaders and to the church body.

When God called Paul and Barnabas to go on the first missionary journey, it was clear to the entire church (Acts 13:1-4). The church recognized God's call upon these two men and supported it.

Many men think they are called to do something when the congregation doesn't see that calling and isn't inclined to support it. Many think of themselves more highly than they ought to think and aren't content with God's gifts and calling (Rom. 12:3).

That is not how God works unless the church is a false or seriously backslidden one. The result is usually confusion rather than peace and blessing.

7. The pillar of fire gave only the light they needed.

As the pillar of fire did not light up the entire wilderness, so God's Word is a light unto our feet (Psa. 119:105). It does not show us our entire lives but leads us step by step, day by day, as we lean not to our own understanding and seek God's will in all our ways (Prov. 3:5-6).

8. The pillar of cloud and pillar of fire were the visible signs of God's presence to Israel, but we must not seek signs. Rather we must be content to live by faith in God's Word.

Matthew 12:39 But he answered and said unto them, An evil and adulterous generation seeketh after a sign; and there shall no sign be given to it, but the sign of the prophet Jonas.

Hebrews 11:6 But without faith *it is* impossible to please *him*: for he that cometh to God must believe that he is, and *that* he is a rewarder of them that diligently seek him.

The Priesthood

Exodus 28-29

The Levites are descendants of Jacob's son Levi (Ge. 29:34).

They were appointed by God to be the priestly tribe (Nu. 1:50; 3:5-9; De. 1-:8-9). They were dedicated to the Lord in the place of Israel's firstborn sons (Nu. 8:13-17). As Creator, God owns all men (Eze. 18:4). And He owns the believer in a double sense--both by right of Creator and by right of Redeemer (1 Cor. 6:19-20).

Moses and Aaron were Levites (Ex. 6:18-20).

Aaron was appointed the first high priest, and this office passed to the eldest son at death.

> Exodus 28:1 And take thou unto thee Aaron thy brother, and his sons with him, from among the children of Israel, that he may minister unto me in the priest's office, *even* Aaron, Nadab and Abihu, Eleazar and Ithamar, Aaron's sons.

> Numbers 20:25-28 Take Aaron and Eleazar his son, and bring them up unto mount Hor: 26 And strip Aaron of his garments, and put them upon Eleazar his son: and Aaron shall be gathered *unto his people*, and shall die there. 27 And Moses did as the LORD commanded: and they went up into mount Hor in the sight of all the congregation. 28 And Moses stripped Aaron of his garments, and put them upon Eleazar his son; and Aaron died there in the top of the mount: and Moses and Eleazar came down from the mount.

Only the high priest could light the lampstand (Num. 8:2-3), burn incense on the golden altar (Ex. 30:7-8), and enter the holy of holies on the Day of Atonement (Lev. 16). The shewbread was to be maintained by the sons of Aaron under Aaron's direction (Lev. 24:5-9). Aaron's sons made the sacrifices (Lev. 1:11; 2:2; 3:2) and blew the silver trumpets (Nu. 10:8).

The high priest and his sons oversaw the work of the other Levites.

> Numbers 8:1-4 And the LORD spake unto Moses, saying, 2 Speak unto Aaron, and say unto him, When thou lightest the lamps, the seven lamps shall give light over against the candlestick. 3 And Aaron did so; he lighted the lamps thereof over against the candlestick, as the LORD commanded Moses. 4 And this work of the candlestick *was of* beaten gold, unto the shaft thereof, unto the flowers thereof, *was* beaten work: according unto the pattern which the LORD had shewed Moses, so he made the candlestick.

Levi had three sons: Gershon, Kohath, and Merari (Ex. 6:16). These became the heads of the three divisions of the Levites who were under the oversight of Aaron and his sons (Nu. 4:22-23, 29-30, 34-35). Their work was assigned by God. Gershon camped on the west and took care of the court hangings and the coverings of the tabernacle (Nu. 3:23-26). Kohath camped on the south and took care of the articles in the tabernacle (Nu. 3:27-31). Merari camped on the north and took care of the tabernacle boards and curtains and pillars and the pillars of the court (Nu. 3;33-37). When Israel traveled in the wilderness, the Gershonites carried the tent hangings and curtains (Nu. 4:24-26), the Kohathites carried the vessels of the tabernacle such as the candlestick and table of shewbread (Nu. 4:15; 3:29-31), and the Merarites carried the boards, bars, pillars, and sockets (Nu. 4:31-32).

The distinction is made in Scripture between the priests the sons of Aaron (Lev. 1:5) and the priests the sons of Levi (De. 21:5). The latter refers to the sons of Gerson, Kohath, and Merari and perhaps at times to the sons of Aaron as well.

These other Levites could do other aspects of the ministry under the oversight of the high priest and his sons. They took down, transported, and set up the tabernacle (Num. 3). In this capacity they doubtless did everything associated with the maintenance of the tabernacle and the physical labor of filling the laver, keeping wood supplied for the brazen altar, etc.

Their work was not limited to physical labor, though. They judged the people (De. 17:8-10; 19:17; 21:5). They were the guardians of Scripture (De. 17:18; 31:9). A book of the law was kept by the Levites in the holy of holies by the ark of the covenant (De. 31:24-26). In their capacity in performing the law of leprosy, they evaluated property (Lev. 27:12, 14; De. 24:8).

The Levite began his ministry of service in the tabernacle at age 25 (Num. 8:24). But he didn't begin the heavy work of transporting the tabernacle until age 30 (Num. 4:3-5). At age 50 he ceased the heavy work but continued to serve in other capacities (Num. 8:25-26). This was a very wise plan, as all of God's plans are!

We are reminded that church leaders should not be novices (1 Tim. 3:6). We are also reminded that when a man gets older he loses some of his abilities, and it is wise for older men to work with younger men in the ministry, both the older and the younger contributing their relative strengths. Multiple men working together in leading churches is what we see in Scripture (e.g., Acts 13:1-2). I have seen cases in which an elderly preacher has harmed a church by keeping full control of the leadership even after he ceased to have the strength, health, and vision to be effective. Sometimes it is out of necessity, but sometimes it is simply the inability to acknowledge one's limitations.

> "They were to have a writ of ease at fifty years old; then they were to return from the warfare, as the phrase is (Nu. 8:25), not cashiered with disgrace, but preferred rather to the rest which their age required, to be loaded with the honours of their office, as hitherto they had been with the

burdens of it. They shall *minister with their brethren in the tabernacle,* to direct the junior Levites, and set them in; and they shall *keep the charge,* as guards upon the avenues of the tabernacle, to see that no stranger intruded, nor any person in his uncleanness, but they shall not be put upon any service which may be a fatigue to them" (Matthew Henry).

The Levites received the tithes of Israel (Nu. 18:21, 24, 26; Ne. 10:37; 12:44). Israel was instructed not to forget the Levites (De. 12:19; 14:-27; 26:11).

The Levites were given 48 cities in Israel (Nu. 35:2-8; Josh. 21). Among these were the six cities of refuge (Nu. 35:6).

In this section we will look at the following:
The typology of the priests
The clothing of the high priest
The clothing of the ordinary priests
The consecration of the priests

THE TYPOLOGY OF THE PRIESTS

The high priest typifies Christ.

Hebrews 5:1-10 For every high priest taken from among men is ordained for men in things *pertaining* to God, that he may offer both gifts and sacrifices for sins: 2 Who can have compassion on the ignorant, and on them that are out of the way; for that he himself also is compassed with infirmity. 3 And by reason hereof he ought, as for the people, so also for himself, to offer for sins. 4 And no man taketh this honour unto himself, but he that is called of God, as *was* Aaron. 5 So also Christ glorified not himself to be made an high priest; but he that said unto him, Thou art my Son, to day have I begotten thee. 6 As he saith also in another *place,* Thou *art* a priest for ever after the order of Melchisedec. 7 Who in the days of his flesh, when he had offered up prayers and supplications with strong crying and tears unto him that was able to save him from death, and was heard in that he feared; 8 Though he were a Son,

> yet learned he obedience by the things which he suffered; 9 And being made perfect, he became the author of eternal salvation unto all them that obey him; 10 Called of God an high priest after the order of Melchisedec.

By meditating upon Aaron in his splendid priestly garments and by examining his ministry, we can learn wonderful things about Christ.

In Aaron we see our High Priest, the One who made the acceptable sacrifice for our sins and now stands in the presence of God for us. We see the One who intercedes for us at the golden altar and feeds us with His bread and enlightens us with His light.

Aaron was the high priest of Israel only, but Christ is the High Priest of all of Abraham's sons in the faith.

Our High Priest is the Second Man who, unlike Adam, is the sinless Man made in God's perfect image (1 Cor. 15:47). This is the Man that God delights in.

Christ is the beloved of the Father, and the believer is "accepted in the beloved" (Eph. 1:6).

Our High Priest is the Christ in whom all things will be gathered together in one (Eph. 1:10). Christ is the head of God's new creation (Rev. 3:14), and the New Testament believer has been born again into that new creation by faith (2 Cor. 5:17). The believer is already in Christ as the firstfruits (Eph. 1:10; Rom. 8:23; Jam. 1:18).

God's eternal plan is that everything will be centered around Christ as Head, and this is how we should live our lives from the moment we are saved. Salvation is not merely about "going to heaven when I die." It is about dying with Christ and rising with Christ to newness of life, a life centered in Christ.

Aaron's sons typify Christians who have been made priests in Christ.

> 1 Peter 2:5 Ye also, as lively stones, are built up a spiritual house, an holy priesthood, to offer up spiritual sacrifices, acceptable to God by Jesus Christ.

> 1 Peter 2:9 But ye *are* a chosen generation, a royal priesthood, an holy nation, a peculiar people; that ye should shew forth the praises of him who hath called you out of darkness into his marvellous light:

The New Testament believer is a member of a holy priesthood. His priestly work is to show forth the praises of Christ by his lips and his testimony. We offer sacrifices, but not sacrifices of sheep and goats. Our sacrifices are spiritual sacrifices: the sacrifice of obedience and holiness and thanksgiving to God and love for our fellow man.

Our priestly sacrifices are described in the New Testament Epistles.

THE HIGH PRIEST'S CLOTHING

The garments of the high priest signify Christ in His glory, having made atonement for man's sin and having risen from the dead. The clothing is for "glory and beauty" (Ex. 28:2).

The garments signify Christ in His three offices (Ex. 28:4): Priest (the ephod), Prophet (the Urim and Thummim), and King (the mitre and crown).

The garments were made with fine white linen and with blue, purple, scarlet, and gold thread (Ex. 28:2-5). These materials picture the Lord Jesus Christ in the various ways that we have seen in the studies on the tabernacle.

The white linen speaks of Christ's purity and sinlessness (1 Pet. 2:22).

The blue thread speaks of Christ's heavenly origin and present position at the right hand of the Father (1 Cor. 15:47).

The purple thread speaks of Jesus' royalty; He is King of kings.

The High Priest - © *GoodSalt*

The scarlet thread speaks of Christ's blood atonement; He is the Saviour.

The gold speaks of Christ's deity; He is "God manifest in the flesh" (1 Tim. 3:16).

All of the priests wore a coat, girdle, and bonnet, with linen breeches as an undergarment (Ex. 28:40, 42).

The rest of the items were unique to the high priest (Ex. 28:3-4).

The Linen Coat

The white linen coat was put on first (Ex. 28:39; 39:27), and the high priest's other garments were put on over it. The white linen depicts Christ's holy, sinless character.

The Robe

> Exodus 28:31-35 And thou shalt make the robe of the ephod all *of* blue. 32 And there shall be an hole in the top of it, in the midst thereof: it shall have a binding of woven work round about the hole of it, as it were the hole of an habergeon, that it be not rent. 33 And *beneath* upon the hem of it thou shalt make pomegranates *of* blue, and *of* purple, and *of* scarlet, round about the hem thereof; and bells of gold between them round about: 34 A golden bell and a pomegranate, a golden bell and a pomegranate, upon the hem of the robe round about. 35 And it shall be upon Aaron to minister: and his sound shall be heard when he goeth in unto the holy *place* before the LORD, and when he cometh out, that he die not.

The robe was put on over the white coat. It was a long robe of blue color, thus signifying that Christ originated from Heaven and is the Lord from Heaven (1 Cor. 15:47). He is the eternal Son of God who came from Heaven to stand between God and man. Had He not been of heavenly, divine origin, had He been a natural man, He would have been a sinner and could not have been our Saviour and Priest.

The Pomegranates

> Exodus 28:33 And *beneath* upon the hem of it thou shalt make pomegranates *of* blue, and *of* purple, and *of* scarlet,

round about the hem thereof; and bells of gold between them round about:

Upon the hem of the high priest's robe were sewn blue, purple, and scarlet pomegranates. This is an attractive, sweet fruit with a profusion of seeds. It is mentioned 33 times in Scripture.

1. The pomegranate signifies fruitfulness.

Deuteronomy 8:8 A land of wheat, and barley, and vines, and fig trees, and pomegranates; a land of oil olive, and honey;

Christ did not die in vain. Through the atonement and by His present work of world evangelism, He is drawing multitudes to Himself (Isa. 53:11). In the Tribulation, even in the midst of God's judgment on this sin-cursed world, souls will be saved without number (Rev. 9:13-14). And Christ will continue to bear fruit throughout eternity!

2. The pomegranate is used in Scripture to signify beauty and pleasure.

Song of Solomon 4:3 Thy lips *are* like a thread of scarlet, and thy speech *is* comely: thy temples *are* like a piece of a pomegranate within thy locks.

Song of Solomon 6:7 As a piece of a pomegranate *are* thy temples within thy locks.

Song of Solomon 8:2 I would lead thee, *and* bring thee into my mother's house, *who* would instruct me: I would cause thee to drink of spiced wine of the juice of my pomegranate.

Thus the pomegranates on the high priest's robe signify the beauty and blessing of Jesus Christ. In his presence is fulness of joy and at his right hand are pleasures for evermore (Psa. 16:11).

The Bells

> Exodus 28:33 And *beneath* upon the hem of it thou shalt make pomegranates *of* blue, and *of* purple, and *of* scarlet, round about the hem thereof; and bells of gold between them round about:

Between the pomegranates were sewn gold bells that rang as the high priest went about his labors. The bells related particularly to the high priest's work in the Holy Place so that the people outside the tabernacle, though unable to see him, could hear the bells and be assured that he was busy in their behalf and that God was accepting his labors.

This beautifully fits this present age, in which Jesus our great High Priest is in heaven and is not visible to human eyes on earth. The bells represent the Word of God and the testimony of the Holy Spirit as He witnesses to men of Jesus' existence and work.

> John 16:12-15 I have yet many things to say unto you, but ye cannot bear them now. 13 Howbeit when he, the Spirit of truth, is come, he will guide you into all truth: for he shall not speak of himself; but whatsoever he shall hear, *that* shall he speak: and he will shew you things to come. 14 He shall glorify me: for he shall receive of mine, and shall shew *it* unto you. 15 All things that the Father hath are mine: therefore said I, that he shall take of mine, and shall shew *it* unto you.

The Holy Spirit has given the Scriptures which tell us of Christ, and He also abides in God's people to witness personally of the things of Christ.

> 1 John 2:20 But ye have an unction from the Holy One, and ye know all things.

The Girdle

> Exodus 28:39 And thou shalt embroider the coat of fine linen, and thou shalt make the mitre *of* fine linen, and thou shalt make the girdle *of* needlework.

To secure the robe, a girdle was used (Ex. 28:39). The girdle was used in service and represents servitude.

> Luke 17:8 And will not rather say unto him, Make ready wherewith I may sup, and gird thyself, and serve me, till I have eaten and drunken; and afterward thou shalt eat and drink?

The girdle represents Jesus as the Servant of the Father. In His incarnation, Christ "took upon him the form of a servant" (Phil. 2:6-8). He came not to do His own will (John 6:38).

The girdle also signifies Christ's compassionate ministry to His people, as when He washed the disciples' feet (John 13:4).

> Matthew 20:28 Even as the Son of man came not to be ministered unto, but to minister, and to give his life a ransom for many.

Christ poured out His earthly life in service, helping multitudes of people, healing them, teaching them, saving them.

> "From morning to night He girded Himself in service and gave Himself up to the claims and needs of others. He was the patient, uncomplaining servant of men, testifying continually that He came not to do His own will" (I.M. Haldeman).

The Ephod

> Exodus 28:6-8 And they shall make the ephod *of* gold, *of* blue, and *of* purple, *of* scarlet, and fine twined linen, with cunning work. 7 It shall have the two shoulderpieces thereof joined at the two edges thereof; and *so* it shall be joined together. 8 And the curious girdle of the ephod,

> which *is* upon it, shall be of the same, according to the work thereof; *even of* gold, *of* blue, and purple, and scarlet, and fine twined linen.

The ephod was placed over the head and shoulders of the high priest.

1. It was made of fine linen with gold, blue, purple, and scarlet colors woven in it.

> Exodus 39:2-5 And he made the ephod *of* gold, blue, and purple, and scarlet, and fine twined linen. 3 And they did beat the gold into thin plates, and cut *it into* wires, to work *it* in the blue, and in the purple, and in the scarlet, and in the fine linen, *with* cunning work. 4 They made shoulderpieces for it, to couple *it* together: by the two edges was it coupled together. 5 And the curious girdle of his ephod, that *was* upon it, *was* of the same, according to the work thereof; *of* gold, blue, and purple, and scarlet, and fine twined linen; as the LORD commanded Moses.

The gold represents Christ's deity; the blue, His heavenly origin; the purple, His royalty; the scarlet, His sacrificial atonement; the white linen, His pure, sinless nature (Heb. 7:26).

2. All of the colors were woven together "with cunning work (Ex. 28:6), signifying the perfection and balance of Christ's character.

This is displayed in the Gospels. In every situation Christ did the right thing and spoke the right thing. He was perfect in His zeal for God's holy law and perfect in His compassion for sinners.

3. The gold thread was woven through the other colors (Ex. 39:2-3), signifying that Christ's divinity permeates His person and is inseparable from His humanity.

Adam was made in God's image, but he fell and that holy image was corrupted. Jesus, the second man, is the Perfect Man, being both the Lord from heaven and man in one

Person (1 Cor. 15:47). He is God manifest in the flesh (1 Tim. 3:16).

> "In Him are inseparably united God and Man; yet He is the One Christ, manifesting that which is altogether new, viz.: that perfect blending of all that is of God, with all that is proper to man" (Henry Soltau).

Pastor I.M. Haldeman comments as follows:

> "His life was unconcealed. He was continually open to inspection. Every eye watched Him, every ear was bent to listen, every word He spoke was weighed and analyzed, every step noted, and yet none dared bring the charge of sin against him. For two thousand years, He has been the object of intensive analysis. He has been subject to the white light of an unparalleled investigation.
>
> "His words have been taken apart, put into the laboratory of critical chemistry, tested in respect to base, to combination and compounded parts, but not an accent, not an emphasis has been found out of place, not a sentence or a word that need be changed, not a thought nor statement that must be reversed or recalled.
>
> "He stands out among men absolutely human, yet of an order entirely new, sinless, God filled, compassionate, sympathetic, going among the outcast and the worthless, among those sick in body, sick in soul, in daily contact with leprosy of body and leprosy of mind, uncovering pollution and shame and iniquity at every step; and yet, even as the sun that reveals the mud, the mire the slime and corruption, and is unstained by them, so He ate with publicans and sinners and shone more resplendently pure because of the contrasted evil and wrong revealed in them.
>
> "He spoke softly, gently, so graciously, that the officers sent by His foes to arrest Him as a disturber of the public peace, enthralled by the sound of His voice, the accent of His words, and the marvelous measure of His thoughts, went back to those who sent them and said, 'Never man spake like this man.'

"There were times, however, when His words had in them the note of distant thunder, and there was an upflash of flame, a light in His eyes as terrible as that which had flashed on Sinai.

"When He saw the multitude He was moved with compassion; they were to Him as sheep without a shepherd; they had been harried and skinned (such is the word in the original) by human wolves, they had been the prey of the avarice, injustice and tyranny of men; but when He spoke of a lost soul in hell, suffering, agonizing, tormented, His voice was cold, calm, emotionless, as the utterance of a judge, as hard as the decrees of eternity. Forgiving a sinful woman taken in the act of a particular treason of sin, He poured forth a tidal sweep of anathema against religious formalism and hypocrisy, against false teaching and tradition, as though indeed the day of unrestrained wrath and anger had come.

"He is unique. There never was anything like Him before. There has never been anything like Him since. He is as a white rose surrounded by scarlet poppies. As a smile of love against a scowl of hate. As a song above discord. As a shaft of light in the blackness of a starless midnight.

"He was pure. He was holy. He was sinless. Not even in death did His body see corruption. There is only collocation of terms that expresses Him; and that is, 'Sinless perfection'" (I.M. Haldeman, *The Tabernacle Priesthood and Offerings*, 1925).

The Onyx Stones

Exodus 28:9-14 And thou shalt take two onyx stones, and grave on them the names of the children of Israel: 10 Six of their names on one stone, and *the other* six names of the rest on the other stone, according to their birth. 11 With the work of an engraver in stone, *like* the engravings of a signet, shalt thou engrave the two stones with the names of the children of Israel: thou shalt make them to be set in ouches of gold. 12 And thou shalt put the two stones upon

> the shoulders of the ephod *for* stones of memorial unto the children of Israel: and Aaron shall bear their names before the LORD upon his two shoulders for a memorial. 13 And thou shalt make ouches *of* gold; 14 And two chains *of* pure gold at the ends; *of* wreathen work shalt thou make them, and fasten the wreathen chains to the ouches.

On the shoulders of the ephod were two onyx stones set in gold with the names of the tribes of Israel engraved therein (Ex. 28:9-12; 39:6-7), thus signifying that God's people are kept secure by Christ's divine strength.

We are carried on His strong shoulders. It is the picture of the lost sheep carried on the shoulders of the shepherd (Lk. 15:4-5). We are secure in Christ because He purchased our salvation and is able to save us to the uttermost. We are kept by Christ's power (1 Pet. 1:5). We can rest in Him (Mat. 11:28) and cast all our cares upon Him (1 Pet. 5:7).

The gold setting depicts Christ as the foundation of our salvation. Gold signifies deity, and the believer is in the divine Person of Christ.

> 1 Corinthians 3:11 For other foundation can no man lay than that is laid, which is Jesus Christ.

The Breastplate

> Exodus 28:15-29 And thou shalt make the breastplate of judgment with cunning work; after the work of the ephod thou shalt make it; *of* gold, *of* blue, and *of* purple, and *of* scarlet, and *of* fine twined linen, shalt thou make it. 16 Foursquare it shall be *being* doubled; a span *shall be* the length thereof, and a span *shall be* the breadth thereof. 17 And thou shalt set in it settings of stones, *even* four rows of stones: *the first* row *shall be* a sardius, a topaz, and a carbuncle: *this shall be* the first row. 18 And the second row *shall be* an emerald, a sapphire, and a diamond. 19 And the third row a ligure, an agate, and an amethyst. 20 And the fourth row a beryl, and an onyx, and a jasper: they shall be set in gold in their inclosings. 21 And the stones shall be

> with the names of the children of Israel, twelve, according to their names, *like* the engravings of a signet; every one with his name shall they be according to the twelve tribes. 22 And thou shalt make upon the breastplate chains at the ends *of* wreathen work *of* pure gold. 23 And thou shalt make upon the breastplate two rings of gold, and shalt put the two rings on the two ends of the breastplate. 24 And thou shalt put the two wreathen *chains* of gold in the two rings *which are* on the ends of the breastplate. 25 And *the other* two ends of the two wreathen *chains* thou shalt fasten in the two ouches, and put *them* on the shoulderpieces of the ephod before it. 26 And thou shalt make two rings of gold, and thou shalt put them upon the two ends of the breastplate in the border thereof, which *is* in the side of the ephod inward. 27 And two *other* rings of gold thou shalt make, and shalt put them on the two sides of the ephod underneath, toward the forepart thereof, over against the *other* coupling thereof, above the curious girdle of the ephod. 28 And they shall bind the breastplate by the rings thereof unto the rings of the ephod with a lace of blue, that *it* may be above the curious girdle of the ephod, and that the breastplate be not loosed from the ephod. 29 And Aaron shall bear the names of the children of Israel in the breastplate of judgment upon his heart, when he goeth in unto the holy *place*, for a memorial before the LORD continually.

Upon the ephod was bound the breastplate, which was placed over the priest's chest. It was a span square (about nine inches). On the breastplate were twelve precious stones set in four rows, each stone engraved with a name of one of the tribes of Israel. The names are not specified in Scripture, and Jewish tradition is not settled on the matter.

1. The breastplate signifies Christ in His multiple offices (with the same fine linen, gold, blue, purple, and scarlet as the ephod).

2. The breastplate signifies Christ's great love for His people. As the breastplate and the jewels were bound over the

high priest's heart, so the Lord's people are permanently engraved upon His heart.

> Jeremiah 31:3 The LORD hath appeared of old unto me, *saying*, Yea, I have loved thee with an everlasting love: therefore with lovingkindness have I drawn thee.

> John 13:1 "... having loved his own which were in the world, he loved them unto the end."

> Ephesians 3:17 That ye ... may be able to comprehend with all saints what *is* the breadth, and length, and depth, and height; 19 And to know the love of Christ, which passeth knowledge, that ye might be filled with all the fulness of God.

3. As the breastplate was securely fastened to the shoulder pieces (Ex. 28:28), so there is no doubt of the believer's secure position in Christ. Nothing can separate us from His love. None of His sheep will ever be lost.

> Romans 8:29 For whom he did foreknow, he also did predestinate *to be* conformed to the image of his Son, that he might be the firstborn among many brethren. 30 Moreover whom he did predestinate, them he also called: and whom he called, them he also justified: and whom he justified, them he also glorified. 31 What shall we then say to these things? If God *be* for us, who *can be* against us? 32 He that spared not his own Son, but delivered him up for us all, how shall he not with him also freely give us all things? 33 Who shall lay any thing to the charge of God's elect? *It is* God that justifieth. 34 Who *is* he that condemneth? *It is* Christ that died, yea rather, that is risen again, who is even at the right hand of God, who also maketh intercession for us. 35 Who shall separate us from the love of Christ? *shall* tribulation, or distress, or persecution, or famine, or nakedness, or peril, or sword?

4. The jewels signify Christ's people as His treasures.

> Malachi 3:16 Then they that feared the LORD spake often one to another: and the LORD hearkened, and heard *it*, and a book of remembrance was written before him for

them that feared the LORD, and that thought upon his name. 17 And they shall be mine, saith the LORD of hosts, in that day when I make up my jewels; and I will spare them, as a man spareth his own son that serveth him.

The church is the treasure that Christ purchased with His blood.

Matthew 13:44 Again, the kingdom of heaven is like unto treasure hid in a field; the which when a man hath found, he hideth, and for joy thereof goeth and selleth all that he hath, and buyeth that field.

Acts 20:28 ... the church of God, which he hath purchased with his own blood.

5. The valuable stones on the high priests breastplate and on his shoulders signify the glory and treasure His people have as adopted sons of God.

We are in Christ and we share His glory. We read of Solomon's glory (Lk. 12:27), a kingdom in which even the shields of the palace guards were made of gold, and silver was counted as nothing (1 Ki. 10:21). We read of Solomon's glorious palaces, his glorious throne, the beautiful apparel of his attendants, his far-flung commercial enterprises, his building projects, his superlative wisdom. His was a kingdom so glorious that the Queen of Sheba, who herself ruled a fabulously wealthy kingdom, was breathless at its sight (1 Ki. 10:5).

Christ's kingdom will be much more glorious, and we will appear with him in that glory (Col. 3:4).

6. As the jewels varied in color and luster, so each believer has his own unique gift and calling in Christ.

Romans 12:3 For I say, through the grace given unto me, to every man that is among you, not to think *of himself* more highly than he ought to think; but to think soberly, according as God hath dealt to every man the measure of faith. 4 For as we have many members in one body, and all

> members have not the same office: 5 So we, *being* many, are one body in Christ, and every one members one of another. 6 Having then gifts differing according to the grace that is given to us, whether prophecy, *let us prophesy* according to the proportion of faith; 7 Or ministry, *let us wait* on *our* ministering: or he that teacheth, on teaching; 8 Or he that exhorteth, on exhortation: he that giveth, *let him do it* with simplicity; he that ruleth, with diligence; he that sheweth mercy, with cheerfulness.

7. The jewels differed in placement on the breastplate. Some were closer to the center of the heart of the high priest.

Whereas the onyx stones on the high priest's shoulders bearing the names of the tribes of Israel were the same, signifying that all of God's people are equally safe by God's power, the jewels on the breastplate were different--in luster and color and value and location.

Though all believers are beloved in Christ and eternally safe in Him, not all occupy the same position in God's affections. This depends on the disciple's passion for Christ.

> John 14:21 He that hath my commandments, and keepeth them, he it is that loveth me: and he that loveth me shall be loved of my Father, and I will love him, and will manifest myself to him.

> John 14:23 Jesus answered and said unto him, If a man love me, he will keep my words: and my Father will love him, and we will come unto him, and make our abode with him.

Consider John. He was more intimate with Christ than the other disciples and is thus called "the disciple that Jesus loved" (John 21:7). He was the one who leaned on Jesus' breast (John 20:2; 21:20). He was the one who stood at the cross and was assigned the care of Jesus' mother (John 19:26). He was the one who outran Peter to the empty tomb and was the first of Christ's disciples to believe in the resurrection (John 20:1-8).

Consider Mary Magdalene, out of whom Jesus cast seven devils, whose love for Jesus kept her at the cross during the crucifixion (Mat. 27:55-56) and took her to the tomb after His death (Mat. 27:61) and then again three days later while it was still dark (Mat. 28:1). It was to Mary that Jesus first appeared that morning (Mark 16:9). John 20 describes the scene in more detail. She saw the stone rolled away and ran and told Peter and John (John 20:1-2). She returned after they left and was weeping at the tomb when she saw Jesus and thought he was a gardener, and He revealed Himself to her in such a touching and intimate manner.

> John 20:10 Then the disciples went away again unto their own home. 11 But Mary stood without at the sepulchre weeping: and as she wept, she stooped down, *and looked* into the sepulchre, 12 And seeth two angels in white sitting, the one at the head, and the other at the feet, where the body of Jesus had lain. 13 And they say unto her, Woman, why weepest thou? She saith unto them, Because they have taken away my Lord, and I know not where they have laid him. 14 And when she had thus said, she turned herself back, and saw Jesus standing, and knew not that it was Jesus. 15 Jesus saith unto her, Woman, why weepest thou? whom seekest thou? She, supposing him to be the gardener, saith unto him, Sir, if thou have borne him hence, tell me where thou hast laid him, and I will take him away. 16 Jesus saith unto her, Mary. She turned herself, and saith unto him, Rabboni; which is to say, Master.

Jesus simply said, "Mary," and she immediately knew who He was.

> "She did not know this supposed gardener who talked to her was the Lord Himself. Then this seeming gardener said just one word: 'Mary.' O the music of it. And mark how she answered: 'Rabboni; which is to say, Master.' All He put into that word, 'Mary,' she put back into that word, 'Master.' All the love that said, 'Mary,' from His lips, from her lips replied in 'Master.' But she said more than just 'Master.' 'Rabboni' is a noun, in the possessive it means: 'My Master.'

> Just as David said, 'My shepherd.' With that same intense accent of personal appropriation she said, 'My Master.' In that supreme moment she forgot everybody, everything else but Him and herself" (I.M. Haldeman).

Consider Paul. He devoted himself passionately to knowing Christ (Phil. 3:7-12).

> "Paul wants to lean on His breast, just above His heartbeat; Paul wants to hear every throb of it. He had Christ already as his Saviour and Lord. He knew his redemption and security in Him, but he wanted more than that; he wanted a closer intimacy with the Lord, a deeper consciousness of Him in his inmost soul. He desired to so walk before the Lord, so serve Him, that he might win a fuller, richer inflow of Him into every essence of his being. To this end he consecrated himself, gave himself up wholly to the Lord and said, 'For me to live is Christ'" (I.M. Haldeman).

Consider Daniel, who was called "greatly beloved" because of his passionate, single-minded devotion to Jehovah God (Dan. 9:23; 10:11, 19).

Since Christ's heart is infinitely large and infinitely loving, there is room for every believer at the very center. He invites each believer to wear His yoke and to learn of Him (Mat. 11:29).

8. The jewels were displayed together so that the glory of each one complimented the others.

Likewise in Christ's church each member is part of the body and all members function together within the body. Ultimately, each living stone is a part of the one glorious eternal temple. "Thus, each had his own peculiar glory and beauty: each differed from, without rivalling the other: and each filled his appointed place in the order of God. There was unity, combined with diversity" (Henry Soltau).

The Urim and Thummim

> Exodus 28:30 And thou shalt put in the breastplate of judgment the Urim and the Thummim; and they shall be upon Aaron's heart, when he goeth in before the LORD: and Aaron shall bear the judgment of the children of Israel upon his heart before the LORD continually.

These objects were placed in the breastplate. Exodus 28:16 says the breastplate was doubled, so it might have formed a pouch or pocket for the urim and thummim.

Some believe that the urim and thummin were the same as the stones on the breastplate. A video published by the Temple Institute in Jerusalem presents this view, but Leviticus 8:8 states that they were separate items.

The appearance of these objects is not described in Scripture, nor was the manner in which they were used. Obviously, then, we do not need to know these things (De. 29:29).

1. The urim and thummim were used to discern God's will (Nu. 27:21; De. 33:8). The words "urim and thummim" mean "lights and perfections" and point to the perfection of revelation in Jesus Christ.

The high priest's Urim and Thummim represent Christ as the Revelation of God (Heb. 1:1-2). He is the Word of God. He is the light and the truth. Those who desire to know the truth about God and life must hear Jesus Christ as recorded in divine Scripture.

2. The urim and thummin represent Christ's omniscience.

The Hebrew word "urim" is the plural of "ore," which means fire. It reminds us of Christ's eyes which appear as a flame of fire in John's vision (Rev. 1:14; 19:12). He knows all things and sees all things. He reminded the churches of this fact ("hath his eyes like unto a flame of fire ... I know thy works," Rev. 2:18-19). The judgment seat of Christ will be a manifestation of the believer's life as seen through the eyes of the omniscient Son of God.

> 1 Corinthians 3:13 Every man's work shall be made manifest: for the day shall declare it, because it shall be revealed by fire; and the fire shall try every man's work of what sort it is.

The urim and thummin within the breastplate remind us that Christ's great love for His people does not mean that He overlooks their sin. "As many as I love, I rebuke and chasten" (Rev. 3:19). Christ not only loves the church, He sanctifies and cleanses it (Eph. 5:25-27). He chastens every one of His sons (Heb. 12:6).

The Mitre and Crown

> Exodus 28:36-39 And thou shalt make a plate *of* pure gold, and grave upon it, *like* the engravings of a signet, HOLINESS TO THE LORD. 37 And thou shalt put it on a blue lace, that it may be upon the mitre; upon the forefront of the mitre it shall be. 38 And it shall be upon Aaron's forehead, that Aaron may bear the iniquity of the holy things, which the children of Israel shall hallow in all their holy gifts; and it shall be always upon his forehead, that they may be accepted before the LORD. 39 And thou shalt embroider the coat of fine linen, and thou shalt make the mitre *of* fine linen, and thou shalt make the girdle *of* needlework.

Upon the high priest's head was a holy golden crown attached to the mitre, which was made of fine white linen (Ex. 28:36-39). This represents Christ as King of kings.

Upon the front of the mitre was attached a golden plate engraved with the words "Holiness to the Lord," signifying the perfect holiness of Christ and His total dedication to the will of the Father.

"Holy" means set apart to God, and this is exemplified by the Lord Jesus. His every thought and desire is to do the will of the Father who had sent Him (John 4:34). He is perfect in thought and deed.

"Holy" means separate from every evil thing, and that, too, characterizes Christ, who is "holy, harmless, undefiled, separate from sinners" (Heb. 7:26).

The crown was not for the high priest; it was for the people. It was "always upon his forehead, that THEY may be accepted before the LORD" (Ex. 28:38).

Our great High Priest bore our sins in His death and continues to intercede for us before the Father on the basis of His atonement. He is the believer's holiness.

Believers, in themselves, are impure even in the holiest things that they do and can be accepted only in Christ. Not for one moment, not in anything that we do, can we find acceptance in ourselves. The very holiest duty we perform must be sanctified by Christ's blood.

This reminds us of John's statement, "If we say that we have no sin, we deceive ourselves" (1 Jn. 1:8).

In his book *Grace Awakening*, Chuck Swindoll says that believers can go for weeks without sinning, but that is not what Scripture teaches. One glorious day we will be saved from the very presence of sin, but that day is yet future. In this present life, the "old man" is with us even as we serve the Lord.

God requires holiness in thought and motive as well as deed; He requires holiness in every public act and every secret counsel; but we are not that holy. We continually fall short of the glory of God. Christ is the New Man that we are to put on; it is His image to which we are to be conformed; but in daily practice we do not yet bear His perfect holiness.

James Gray comments:

> "The 'holy things' are described in the context as the sacrifices and offerings of Israel. Whatever they presented to God in worship were holy in the sense that they were

> consecrated to and appointed by Him. And yet these things themselves had iniquity. When the worshipper brought his bleeding victim as an offering for his sins, his very act of bringing it had in it additional sin which required to be atoned for. ... We are by nature children of wrath, and now, although as believers on our Lord Jesus Christ we are regenerated by His Spirit, still in our flesh there dwelleth no good thing (Rom. 7:18; 8:7). ... In every act of our worship there are imperfection and defilement, because there is present in that act the old evil nature along with the new. ... Bishop Beveridge said: 'I cannot pray but I sin; I cannot hear or preach a sermon but I sin; I cannot give alms or receive the sacrament but I sin; no, I cannot so much as confess my sins but my very confessions are still aggravations of them; my repentance needs to be repented of; my tears need washing; and the very washing of my tears needs still to be washed over again with the blood of my Redeemer'" (James Gray's Commentary).

Thank God, the day of full deliverance from the presence and power of sin is drawing nigh!

The fact that the golden plate was *always* upon Aaron's forehead (Ex. 28:38), reminds us that believers are accepted in Christ at every moment and forever!

THE CLOTHING OF THE ORDINARY PRIESTS

> Exodus 28:40-43 And for Aaron's sons thou shalt make coats, and thou shalt make for them girdles, and bonnets shalt thou make for them, for glory and for beauty. 41 And thou shalt put them upon Aaron thy brother, and his sons with him; and shalt anoint them, and consecrate them, and sanctify them, that they may minister unto me in the priest's office. 42 And thou shalt make them linen breeches to cover their nakedness; from the loins even unto the thighs they shall reach: 43 And they shall be upon Aaron, and upon his sons, when they come in unto the tabernacle of the congregation, or when they come near unto the altar to minister in the holy *place*; that they bear not iniquity,

> and die: *it shall be* a statute for ever unto him and his seed after him.
>
> Exodus 39:27-28 And they made coats *of* fine linen *of* woven work for Aaron, and for his sons, 28 And a mitre *of* fine linen, and goodly bonnets *of* fine linen, and linen breeches *of* fine twined linen,

Aaron's sons, the "common" priests, wore four pieces of clothing: linen breeches, coats, girdles, and bonnets.

The garments were made "for glory and for beauty" (Ex. 28:40). They signify the believer's clothing as a priest of God.

> Isaiah 61:10 I will greatly rejoice in the LORD, my soul shall be joyful in my God; for he hath clothed me with the garments of salvation, he hath covered me with the robe of righteousness, as a bridegroom decketh *himself* with ornaments, and as a bride adorneth *herself* with her jewels.

Like Adam and Eve after the fall, we are clothed in the holy garments provided through the sacrifice of God's holy Lamb (Ge. 3:21).

Not one sin can enter into God's holy presence. In our natural condition before God, we wear filthy garments of sin and self-righteousness (Isa. 64:6). When we come to Christ and believe on Him, He removes our filthy garments and replaces them with the beautiful garments of His own perfect holiness. This is the meaning of justification: *declared righteous* by God because of Christ's atonement.

The coats

1. The coats were made of white linen, which depicts the righteousness of Christ that is imputed to His saints (Rev. 19:8). He is made unto us "righteousness" (1 Cor. 1:30; 2 Cor. 5:21).

2. The white linen will apparently be our clothing even in eternity, and angels are clothed similarly.

Revelation 4:4 And round about the throne *were* four and twenty seats: and upon the seats I saw four and twenty elders sitting, clothed in white raiment; and they had on their heads crowns of gold.

Revelation 7:9 After this I beheld, and, lo, a great multitude, which no man could number, of all nations, and kindreds, and people, and tongues, stood before the throne, and before the Lamb, clothed with white robes, and palms in their hands.

Revelation 7:9 After this I beheld, and, lo, a great multitude, which no man could number, of all nations, and kindreds, and people, and tongues, stood before the throne, and before the Lamb, clothed with white robes, and palms in their hands.

Revelation 15:6 And the seven angels came out of the temple, having the seven plagues, clothed in pure and white linen, and having their breasts girded with golden girdles.

3. That the saints' coats are long robes is obvious from many passages. Modest dress is long and loose.

Mark 16:5 And entering into the sepulchre, they saw a young man sitting on the right side, clothed in a long white garment; and they were affrighted.

Revelation 1:13 And in the midst of the seven candlesticks one like unto the Son of man, clothed with a garment down to the foot, and girt about the paps with a golden girdle.

4. The white linen coats also teach us that we can only serve God in Christ's power. Paul said that the Christian life that he lived was really Christ living the life through him (Galatians 2:20). We must walk in Christ, the New Man, and renounce the old man.

The girdle

1. The girdle represents service.

It was used like a belt to tie the robe to one's waist so that the individual could move about more freely, as when the Jews prepared to journey from Egypt (Ex. 12:11) and as when the servant girded himself to serve his master (Luke 17:8). Every believer is a priest who is called to God's service. We are saved to serve. Christ has emphasized His will in this present age that His people preach the gospel to every person in every nation, that we baptize those who believe, and that we teach them to observe all things that He has commanded (Mat. 28:29-30; Mark 16:15). This is a massive job; there is a lot of work to do; and it requires the participation of every saint. Each is given gifts and appointed a ministry.

2. The girdle was also used for military equipment (2 Sam. 20:8).

This depicts the believer as a soldier in God's army. We are engaged in spiritual warfare against the forces of darkness (Eph. 6:10-18). The girdle in the Christian's armor is "truth" (Eph. 6:14). It is by the truth of Christ and by the truth of God's Word and by the truth of our personal testimony that we overcome the devil.

3. The girdle reminds us of Christ's imminent return.

> Luke 12:35-36 Let your loins be girded about, and *your* lights burning; 36 And ye yourselves like unto men that wait for their lord, when he will return from the wedding; that when he cometh and knocketh, they may open unto him immediately.

Christ can come at any time, and we are to be ready to meet Him.

These two things are intimately connected. By staying busy in the Lord's service we are kept reminded about His coming and are ready for His return, whereas when we grow slack and worldly and spiritually lazy, the truth of Christ's return grows dim in our vision and the world with its enticements grows large.

> "The hope of the Lord's return will not really abide in the heart, unless we keep our loins girded as engaged in our Master's work, and let our light shine out before men. An inactive believer is sure to become a worldly minded one, and he will begin to eat and drink with the drunken. He will have companionship with the men of the world, whose intoxicating pursuits of avarice, ambition, and pleasure, deaden their hearts and consciences to all the truth of God" (Henry Soltau).

4. The girdle reminds us of the necessity of controlling our thoughts.

> 1 Peter 1:13 Wherefore gird up the loins of your mind, be sober, and hope to the end for the grace that is to be brought unto you at the revelation of Jesus Christ;

We are to gird up the loins of our minds. The mind is the chief battleground of the believer's life. We must fill it with God's Word and reject everything that is contrary to this holy Standard (Psalm 1:1-3).

A great many believers are slothful in their pursuit of the knowledge of God's Word and careless about what they read and study, what they meditate on, what they watch on television and view on the Internet, what they talk about. This is reflected in weak Christian living, weak families, and weak churches.

We must keep our minds "sober," which means that we are not intoxicated with and captivated by anything contrary to God's will and anything that detracts from right thinking, whether liquor, drugs, worldly music, the vain world of professional sports, the entertainment of the pop culture, or science falsely so called. Even romance novels and "conservative politics" can be an unholy intoxication that detracts from what we should be thinking about, which is Jesus Christ and His glory and His will and His coming kingdom. Rush Limbaugh and FoxNews are "conservative" by the standard of today's politics, but they aren't godly by any standard, and they are enemies of the holy laws and perfect standards of God's Word.

We must gird up the loins of our mind and keep ourselves from being intoxicated by the exciting but perverse elements of the electronic pop culture which is racing on jet engines toward eternal destruction.

5. The girded Christian is true New Testament Christianity, as we see in Thessalonians.

> 1 Thessalonians 1:9-10 For they themselves shew of us what manner of entering in we had unto you, and how ye turned to God from idols to serve the living and true God; 10 And to wait for his Son from heaven, whom he raised from the dead, *even* Jesus, which delivered us from the wrath to come.

The church at Thessalonica is upheld in God's Word as a model church. Its members had turned to God from idols in true repentance and saving faith. And they were busy serving God and waiting for Christ's return.

The bonnet

> Exodus 28:40 And for Aaron's sons thou shalt make coats, and thou shalt make for them girdles, and bonnets shalt thou make for them, for glory and for beauty.

> Exodus 39:28 And a mitre *of* fine linen, and goodly bonnets *of* fine linen, and linen breeches *of* fine twined linen,

The bonnet was for glory and for beauty (Ex. 28:40). It was made of fine linen and was called "goodly" (Ex. 39:28). It therefore depicts the believer's glory in Christ.

The linen breeches

> Exodus 28:42-43 And thou shalt make them linen breeches to cover their nakedness; from the loins even unto the thighs they shall reach: 43 And they shall be upon Aaron,

and upon his sons, when they come in unto the tabernacle of the congregation, or when they come near unto the altar to minister in the holy *place*; that they bear not iniquity, and die: *it shall be* a statute for ever unto him and his seed after him.

These were undergarments. They covered from the loins to the thighs and were intended to hide the priest's nakedness as he served the Lord.

Spiritually, the priest's breeches remind us that the believer is fully clothed in Christ's righteousness, and his sinful nakedness is covered (Rev. 3:18).

The priest's breeches also remind us of the importance of modesty in the Christian life. After the fall, man's heart became evil, and since then nakedness is a path to sin. Men, especially, are enticed easily through sight (Mat. 5:28). Thus, after the fall God clothed Adam and Eve in robes to replace the aprons which were not sufficient to hide their nakedness.

THE CONSECRATION OF THE PRIESTS

See Exodus 29 and Leviticus 8.

The consecration of the priests represents wonderful spiritual truths, especially as a picture of the consecration of believers. None of this typifies salvation; consecration is the process of dedication and sanctification following salvation.

The difference between Aaron and his sons is noted in the following statement:

> "Aaron alone was anointed before the blood was shed; he was clad in his robes of office and anointed with the holy oil before ever his sons were clothed or anointed. The reason for this is obvious. Aaron, when spoken of by himself, typifies Christ in His own peerless excellency and dignity; and, as we know, Christ appeared in all His own personal worth and was anointed by the Holy Ghost previous to the accomplishment of His atoning work. In all things He has the pre-eminence (Col. 1:18). Still, there is

> the fullest identification afterwards between Aaron and his sons, as there is the fullest identification between Christ and His people. 'The Sanctifier and the sanctified are all of one' (Heb. 2:11). The personal distinctness enhances the value of the mystic oneness" (C.H. Mackintosh, *Notes on the Pentateuch*, p. 340).

Washing with water

> Exodus 29:4 And Aaron and his sons thou shalt bring unto the door of the tabernacle of the congregation, and shalt wash them with water.

The washing with water typifies God's demand that His people be pure and put away sin from their lives. In the New Testament, the Word of God is identified as the water that God uses to cleanse His saints.

> Ephesians 5:26 That he might sanctify and cleanse it with the washing of water by the word,

> John 15:3 Now ye are clean through the word which I have spoken unto you.

> John 17:17 Sanctify them through thy truth: thy word is truth.

> James 1:21 Wherefore lay apart all filthiness and superfluity of naughtiness, and receive with meekness the engrafted word, which is able to save your souls.

The Bible is the living Word of God (Heb. 4:12), and it not only shows the way of righteousness but also supplies the believer with power to walk in that way.

We see the necessity of believers letting the Word of God dwell in them richly through reading, studying, singing, hearing, meditating in, and memorizing the Scriptures (Col. 3:16).

Aaron was clothed and anointed with oil

> Exodus 29:5-7 And thou shalt take the garments, and put upon Aaron the coat, and the robe of the ephod, and the ephod, and the breastplate, and gird him with the curious girdle of the ephod: 6 And thou shalt put the mitre upon his head, and put the holy crown upon the mitre. 7 Then shalt thou take the anointing oil, and pour *it* upon his head, and anoint him.

1. The anointing oil represents the Holy Spirit, and Aaron's anointing signifies the anointing of Christ by the Spirit of God.

The name *Messiah* (Hebrew) or *Christ* (Greek) means *Anointed* (Isaiah 11:1-3).

Jesus was conceived by the Spirit (Mat. 1:18-20) and was anointed by the Spirit at His baptism (Luke 3:21-22).

When Jesus began His public ministry in Nazareth, He preached from Isaiah 61:1, identifying Himself as the Anointed One, the Messiah (Lk. 4:16-21).

He ministered in the power of the Spirit (Luke 4:14).

Peter said that Jesus was anointed with the Holy Spirit and with power (Acts 10:38).

Christ was also raised up from the dead by the Spirit (Rom. 8:11).

2. As Aaron was anointed before the blood of the sacrifices was shed and applied (Ex. 29:5-7, 10-14), so Jesus was sinless and had no need of an atonement for Himself.

On the other hand, the sons of Aaron, typifying Christ's priestly people, could not be anointed until first they had been cleansed by the blood.

3. The anointing oil was sprinkled on Aaron's sons (Ex. 29:21).

This signifies the anointing of believer-priests by the Holy Spirit.

2 Corinthians 1:21-22 Now he which stablisheth us with you in Christ, and hath anointed us, *is* God; 22 Who hath also sealed us, and given the earnest of the Spirit in our hearts.

By the Spirit of God, the believer has wisdom and understanding (1 John 2:20, 27), comfort and encouragement (John 14:16), power to overcome the devil (Eph. 6:12-18), conviction of sin (Eph. 4:30; Jam. 4:5), help in prayer (Rom. 8:26), divine guidance (Acts 8:29), spiritual gifts for service (1 Cor. 12:7-11), and power for evangelism (Acts 1:8).

4. As the priests were anointed both with blood and oil *at the same time.*

Likewise the believer is washed by the blood of Christ and indwelt with the Holy Spirit at the time of his conversion. There is no time gap between regeneration and the coming of the Holy Spirit into the believer's life. When we believe the gospel and trust Christ, we receive the Spirit.

Ephesians 1:12-13 That we should be to the praise of his glory, who first trusted in Christ. 13 In whom ye also *trusted*, after that ye heard the word of truth, the gospel of your salvation: in whom also after that ye believed, ye were sealed with that holy Spirit of promise,

5. The anointing oil was a mixture of four spices compounded in oil.

Exodus 30:22-25 Moreover the LORD spake unto Moses, saying, 23 Take thou also unto thee principal spices, of pure myrrh five hundred *shekels*, and of sweet cinnamon half so much, *even* two hundred and fifty *shekels*, and of sweet calamus two hundred and fifty *shekels*, 24 And of cassia five hundred *shekels*, after the shekel of the sanctuary, and of oil olive an hin: 25 And thou shalt make it an oil of holy ointment, an ointment compound after the art of the apothecary: it shall be an holy anointing oil.

The spices were blended together to make one holy oil. This is a powerful picture of the Holy Spirit. The fruit of the Holy Spirit is one fruit with multiple characteristics.

> Galatians 5:22-23 But the fruit of the Spirit is love, joy, peace, longsuffering, gentleness, goodness, faith, 23 Meekness, temperance: against such there is no law.

> Ephesians 5:9 (For the fruit of the Spirit *is* in all goodness and righteousness and truth;)

Its essence is holy love as defined in 1 Corinthians 13:4-7.

The fruit of the Spirit is found in its perfection in Jesus Christ. Even as the oil flowed down Aaron in an abundance and covered his entire person (Psa. 133:2), so Christ our High Priest has the fulness of the Spirit.

> John 3:34 For he whom God hath sent speaketh the words of God: for God giveth not the Spirit by measure *unto him*.

Christ is full of grace (John 1:14), and the believer partakes of Christ's fulness insofar as he yields to His control (John 1:16).

> John 1:14 And the Word was made flesh, and dwelt among us, (and we beheld his glory, the glory as of the only begotten of the Father,) full of grace and truth.

> John 1:16 And of his fulness have all we received, and grace for grace.

6. The anointing oil had a pleasing smell. This speaks of the joy of the Lord that is produced by the Spirit.

Jesus is anointed with the oil of gladness above His fellows (Psa. 45:7). He is the happiest Man in the universe! In Christ's presence is fullness of joy (Psa. 16:11) and in His kingdom His people will trade the oil of mourning for joy (Isa. 61:3).

The oil's pleasant texture and smell also speak of the incalculable blessings in Christ. He has given us all things to enjoy (1 Tim. 6:17). He made a delightful garden for the first man, and He has made an even more delightful garden for the eternal dwelling of the Second Man.

7. The oil was holy; it was distinct and set apart to God.

> Exodus 30:31-33 And thou shalt speak unto the children of Israel, saying, This shall be an holy anointing oil unto me throughout your generations. 32 Upon man's flesh shall it not be poured, neither shall ye make *any other* like it, after the composition of it: it *is* holy, *and* it shall be holy unto you. 33 Whosoever compoundeth *any* like it, or whosoever putteth *any* of it upon a stranger, shall even be cut off from his people.

The oil was unlike anything in this world and was not to be imitated. Likewise there is one true Holy Spirit but many false spirits (2 Cor. 11:4; 1 Tim. 4:1; 1 John 4:1). There is the spirit of the prince of this world that is active in every unsaved person (Eph. 2:2).

The true Spirit of God is called "the Spirit of truth" four times in Scripture (John 14:17; 15:26; 16:13; 1 John 4:6). Repetition is for emphasis, and God is warning us to try the spirits and to reject any spirit that is not according to the truth of God's Word.

In this day, contemporary worship is a major example of false oil. In 1987 I attended one of the largest charismatic conferences ever held. Called the North American Congress on the Holy Spirit & World Evangelization and attended by about 40,000, it represented the ecumenical charismatic movement of our times. It represented the heart and soul of contemporary worship music. The attendees came from 40 different denominations. Fifty percent were Roman Catholic, and there were many Roman Catholic speakers. There were Roman Catholic ministries in attendance that promoted the papacy and Mary veneration. A Catholic mass was held every morning, and the Pentecostal chairman of the meeting, Vincent Synan, urged everyone to attend. One of the Catholic speakers, Tom Forrest, said that the only way he could get to heaven was through purgatory.

I attended this conference with media credentials and talked to many of the speakers and attendees and participated in the official media sessions, and I met no one who had a problem with yoking together with Roman Catholics in ministry and worship.

Beware. This is not the pure oil of the Lord's holy tabernacle!

8. The oil was used to anoint the tabernacle and every object in it to sanctify them.

> Exodus 30:25-29 And thou shalt make it an oil of holy ointment, an ointment compound after the art of the apothecary: it shall be an holy anointing oil. 26 And thou shalt anoint the tabernacle of the congregation therewith, and the ark of the testimony, 27 And the table and all his vessels, and the candlestick and his vessels, and the altar of incense, 28 And the altar of burnt offering with all his vessels, and the laver and his foot. 29 And thou shalt sanctify them, that they may be most holy: whatsoever toucheth them shall be holy.

> Leviticus 8:10 And Moses took the anointing oil, and anointed the tabernacle and all that *was* therein, and sanctified them.

Just as everything had to be anointed by the holy oil before it could be used for ministry, it is the Holy Spirit who sets the believer apart to God and seals and anoints him for service (Ephesians 1:13-14; 1 John 2:27).

The believers did not begin to fulfill Christ's command for world evangelism until the Spirit came at Pentecost (Acts 1:8).

9. The oil was not to be put upon a stranger.

> Exodus 30:33 ... whosoever putteth *any* of it upon a stranger, shall even be cut off from his people.

Likewise the Bible says that those who do not have the Spirit of God do not have Christ (Rom. 8:9). Those who do not have the Spirit are unregenerate and have no part in the things of God. They are strangers. They are still in their sins and are unclean before God. They should not be allowed to join the church as members or to serve in the church in any position. Their service is not acceptable to God.

10. The oil was not to be poured upon man's flesh.

> Exodus 30:32 Upon man's flesh shall it not be poured...

Likewise the Bible teaches us that the fallen flesh cannot be sanctified. It must die, being under God's judgment (Rom. 6:23). The old man was put to death by Christ on the cross, and the believer is dead positionally. In practice, the flesh is still present and active, and there is a battle between the flesh and the Spirit in the Christian life.

> Galatians 5:16-17 *This* I say then, Walk in the Spirit, and ye shall not fulfil the lust of the flesh. 17 For the flesh lusteth against the Spirit, and the Spirit against the flesh: and these are contrary the one to the other: so that ye cannot do the things that ye would.

The Offerings

The sin offering (Ex. 29:10-14) and the burnt offering (Ex. 29:15-18) represent the two-fold aspect of Christ's atonement.

The sin offering signifies the man-ward aspect: the payment of man's sin debt through Christ's blood and death (Rom. 5:9-10).

The burnt offering signifies the God-ward aspect: Christ's complete devotion to the Father (John 4:34; 18:11) and the Father's complete acceptance of Christ and His Sacrifice (Mat. 3:17; 17:5).

The Sin Offering

> Exodus 29:10-14 And thou shalt cause a bullock to be brought before the tabernacle of the congregation: and Aaron and his sons shall put their hands upon the head of the bullock. 11 And thou shalt kill the bullock before the LORD, *by* the door of the tabernacle of the congregation. 12 And thou shalt take of the blood of the bullock, and put *it* upon the horns of the altar with thy finger, and pour all the blood beside the bottom of the altar. 13 And thou shalt take all the fat that covereth the inwards, and the caul *that is* above the liver, and the two kidneys, and the fat that *is* upon them, and burn *them* upon the altar. 14 But the flesh of the bullock, and his skin, and his dung, shalt thou burn with fire without the camp: it *is* a sin offering.

> Leviticus 8:14-17 And he brought the bullock for the sin offering: and Aaron and his sons laid their hands upon the head of the bullock for the sin offering. 15 And he slew *it*; and Moses took the blood, and put *it* upon the horns of the altar round about with his finger, and purified the altar, and poured the blood at the bottom of the altar, and sanctified it, to make reconciliation upon it. 16 And he took all the fat that *was* upon the inwards, and the caul *above* the liver, and the two kidneys, and their fat, and Moses burned *it* upon the altar. 17 But the bullock, and his hide, his flesh, and his dung, he burnt with fire without the camp; as the LORD commanded Moses.

The *sin offering* depicts Christ as our sin-bearer. It depicts justification and eternal salvation through Christ's offering on the cross. It signifies Christ as "the lamb of God, which taketh away the sin of the world" (John 1:29).

1. The bullock portrays Christ as the Servant of God, the One who came to do God's will.

This is the theme of the Gospel of Mark. Christ summarized it as follows: "For even the Son of man came not to be ministered unto, but to minister, and to give his life a ransom for many" (Mk. 10:45).

"The bullock is typical of the Lord Jesus Christ in His life of perfect service, as well as in His atoning death. The bullock ploughed the land, brought home the sheaves from the harvest field, trod out the corn for the household" (Thomas Newberry, *Types of the Levitical Offerings*).

2. The sacrificial animals were "without blemish" (Ex. 29:1).

This signifies Christ's sinless character. He is "as a lamb without blemish and without spot" (1 Pet. 1:19).

3. The priests laid their hands on the sacrifice (Ex. 29:10, 15).

This signifies the two-fold action of transferring the offerer's sin to the sacrifice and transferring the sacrifice's atoning value to the offerer. This is the two-fold action of justification as seen in the following verse:

> 2 Corinthians 5:21 For he hath made him *to be* sin for us, who knew no sin; that we might be made the righteousness of God in him.

The sin offering died in the place of the priests, as Christ died *in the place of* the sinner. He is our sin-bearer (Isa. 53:5-6).

The burnt offering was accepted as a sweet savour by God *in the place of* the priests (Ex. 29:18). Likewise Christ is the sinless One who is well-pleasing before God the Father, and believers are accepted in Him.

The laying on of hands signifies repentance and faith, which is the means of receiving Christ's salvation. The sinner must symbolically place his hands on Christ, admitting that he is a sinner deserving of God's judgment and believing that Christ, the innocent, sinless Substitute, paid the full punishment that we deserve.

4. The sacrifice was killed before the Lord (Ex. 29:11).

Christ's sacrifice was a sacrifice made *unto God*; it was made to satisfy God's holy law (Isa. 53:10-11).

5. Blood was shed (Ex. 29:12).

Christ had to die but He also had to shed His blood. God's law says that without the shedding of blood, there is no remission of sin (Heb. 9:22). Had Christ died by strangling, He would not have atoned for our sin. The saints will sing of Christ's blood forever.

> Revelation 5:9 And they sung a new song, saying, Thou art worthy to take the book, and to open the seals thereof: for thou wast slain, and hast redeemed us to God by thy blood out of every kindred, and tongue, and people, and nation;

6. The blood of the sin offering was put on the horns of the altar (Ex. 29:12).

Horns signify power.

> Psalms 75:4-5 I said unto the fools, Deal not foolishly: and to the wicked, Lift not up the horn: 5 Lift not up your horn on high: speak *not with* a stiff neck.

See also Psalm 89:24; 91:10; 112:9.

The blood-anointed altar signifies the power of the cross of Christ to take away sin. The horns picture Christ's authority. He is the eternal Son of God. He has all power in heaven and in earth (Mat. 28:18). All things have been put under His feet (Eph. 1:22). The fact that this is the One who made the sacrifice teaches us that the sacrifice was perfectly acceptable before God and perfectly efficacious in its power to save.

7. The blood was poured out beside the altar (Ex. 29:12).

This signifies Christ pouring out all of His life's blood for our sins by means of the beatings, the crucifixion, and the terrible wound in his side (John 19:34). Isaiah prophesied that he "poured out his soul unto death" (Isa. 53:12). Jesus said, "this is my blood of the new testament WHICH IS SHED for many for the remission of sins" (Mat. 26:28).

8. The inner part of the sacrifice was burned on the altar (Ex. 29:13).

This signifies Christ's love for and total devotion to God the Father and God's acceptance of His devotion, as we will see in the study on the burnt offering. When Christ died, God the Father saw Christ's innermost devotion and suffering.

As the offering was consumed on the fire, so Christ was consumed on the cross. He died and was buried for three days.

9. The flesh of the sacrifice was burned without the camp (Ex. 29:14).

This signifies Christ rejected by His own people Israel and crucified outside of the city of Jerusalem as a common criminal.

> Hebrews 13:11-13 For the bodies of those beasts, whose blood is brought into the sanctuary by the high priest for sin, are burned without the camp. 12 Wherefore Jesus also, that he might sanctify the people with his own blood, suffered without the gate. 13 Let us go forth therefore unto him without the camp, bearing his reproach.

The "camp" also signifies Israel's Pharisaical system of religious legalism. Christ died outside of every religious system, and those who will be saved must turn from false religions of human works and receive Christ alone as Lord and Saviour.

The Burnt Offering

> Exodus 29:15-18 Thou shalt also take one ram; and Aaron and his sons shall put their hands upon the head of the ram. 16 And thou shalt slay the ram, and thou shalt take his blood, and sprinkle *it* round about upon the altar. 17 And thou shalt cut the ram in pieces, and wash the inwards of him, and his legs, and put *them* unto his pieces, and

unto his head. 18 And thou shalt burn the whole ram upon the altar: it *is* a burnt offering unto the LORD: it *is* a sweet savour, an offering made by fire unto the LORD.

Leviticus 8:18-29 And he brought the ram for the burnt offering: and Aaron and his sons laid their hands upon the head of the ram. 19 And he killed *it*; and Moses sprinkled the blood upon the altar round about. 20 And he cut the ram into pieces; and Moses burnt the head, and the pieces, and the fat. 21 And he washed the inwards and the legs in water; and Moses burnt the whole ram upon the altar: it *was* a burnt sacrifice for a sweet savour, *and* an offering made by fire unto the LORD; as the LORD commanded Moses. 22 And he brought the other ram, the ram of consecration: and Aaron and his sons laid their hands upon the head of the ram. 23 And he slew *it*; and Moses took of the blood of it, and put *it* upon the tip of Aaron's right ear, and upon the thumb of his right hand, and upon the great toe of his right foot. 24 And he brought Aaron's sons, and Moses put of the blood upon the tip of their right ear, and upon the thumbs of their right hands, and upon the great toes of their right feet: and Moses sprinkled the blood upon the altar round about. 25 And he took the fat, and the rump, and all the fat that *was* upon the inwards, and the caul *above* the liver, and the two kidneys, and their fat, and the right shoulder: 26 And out of the basket of unleavened bread, that *was* before the LORD, he took one unleavened cake, and a cake of oiled bread, and one wafer, and put *them* on the fat, and upon the right shoulder: 27 And he put all upon Aaron's hands, and upon his sons' hands, and waved them *for* a wave offering before the LORD. 28 And Moses took them from off their hands, and burnt *them* on the altar upon the burnt offering: they *were* consecrations for a sweet savour: it *is* an offering made by fire unto the LORD. 29 And Moses took the breast, and waved it *for* a wave offering before the LORD: *for* of the ram of consecration it was Moses' part; as the LORD commanded Moses.

The *burnt offering* depicts Christ's complete devotion to God and God's acceptance of Him. The burnt offering is burnt wholly on the altar (Ex. 29:18). It signifies Christ offering "himself without spot to God" (Heb. 9:14). It signifies Christ as God's (1 Cor. 3:23).

1. The offering was a ram, which was a male sheep and was an expensive sacrifice.

The first mention of a ram in the Bible was the ram that Abraham was instructed to kill along with other sacrifices (Ge. 15:9-10). The sacrifices on that occasion signified God's eternal, sure covenant with Abraham. God walked through the sacrifices alone, signifying the unconditional nature of the covenant (Ge. 15:17-21). Likewise Christ is the sacrifice that makes God's promise of salvation sure to every believer, and Christ died alone to purchase this salvation. The sinner does nothing to earn the gift; his part is to receive it and enjoy it forever.

The second mention of a ram in the Bible is the one that was provided by God to die in the place of Isaac (Ge. 22:13). The ram was caught in the thorn bushes. What a wonderful lesson! Christ is the thorn-crowned Saviour who died in the sinner's place.

2. The priests laid their hands on the burnt offering (Ex. 29:15).

As we have seen, this means that the offering became their substitute. As Jesus is our substitute for the payment of sin, He is also our substitute for devotion to God. We are never accepted in ourselves. Our standing before God is only and always because of Jesus, and our service to God is only because of Him. Our acceptance is "in Christ." Our very best service is impure, but God accepts it because of Christ and even rewards us for it.

It is because we are in Christ that we are invited to present our bodies a "living sacrifice, holy, acceptable unto God" (Rom. 12:1).

Our labor is not in vain because it is "in the Lord" (1 Cor. 15:58).

3. The ram's blood was sprinkled "round about upon the altar" (Ex. 29:16; Lev. 8:19).

The blood of Christ is not only the basis of forgiveness of sin and eternal life, it is the basis of our acceptable service and worship.

The sprinkling round about signifies the power of the blood to save men of all nations: east, west, north, and south. It signifies the preaching of the gospel to every creature (Mark 16:15).

"The blood has a voice of invitation to sinners of every clime" (Thomas Newberry).

4. The ram's inwards and legs were washed and placed with the head upon the altar (Ex. 29:17).

This signifies Christ's complete holiness and sinless perfection. He was perfect in every way: in his actions (the legs), in his thoughts, in the very secrets of his deepest motives (the head), and in his affections (the heart and other inward organs).

Christ did not sin (1 Pet. 2:22) and there was no sin in Him (1 Jn. 3:5). He was pure in thought and deed.

Had Christ not been sinlessly perfect, He could not have been our substitute. If He had any sin whatsoever, He would have died for His own sin rather than for our sin. To break even one of God's laws brings death (Jam. 2:10).

> "Every portion of the ram came under the eye of Moses. The head, the seat of mind and intellect: the inwards, the seat of the will and affections: the legs, the tokens of the outward walk and conduct. All were scrutinized, and

presented in perfect cleanness to God, upon the altar. This is the type of the unblemished ways, and spotless intrinsic purity of Christ" (Henry Soltau).

5. The ram was wholly burnt on the altar as a sweet savour unto the LORD (Ex. 29:18).

This *signifies Christ's complete devotion to the Father.*

> Psalms 40:6-8 Sacrifice and offering thou didst not desire; mine ears hast thou opened: burnt offering and sin offering hast thou not required. 7 Then said I, Lo, I come: in the volume of the book *it is* written of me, 8 I delight to do thy will, O my God: yea, thy law *is* within my heart.

In this Messianic Psalm, the opening of the ear refers to the boring of the ear of a servant who loves his master and wife and children so much that he wants to stay with them rather than accept his freedom (Ex. 21:5-6). This represents the sweet devotion that Christ has to the Father.

> John 4:34 Jesus saith unto them, My meat is to do the will of him that sent me, and to finish his work.

> John 5:30 I can of mine own self do nothing: as I hear, I judge: and my judgment is just; because I seek not mine own will, but the will of the Father which hath sent me.

> John 6:38 For I came down from heaven, not to do mine own will, but the will of him that sent me.

> John 8:29 And he that sent me is with me: the Father hath not left me alone; for I do always those things that please him.

The burnt offering is depicted by Abraham's offering of Isaac (Ge. 22:1-2). As Isaac was willing to be offered and made no protest or resistancc, so Christ was willing to leave His heavenly glory and come into this sin-cursed world and suffer and die for man's sins.

His death was an act of devotion to the Father as much as an act of love for sinners. He "offered himself without spot to God" (Heb. 9:14).

The ram wholly burnt on the altar *also signifies the Father's complete satisfaction with the Son*. The ram was "a sweet savour, an offering made by fire unto the LORD" (Ex. 29:18).

At Christ's baptism and again at His transfiguration, the Father said, "This is my beloved Son in whom I am well pleased (Mat. 3:17; 17:5).

As the ram was placed on the fire of the altar (Ex. 29:18), so Christ endured every trial and tribulation in this sin-cursed world, including the devil's temptations, the rejection by His own people, and the shame and suffering of the cross, yet He never wavered in His devotion to the Father.

This is the perfect devotion that Adam failed to give to His loving Creator, but which characterizes the Second Man. In all of this we see the Trinity. The Son was with the Father from all eternity (John 1:1). The Son is in the bosom of the Father, meaning at the heart of His affections (Jn. 1:18). Jesus spoke of the glory that He had with the Father before the world was made (John 17:5).

The Consecration Offering

> Exodus 29:19-28 And thou shalt take the other ram; and Aaron and his sons shall put their hands upon the head of the ram. 20 Then shalt thou kill the ram, and take of his blood, and put *it* upon the tip of the right ear of Aaron, and upon the tip of the right ear of his sons, and upon the thumb of their right hand, and upon the great toe of their right foot, and sprinkle the blood upon the altar round about. 21 And thou shalt take of the blood that *is* upon the altar, and of the anointing oil, and sprinkle *it* upon Aaron, and upon his garments, and upon his sons, and upon the garments of his sons with him: and he shall be hallowed, and his garments, and his sons, and his sons' garments with him. 22 Also thou shalt take of the ram the fat and the rump, and the fat that covereth the inwards, and the caul *above* the liver, and the two kidneys, and the fat that *is* upon them, and the right shoulder; for it *is* a ram of

> consecration: 23 And one loaf of bread, and one cake of oiled bread, and one wafer out of the basket of the unleavened bread that *is* before the LORD: 24 And thou shalt put all in the hands of Aaron, and in the hands of his sons; and shalt wave them *for* a wave offering before the LORD. 25 And thou shalt receive them of their hands, and burn *them* upon the altar for a burnt offering, for a sweet savour before the LORD: it *is* an offering made by fire unto the LORD. 26 And thou shalt take the breast of the ram of Aaron's consecration, and wave it *for* a wave offering before the LORD: and it shall be thy part. 27 And thou shalt sanctify the breast of the wave offering, and the shoulder of the heave offering, which is waved, and which is heaved up, of the ram of the consecration, *even* of *that* which *is* for Aaron, and of *that* which is for his sons: 28 And it shall be Aaron's and his sons' by a statute for ever from the children of Israel: for it *is* an heave offering: and it shall be an heave offering from the children of Israel of the sacrifice of their peace offerings, *even* their heave offering unto the LORD.

The consecration offering represents the believer's devotion and service to God as accepted in Christ.

1. The priests laid their hands on the head of the offering (Ex. 29:19), signifying that Christ died in their place and is the Substitute for them before God.

2. The blood was put on the right ear, the right thumb, and the right big toe (Ex. 29:20).

This signifies the cleansing of the whole man by Christ's blood. He cleanses our hearing, our actions, and our goings so that we can offer acceptable service to God.

We are to dedicate our hearing wholly to the Lord, so that we hear only that which is conformable to His Word and reject those things which are false and evil.

We are to dedicate our hands to the Lord so that we only do those things that please Him. The right hand signifies strength and skill (Ex. 15:6; Psa. 137:5). We should give our very best to the Lord.

And we are to dedicate our feet to the Lord so that we only go where God leads. We should use our feet to carry the good news of salvation (Rom. 10:15).

It is only through Christ's blood that we can do any of these. The ear can only be opened by salvation. Before that we cannot understand the things of God (1 Cor. 2:14). Before we are cleansed by Christ's blood our entire thoughts and actions are unclean before God and unacceptable to Him.

3. The blood and anointing oil were sprinkled on the priests (Ex. 29:21).

This signifies the Holy Spirit's consecration of the believer and His work in the believer.

4. The rump, inwards, and right shoulder were taken from the sacrifice. These are waved before the Lord together with one loaf of bread, one cake, and one wafer (Ex. 29:22-24).

The sacrifice with its bread offerings signifies Christ. The unleavened bread signifies His sinless perfection. Leaven is always used as a symbol for sin or error in the Bible (e.g., Lk. 12:1; 1 Cor. 5:6-8; Gal. 5:9).

The cakes mingled with oil (Ex. 29:2) signify Christ born of the Spirit and thus perfectly holy in His nature (Luke 1:35).

The wafers anointed with oil (Ex. 29:2) signify Christ anointed by the Spirit at His baptism and thereafter led by and empowered by the Spirit during His earthly ministry (Mat. 3:16; Lk. 4:18).

Observe that many types are required to picture Christ. He is eternal and infinite, and we will learn about Him forever.

The waving signifies the complete devotion of Christ to God ("I do always those things that please him," John 8:29).

"Blessed perfectness, sinless purity, unswerving obedience! How contrasted with the mixed motives, the unclean desires, the constant unbelief and disobedience which meet the eye of our heavenly Father, as He marks *our* thoughts and intents, as He searches *our* purposes and ways" (Henry Soltau).

The waving of the consecration offering also signifies the devotion of the believer to God. We can offer ourselves to God and serve him acceptably because we are sanctified in Christ. We should therefore offer our lives to the Lord in complete surrender to His service (Romans 12:1-2). The waving of the offering depicts the believer saying to God, "Here am I, send me" (Isa. 6:8). To surrender to God's will is only our reasonable duty in light of what He has done for us. Having saved us, He owns us by right of creation and by right of redemption.

We should continually fill our hands with and wave those things before the Lord which are acceptable to Him.

> "We may be assured that our hands and hearts will be occupied with one thing, or another. Either the world with its vanities, and the flesh with its lusts will take their place within--or Christ and His comeliness, His beauty, His perfections, will fill our souls" (Soltau).

5. The consecration offering was burned on the altar as a burnt offering before the Lord (Ex. 29:25).

This signifies Christ's complete surrender to the Father as a pleasing and acceptable offering and the believer's acceptance in Him.

6. The breast of the offering was waved before the Lord (Ex. 29:26).

This signifies the heart and affections of Christ completely devoted to the Father. Only the Father can fully understand the heart of Christ. Only the Father knows the Son and the Son the Father (Mat. 11:27). There are mysteries here, and depth of knowledge here, that we will never plumb.

The waving of the breast also signifies the heart and affections of the believer devoted to God as accepted in

Christ. We are to set our affections on things above, not on things on the earth (Col. 3:1-2).

We are not to serve God out of a mere sense of duty. We are to love God with all the heart because He is worthy of our deepest and most passionate affection.

> Deuteronomy 6:5 And thou shalt love the LORD thy God with all thine heart, and with all thy soul, and with all thy might.

John says that "we love him because he first loved us" (1 John 4:19), and the better we know Him, the more we love Him.

7. The breast and shoulder of the consecration ram together with the bread were to be eaten by Aaron and his sons (Ex. 29:27-28, 31-34).

The eating first represents believing on Christ for salvation (John 6:35). Secondly, it represents communing with Christ after salvation.

The same picture is seen in the Lord's Supper. The bread and wine depict Christ's broken body and shed blood for our salvation, and by eating and drinking we signify our faith in the gospel and our ongoing communion with Christ.

The priests were to eat the breast and right shoulder of the offering, signifying the heart and strength of Christ. The more we commune with the Lord, the more we reflect His character and the more we share His strength.

8. The meat and bread remind us that communion with Christ is not only life-giving and life sustaining, but it is satisfying and enjoyable.

God gives us richly all things to enjoy (1 Tim. 6:17), yet as we grow in the Christian life we learn that communion with the Saviour is more satisfying and enjoyable than any physical pleasure. And the experience we have in this present life, regardless of how deep it might be, is nothing compared to that which we will experience in eternity in a redeemed body and in the midst of a glorious city.

> Psalms 16:11 Thou wilt shew me the path of life: in thy presence *is* fulness of joy; at thy right hand *there are* pleasures for evermore.

The priest's part of the offerings (Ex. 29:27-28, 31-34) also teaches the practical lesson that those who serve in the Lord's work should be rewarded.

> 1 Corinthians 9:13-14 Do ye not know that they which minister about holy things live *of the things* of the temple? and they which wait at the altar are partakers with the altar? 14 Even so hath the Lord ordained that they which preach the gospel should live of the gospel.

The Seven-day Waiting

> Leviticus 8:33-36 And ye shall not go out of the door of the tabernacle of the congregation *in* seven days, until the days of your consecration be at an end: for seven days shall he consecrate you. 34 As he hath done this day, *so* the LORD hath commanded to do, to make an atonement for you. 35 Therefore shall ye abide *at* the door of the tabernacle of the congregation day and night seven days, and keep the charge of the LORD, that ye die not: for so I am commanded. 36 So Aaron and his sons did all things which the LORD commanded by the hand of Moses.

> Leviticus 9:1-6 And it came to pass on the eighth day, *that* Moses called Aaron and his sons, and the elders of Israel; 2 And he said unto Aaron, Take thee a young calf for a sin offering, and a ram for a burnt offering, without blemish, and offer *them* before the LORD. 3 And unto the children of Israel thou shalt speak, saying, Take ye a kid of the goats for a sin offering; and a calf and a lamb, *both* of the first year, without blemish, for a burnt offering; 4 Also a bullock and a ram for peace offerings, to sacrifice before the LORD; and a meat offering mingled with oil: for to day the LORD will appear unto you. 5 And they brought *that*

> which Moses commanded before the tabernacle of the congregation: and all the congregation drew near and stood before the LORD. 6 And Moses said, This *is* the thing which the LORD commanded that ye should do: and the glory of the LORD shall appear unto you.

After the priests were clothed and anointed and had offered the required offerings, they were instructed to remain in the holy place of the tabernacle for seven days. On the eighth day the Lord appeared to them in glory.

This is a wonderful type of the church caught away to heaven and disappearing for seven years, then returning to dwell in Christ's glory in His millennial kingdom.

The eighth day is the day of resurrection. It is Sunday, the day that Christ rose from the dead. When Christ returns the saints will be raised to immortality.

The Ransom Money

Exodus 30:11-16 And the LORD spake unto Moses, saying, 12 When thou takest the sum of the children of Israel after their number, then shall they give every man a ransom for his soul unto the LORD, when thou numberest them; that there be no plague among them, when *thou* numberest them. 13 This they shall give, every one that passeth among them that are numbered, half a shekel after the shekel of the sanctuary: (a shekel *is* twenty gerahs:) an half shekel *shall be* the offering of the LORD. 14 Every one that passeth among them that are numbered, from twenty years old and above, shall give an offering unto the LORD. 15 The rich shall not give more, and the poor shall not give less than half a shekel, when *they* give an offering unto the LORD, to make an atonement for your souls. 16 And thou shalt take the atonement money of the children of Israel, and shalt appoint it for the service of the tabernacle of the congregation; that it may be a memorial unto the children of Israel before the LORD, to make an atonement for your souls.

The silver ransom money is another beautiful picture of salvation in Jesus Christ. It is another way that the law of Moses points to the grace of Christ (Rom. 3:21-22).

The ransom money points to the blood of Christ.

1 Peter 1:18 Forasmuch as ye know that ye were not redeemed with corruptible things, *as* silver and gold, from your vain conversation *received* by tradition from your fathers;

The word "ransom" means to satisfy a debt with a full payment (Psa. 49:7). It means to appease an offended party (Ex. 21:30).

Psalms 49:7 None *of them* can by any means redeem his brother, nor give to God a ransom for him:

> Exodus 21:30 If there be laid on him a sum of money, then he shall give for the ransom of his life whatsoever is laid upon him.

Following are some of the lessons of the ransom money:

1. Every person needed the ransom ("every man," Ex. 30:12).

Likewise the Bible says that all have sinned and come short of the glory of God (Rom. 3:23). Every individual needs the salvation that is offered by Christ.

2. The ransom was required of those who were "of age" (Ex. 30:14).

Jesus said that salvation is for those who "believe" (Mark 16:15). The "age of accountability" doubtless differs according to the individual, but there is a point in an individual's life when he or she comes of age and is accountable before God for accepting or rejecting Christ.

3. The ransom was offered to God ("unto the LORD," Ex. 30:12).

It is God that we have offended by breaking His holy laws, and it is God who must be appeased by the acceptable sacrifice.

4. The ransom price was set by God ("after the shekel of the sanctuary," Ex. 30:13).

God will only accept the sacrifice of His own holy Son. He will not accept anything that man offers, such as good works and religious deeds and the "sincerity of heart."

5. The price was the same for every person ("The rich shall not give more, and the poor shall not give less," Ex. 30:15).

The Bible says that all have sinned against God, and the way of salvation is the same for all.

6. The ransom was available for all and within the reach of all.

The amount was only one-half shekel, which was available to every person. Likewise Jesus "gave himself a ransom for all" (1 Tim. 2:6).

7. The price had been provided by God (Ex. 30:15).

The silver ransom price was available for every person because God had provided it for them from the Egyptians (Ex. 11:2). Likewise God has provided the ransom price Himself by the blood of His own Son. God ransomed sinners by becoming sin for us.

> Hosea 13:14 I will ransom them from the power of the grave; I will redeem them from death: O death, I will be thy plagues; O grave, I will be thy destruction: repentance shall be hid from mine eyes.

Just as God provided a ram in the place of Isaac, so He has provided His Son as a ransom for sinners. We are invited to come and receive God's banquet "without money and without price" (Isa. 55:1). We are invited to drink the water of life freely (Rev. 22:17). There are no glorious invitations like these in any "religion" other than the Bible.

8. The ransom price was sufficient.

Nothing had to be added by the supplicant. Likewise Christ purchased our full and eternal salvation through His blood. Salvation is a free gift by which the believer is perfected forever through Christ's offering (Heb. 10:14).

9. Each individual bringing the ransom price was counted ("every one that passeth among them," Ex. 30:14).

The individuals passed under the watchcare of the priest, acting as a shepherd counting his sheep as they enter the fold.

> Ezekiel 20:37 And I will cause you to pass under the rod, and I will bring you into the bond of the covenant:

The Lord knows His sheep, and none of them will perish (John 10:27-29). As the redeemed Israelites were known by name and tribe in the Jewish records, so the believer's name is entered into the Lamb's book of life.

10. The ransom money brought the individual into God's family and gave him a place as a servant and soldier.

Likewise through salvation the believing sinner is adopted into God's family and becomes an ambassador for Christ (2 Cor. 5:20) and a soldier in Christ's army (Eph. 6:10-18; 2 Tim. 2:3-4).

> "The Israelite, who paid his ransom-money, was numbered as a soldier and a servant for God. A place was assigned him in the battlefield: and he had his position in the camp, appointed with reference to the tabernacle, the dwelling-place of God in the midst of the hosts. From henceforth Jehovah was his Leader, his Lord, his King. In like manner, the believer is redeemed to God, by the blood of Christ, from the world, and from slavery to sin and Satan; that he may be a soldier and a servant of the Most High; to be led, guided, and sustained by Him, who has called him out of darkness, into His marvellous light" (Henry Soltau, *The Tabernacle the Priesthood and the Offerings*).

The Golden Calf

Exodus 32:1-6 And when the people saw that Moses delayed to come down out of the mount, the people gathered themselves together unto Aaron, and said unto him, Up, make us gods, which shall go before us; for *as for* this Moses, the man that brought us up out of the land of Egypt, we wot not what is become of him. 2 And Aaron said unto them, Break off the golden earrings, which *are* in the ears of your wives, of your sons, and of your daughters, and bring *them* unto me. 3 And all the people brake off the golden earrings which *were* in their ears, and brought *them* unto Aaron. 4 And he received *them* at their hand, and fashioned it with a graving tool, after he had made it a molten calf: and they said, These *be* thy gods, O Israel, which brought thee up out of the land of Egypt. 5 And when Aaron saw *it*, he built an altar before it; and Aaron made proclamation, and said, To morrow *is* a feast to the LORD. 6 And they rose up early on the morrow, and offered burnt offerings, and brought peace offerings; and the people sat down to eat and to drink, and rose up to play.

While Moses was on Mt. Sinai for 40 days receiving the law from God, the Israelites grew weary of waiting. They demanded that Aaron make them "gods" because "as for this Moses ... we wot not what is become of him" (Ex. 32:1).

Introductory Lessons

1. Observe how disrespectfully the people spoke of Moses -- "as for this man Moses..." (Ex. 32:1).

After all he had done for them, Moses was just another man. Preachers should not be surprised at the fickleness of people. They should not be surprised at how quickly people can forget attempts to help them.

My wife and I have often commented to one another that it seems that the people we help the most are the first to turn on us or to turn away from us. This is not an absolute law, thank the Lord, but it does happen often, and it is because of the weakness of fallen human nature.

2. Observe that the people didn't mention Jehovah God.

They only knew Him from a distance. They didn't know Him personally and didn't love Him, and they easily forgot Him. Instead, they said that *Moses* had brought them out of Egypt.

After all of the amazing miracles, the people still disbelieved and disobeyed. After all of God's blessings on them, they still didn't love Him.

This was the root of the people's problem. They didn't know God personally. A large percentage of them had not personally believed God's promises.

> Hebrews 4:1-2 Let us therefore fear, lest, a promise being left *us* of entering into his rest, any of you should seem to come short of it. 2 For unto us was the gospel preached, as well as unto them: but the word preached did not profit them, not being mixed with faith in them that heard *it*.

3. We see that signs and miracles cannot produce salvation.

> Luke 16:31 And he said unto him, If they hear not Moses and the prophets, neither will they be persuaded, though one rose from the dead.

From Moses' day until the time of Jesus, the Jews demanded signs from God, and Christ told them, "An evil and adulterous generation seeketh after a sign; and there shall no sign be given to it, but the sign of the prophet Jonas: For as Jonas was three days and three nights in the whale's belly; so shall the Son of man be three days and three nights in the heart of the earth" (Mat. 12:39-40).

If men will not believe the preaching of the gospel--the death, burial, and resurrection of Christ for sin--they will not believe even if an angel were to appear to them personally.

4. We see, too, that man is corrupt in the depths of his very nature.

No amount of external religion can make him holy and right with God. This is why Jesus said, "Ye must be born again" (John 3:3). To be born again means to be converted and to have a new holy nature imparted into one's being by the supernatural act of God in response to saving faith.

Lessons about the Golden Calf

1. Observe how that the people easily returned to Egyptian idols.

The unsaved man loves false gods because he is not accountable to them.

2. In their hearts, the Israelites had not left Egypt.

> Acts 7:39 To whom our fathers would not obey, but thrust *him* from them, and IN THEIR HEARTS turned back again into Egypt,

Nominal Christians are in the same condition. They profess Christ with their mouth but their hearts have never left the world. They haven't repented and been born again. They have adopted Christ as a new religion rather than as a new life. Paul described the true Christian as follows:

> Galatians 6:14-15 But God forbid that I should glory, save in the cross of our Lord Jesus Christ, by whom the world is crucified unto me, and I unto the world. 15 For in Christ Jesus neither circumcision availeth any thing, nor uncircumcision, but a new creature.

The true Christian has been crucified WITH Christ and FROM the world.

This is the picture of baptism. It depicts true faith and repentance. The believer has died with Jesus and risen to new life with Jesus. But baptism is only a dead ritual for many because their lives demonstrate that they haven't experienced the reality of what it represents.

3. The Israelites were living by sight rather than by faith; they stopped looking for Moses' return (Ex. 32:1).

> Exodus 24:18 And Moses went into the midst of the cloud, and gat him up into the mount: and Moses was in the mount forty days and forty nights.

Moses was on the mountain for more than a month, and the people could not see him so they started following their own thinking. Likewise if believers today are not looking for Christ's return, they start living according to the flesh, as Jesus warned about in His parable.

> Luke 12:45 But and if that servant say in his heart, My lord delayeth his coming; and shall begin to beat the menservants and maidens, and to eat and drink, and to be drunken;

The doctrine of the imminent coming of Christ is very important for godly Christian living, and it is strongly emphasized in Scripture. It helps us to live expectantly and to be ready to stand before the Lord.

> Matthew 24:44 Therefore be ye also ready: for in such an hour as ye think not the Son of man cometh.

> 1 Corinthians 1:7 So that ye come behind in no gift; waiting for the coming of our Lord Jesus Christ:

> Philippians 3:20 For our conversation is in heaven; from whence also we look for the Saviour, the Lord Jesus Christ.

> Philippians 4:5 Let your moderation be known unto all men. The Lord *is* at hand.

> 1 Thessalonians 1:9-10 For they themselves shew of us what manner of entering in we had unto you, and how ye turned to God from idols to serve the living and true God;

10 And to wait for his Son from heaven, whom he raised from the dead, *even* Jesus, which delivered us from the wrath to come.

2 Timothy 4:8 Henceforth there is laid up for me a crown of righteousness, which the Lord, the righteous judge, shall give me at that day: and not to me only, but unto all them also that love his appearing.

Titus 2:13 Looking for that blessed hope, and the glorious appearing of the great God and our Saviour Jesus Christ;

Hebrews 9:27 And as it is appointed unto men once to die, but after this the judgment.

Hebrews 10:25 Not forsaking the assembling of ourselves together, as the manner of some *is*; but exhorting *one another*: and so much the more, as ye see the day approaching.

James 5:8-9 Be ye also patient; stablish your hearts: for the coming of the Lord draweth nigh. 9 Grudge not one against another, brethren, lest ye be condemned: behold, the judge standeth before the door.

1 Peter 4:7 But the end of all things is at hand: be ye therefore sober, and watch unto prayer.

Revelation 22:7 Behold, I come quickly: blessed *is* he that keepeth the sayings of the prophecy of this book.

Aaron, the Weak Leader

1. Instead of leading the people, Aaron followed them.

Exodus 32:1-2 And when the people saw that Moses delayed to come down out of the mount, the people gathered themselves together unto Aaron, and said unto him, Up, make us gods, which shall go before us; for *as for* this Moses, the man that brought us up out of the land of Egypt, we wot not what is become of him. 2 And Aaron said unto them, Break off the golden earrings, which *are* in the ears of your wives, of your sons, and of your daughters, and bring *them* unto me.

> Exodus 32:21-24 And Moses said unto Aaron, What did this people unto thee, that thou hast brought so great a sin upon them? 22 And Aaron said, Let not the anger of my lord wax hot: thou knowest the people, that they *are set* on mischief. 23 For they said unto me, Make us gods, which shall go before us: for *as for* this Moses, the man that brought us up out of the land of Egypt, we wot not what is become of him. 24 And I said unto them, Whosoever hath any gold, let them break *it* off. So they gave *it* me: then I cast it into the fire, and there came out this calf.

Aaron feared the people more than he feared God.

> Proverbs 29:25 The fear of man bringeth a snare: but whoso putteth his trust in the LORD shall be safe.

Many pastors are cut from this same cloth. They give the people what they want instead of what they need, which is the uncompromised preaching of the Word of God. They water down God's Word so that it won't offend the people instead of preaching the whole counsel of God.

If the people want to dress like the world and listen to the world's music and send their children to be educated by the world, etc., the pastor will not rebuke them.

Paul did not follow Aaron's weak example.

> Acts 20:27 For I have not shunned to declare unto you all the counsel of God.

Paul instructed the preachers to preach God's Word with boldness.

> 2 Timothy 4:1-2 I charge *thee* therefore before God, and the Lord Jesus Christ, who shall judge the quick and the dead at his appearing and his kingdom; 2 Preach the word; be instant in season, out of season; reprove, rebuke, exhort with all longsuffering and doctrine.

> Titus 2:15 These things speak, and exhort, and rebuke with all authority. Let no man despise thee.

James warned that preachers will give greater account to God.

> James 3:1 My brethren, be not many masters, knowing that we shall receive the greater condemnation.

The compromising preacher might give some general warning in his preaching, but he won't confront the people one on one, and he won't discipline them for their sins, and he won't require God's holy standards of living for those who serve as officers and teachers in the church. This is like Eli who reproved his sons but did nothing more.

> 1 Samuel 2:22-29 Now Eli was very old, and heard all that his sons did unto all Israel; and how they lay with the women that assembled *at* the door of the tabernacle of the congregation. 23 And he said unto them, Why do ye such things? for I hear of your evil dealings by all this people. 24 Nay, my sons; for *it is* no good report that I hear: ye make the LORD'S people to transgress. 25 If one man sin against another, the judge shall judge him: but if a man sin against the LORD, who shall intreat for him? Notwithstanding they hearkened not unto the voice of their father, because the LORD would slay them. 26 And the child Samuel grew on, and was in favour both with the LORD, and also with men. 27 And there came a man of God unto Eli, and said unto him, Thus saith the LORD, Did I plainly appear unto the house of thy father, when they were in Egypt in Pharaoh's house? 28 And did I choose him out of all the tribes of Israel *to be* my priest, to offer upon mine altar, to burn incense, to wear an ephod before me? and did I give unto the house of thy father all the offerings made by fire of the children of Israel? 29 Wherefore kick ye at my sacrifice and at mine offering, which I have commanded *in my* habitation; and honourest thy sons above me, to make yourselves fat with the chiefest of all the offerings of Israel my people?

2. Aaron refused to take responsibility for his actions.

He encouraged the people to bring the gold ornaments and he made them naked (Ex. 32:2, 25), yet he blamed them for his actions (Ex. 32:22).

In one of the most ridiculous acts of self-justification in human history, Aaron even blamed the calf itself!

> Exodus 32:24 And I said unto them, Whosoever hath any gold, let them break *it* off. So they gave *it* me: then I cast it into the fire, and there came out this calf.

Moses, though, charged Aaron with the sin (Ex. 32:21). As we have seen, the Bible warns that church leaders will face a greater judgment; therefore, they must fear God more than they fear man and teach the people to fear God and walk in His ways.

The Rock Party in the Wilderness

> Exodus 32:5-6 And when Aaron saw *it*, he built an altar before it; and Aaron made proclamation, and said, To morrow *is* a feast to the LORD. 6 And they rose up early on the morrow, and offered burnt offerings, and brought peace offerings; and the people sat down to eat and to drink, and rose up to play.

> Exodus 32:18-19 And he said, *It is* not the voice of *them that* shout for mastery, neither *is it* the voice of *them that* cry for being overcome: *but* the noise of *them that* sing do I hear. 19 And it came to pass, as soon as he came nigh unto the camp, that he saw the calf, and the dancing: and Moses' anger waxed hot, and he cast the tables out of his hands, and brake them beneath the mount.

> Exodus 32:25 And when Moses saw that the people *were* naked; (for Aaron had made them naked unto *their* shame among their enemies:)

1. There was false worship patterned after the Egyptian culture (Ex. 32:4-6).

The Israelites were worshipping God with pagan methods, and it was not acceptable. They were worshiping Jehovah, but they were worshiping Him under the image of Egyptian idols.

Christian rock worship is an exact imitation of this. Christian rockers are disobeying the clear Scripture warnings against being conformed to this world.

> Romans 12:2 And be not conformed to this world: but be ye transformed by the renewing of your mind, that ye may prove what *is* that good, and acceptable, and perfect, will of God.

> 2 Corinthians 6:14 Be ye not unequally yoked together with unbelievers: for what fellowship hath righteousness with unrighteousness? and what communion hath light with darkness?

> James 4:4 Ye adulterers and adulteresses, know ye not that the friendship of the world is enmity with God? whosoever therefore will be a friend of the world is the enemy of God.

> 1 John 2:15-16 Love not the world, neither the things *that are* in the world. If any man love the world, the love of the Father is not in him. 16 For all that *is* in the world, the lust of the flesh, and the lust of the eyes, and the pride of life, is not of the Father, but is of the world.

2. There was loud sensual music (Ex. 32:18).

It was raucous noise that sounded like war and was fitting for the sensual activities.

3. There was dancing and nakedness (Ex. 32:19, 25).

Sensual dancing and sensual music go hand-in-hand with immorality. The description of the idolatrous party in Exodus 32 is a perfect description of a modern rock & roll party.

Moses' Intercession for Israel

> Exodus 32:7-14 And the LORD said unto Moses, Go, get thee down; for thy people, which thou broughtest out of the land of Egypt, have corrupted *themselves*: 8 They have

> turned aside quickly out of the way which I commanded them: they have made them a molten calf, and have worshipped it, and have sacrificed thereunto, and said, These *be* thy gods, O Israel, which have brought thee up out of the land of Egypt. 9 And the LORD said unto Moses, I have seen this people, and, behold, it *is* a stiffnecked people: 10 Now therefore let me alone, that my wrath may wax hot against them, and that I may consume them: and I will make of thee a great nation. 11 And Moses besought the LORD his God, and said, LORD, why doth thy wrath wax hot against thy people, which thou hast brought forth out of the land of Egypt with great power, and with a mighty hand? 12 Wherefore should the Egyptians speak, and say, For mischief did he bring them out, to slay them in the mountains, and to consume them from the face of the earth? Turn from thy fierce wrath, and repent of this evil against thy people. 13 Remember Abraham, Isaac, and Israel, thy servants, to whom thou swarest by thine own self, and saidst unto them, I will multiply your seed as the stars of heaven, and all this land that I have spoken of will I give unto your seed, and they shall inherit *it* for ever. 14 And the LORD repented of the evil which he thought to do unto his people.

This is one of the most amazing prayers in the Bible. It literally changed the course of history.

1. Moses based his prayer upon his concern for God's testimony in the world (Ex. 32:11-12) and upon God's covenant with Abraham (Ex. 32:13).

Moses was petitioning God on the basis of God's promises. This is the solid foundation for answered prayer.

2. Prayer changes things both in heaven and on earth (Ex. 32:14)!

Moses' petition changed God's mind and literally changed the course of history. God intended to destroy Israel and raise up a new nation from Moses, and He could have done that, but because of Moses' petition He did not.

We don't have to understand how God can change His mind. All we have to do is believe God's own Word! (We deal more with this subject in the book *Things Hard to Be Understood: A Handbook of Biblical Difficulties.*)

3. Moses fasted and prayed for 40 days for Israel (Ex. 32:30-34; De. 9:18-19).

Compare Matthew 17:21, which teaches that prayer with fasting is a necessary part of defeating the devil.

4. Moses was willing to go to hell for Israel's sake (Ex. 32:31-32).

Compare the apostle Paul's testimony in Romans 9:3. Moses and Paul reflect the compassion of Christ, who was willing to suffer in the place of sinners.

5. Note that there is a book of life.

It is the book that was written by God's foreknowledge and contains the names of those who trust in the blood of Christ.

> Philippians 4:3 And I intreat thee also, true yokefellow, help those women which laboured with me in the gospel, with Clement also, and *with* other my fellowlabourers, whose names *are* in the book of life.
>
> Revelation 13:8 And all that dwell upon the earth shall worship him, whose names are not written in the book of life of the Lamb slain from the foundation of the world.
>
> Revelation 17:8 The beast that thou sawest was, and is not; and shall ascend out of the bottomless pit, and go into perdition: and they that dwell on the earth shall wonder, whose names were not written in the book of life from the foundation of the world, when they behold the beast that was, and is not, and yet is.
>
> Revelation 20:12 And I saw the dead, small and great, stand before God; and the books were opened: and another book was opened, which is *the book* of life: and the dead were judged out of those things which were written in the books, according to their works.

Revelation 20:15 And whosoever was not found written in the book of life was cast into the lake of fire.

6. Moses' prayer also stayed God's judgment upon Aaron.

Deuteronomy 9:20 And the LORD was very angry with Aaron to have destroyed him: and I prayed for Aaron also the same time.

What a powerful prayer warrior Moses was, and what a tremendous example he is to us in this most essential business!

God's Judgment on Israel

Exodus 32:25-28 And when Moses saw that the people *were* naked; (for Aaron had made them naked unto *their* shame among their enemies:) 26 Then Moses stood in the gate of the camp, and said, Who *is* on the LORD'S side? *let him come* unto me. And all the sons of Levi gathered themselves together unto him. 27 And he said unto them, Thus saith the LORD God of Israel, Put every man his sword by his side, *and* go in and out from gate to gate throughout the camp, and slay every man his brother, and every man his companion, and every man his neighbour. 28 And the children of Levi did according to the word of Moses: and there fell of the people that day about three thousand men.

1. The sons of Levi distinguished themselves in the work of exercising God's judgment (Ex. 32:26).

God rewarded them for their zeal against sin and error.

Exodus 32:29 For Moses had said, Consecrate yourselves to day to the LORD, even every man upon his son, and upon his brother; that he may bestow upon you a blessing this day.

Malachi 2:4-6 And ye shall know that I have sent this commandment unto you, that my covenant might be with Levi, saith the LORD of hosts. 5 My covenant was with him of life and peace; and I gave them to him *for* the fear

> wherewith he feared me, and was afraid before my name. 6 The law of truth was in his mouth, and iniquity was not found in his lips: he walked with me in peace and equity, and did turn many away from iniquity.

Those who were killed appear to be those who were leading in the idolatry and immorality (Ex. 32:25-26).

> "When Moses stood in the camp of Israel and made proclamation for those who were on Jehovah's side, we read that 'he saw that the people were naked' (ver. 25), or unreined, licentious (comp. ver. 6; 1 Cor. 10:7, 8). In short, there stood before him a number of men, fresh from their orgies, in a state of licentious attire, whom even his appearance and words had not yet sobered into quietness, shame, and repentance. ... while the vast multitude had retired to the quietness of their tents in tardy repentance and fear" (Alfred Edersheim, *Bible History of the Old Testament*).

2. Discipline of sin and error in the house of God is a difficult work but a necessary one.

It results in a proper fear of God.

> Acts 5:9-11 Then Peter said unto her, How is it that ye have agreed together to tempt the Spirit of the Lord? behold, the feet of them which have buried thy husband *are* at the door, and shall carry thee out. 10 Then fell she down straightway at his feet, and yielded up the ghost: and the young men came in, and found her dead, and, carrying *her* forth, buried *her* by her husband. 11 And great fear came upon all the church, and upon as many as heard these things.

It keeps the church pure.

> 1 Corinthians 5:6-8 Your glorying *is* not good. Know ye not that a little leaven leaveneth the whole lump? 7 Purge out therefore the old leaven, that ye may be a new lump, as ye are unleavened. For even Christ our passover is sacrificed for us: 8 Therefore let us keep the feast, not with old leaven, neither with the leaven of malice and

wickedness; but with the unleavened *bread* of sincerity and truth.

It can result in the repentance of sinners.

2 Corinthians 7:9-11 Now I rejoice, not that ye were made sorry, but that ye sorrowed to repentance: for ye were made sorry after a godly manner, that ye might receive damage by us in nothing. 10 For godly sorrow worketh repentance to salvation not to be repented of: but the sorrow of the world worketh death. 11 For behold this selfsame thing, that ye sorrowed after a godly sort, what carefulness it wrought in you, yea, *what* clearing of yourselves, yea, *what* indignation, yea, *what* fear, yea, *what* vehement desire, yea, *what* zeal, yea, *what* revenge! In all *things* ye have approved yourselves to be clear in this matter.

The Levitical Offerings

Leviticus 1-9

The book of Leviticus is a continuation of the Law of Moses and was written while Israel was encamped at Mt. Sinai for nearly a year.

It was given to Moses by God after the tabernacle was set up. The words were spoken directly by God who was dwelling in the holy of holies

> Leviticus 1:1 And the LORD called unto Moses, and spake unto him out of the tabernacle of the congregation, saying,

God spoke to Moses in a voice from above the mercy seat.

> Numbers 7:89 And when Moses was gone into the tabernacle of the congregation to speak with him, then he heard the voice of one speaking unto him from off the mercy seat that *was* upon the ark of testimony, from between the two cherubims: and he spake unto him.

This signifies that God was speaking to Moses by grace. God spoke from above the blood-sprinkled mercy seat that covered the broken law. This is the only way that God can speak to man apart from eternal judgment.

MAJOR TEACHINGS OF THE OFFERINGS

There were five offerings --
- The Burnt offering (Leviticus 1)
- The Meal offering (Leviticus 2)
- The Peace offering (Leviticus 3)
- The Sin offering (Leviticus 4)
- The Trespass offering (Leviticus 5:1 - 6:7)

The Levitical offerings are a continuation of the laws pertaining to the tabernacle. In fact, the priestly offerings lie at the heart and soul of the tabernacle. Without the offerings the Lord would be in His holy temple and man would be eternally shut out from His presence. The offerings perfect the teaching of the tabernacle, adding layer after layer of instruction about Christ and salvation.

1. First and foremost, the offerings depict Jesus Christ the Lamb of God.

He is the sinless Son of God, the God-Man whose life is acceptable and well-pleasing to the Father. His redemption is the foundation of the new creation, and He is worthy to receive all honor and glory and praise forever.

> Revelation 5:8-13 And when he had taken the book, the four beasts and four *and* twenty elders fell down before the Lamb, having every one of them harps, and golden vials full of odours, which are the prayers of saints. 9 And they sung a new song, saying, Thou art worthy to take the book, and to open the seals thereof: for thou wast slain, and hast redeemed us to God by thy blood out of every kindred, and tongue, and people, and nation; 10 And hast made us unto our God kings and priests: and we shall reign on the earth. 11 And I beheld, and I heard the voice of many angels round about the throne and the beasts and the elders: and the number of them was ten thousand times ten thousand, and thousands of thousands; 12 Saying with a loud voice, Worthy is the Lamb that was slain to receive power, and riches, and wisdom, and strength, and honour, and glory, and blessing. 13 And every creature which is in heaven, and on the earth, and under the earth, and such as are in the sea, and all that are in them, heard I saying, Blessing, and honour, and glory, and power, *be* unto him that sitteth upon the throne, and unto the Lamb for ever and ever.

The major objective of the Scripture, in whole and in every part, is to reveal God in Christ. Every believer is predestined to be conformed to His image (Rom. 8:29), and this process begins in this life as we see Christ in Scripture (2 Cor. 3:18).

Ultimately all things will be gathered together in one in Christ (Eph. 1:10).

2. The offerings picture Christ from the perspective of God the Father.

At least 59 times in Leviticus 1-7 the expressions "unto the Lord" or "before the Lord" appear. This refers to God's part in Christ.

Jesus came to earth to do the Father's will, and He was well-pleasing to the Father in all things (Mat. 3:17; 12:18). This is the mystery of the Trinity. The Bible says "Christ is God's" (1 Cor. 3:23).

Jesus' sacrifice on the cross was made unto God to satisfy God's holy law. He gave himself "to God for a sweetsmelling savour" (Eph. 5:2).

3. The offerings picture Christ from the perspective of the believer receiving and enjoying salvation.

Without Christ, we have no relationship with God. With Him, we have an intimate, eternal relationship, and from beginning to end Christ is the basis of that relationship. Christ is our burnt offering, our meal offering, our peace offering, our sin offering, our trespass offering.

The highest object of the Christian life is to grow in knowledge of Him.

> John 17:3 And this is life eternal, that they might know thee the only true God, and Jesus Christ, whom thou hast sent.
>
> Ephesians 1:17 That the God of our Lord Jesus Christ, the Father of glory, may give unto you the spirit of wisdom and revelation in the knowledge of him:
>
> Philippians 3:8 Yea doubtless, and I count all things *but* loss for the excellency of the knowledge of Christ Jesus my Lord: for whom I have suffered the loss of all things, and do count them *but* dung, that I may win Christ,
>
> 2 Peter 3:18 But grow in grace, and *in* the knowledge of our Lord and Saviour Jesus Christ. To him *be* glory both now and for ever. Amen.

Too many believers are content to understand Christ as their sin offering, to know that they are saved and have eternal salvation. But they aren't passionate to learn more of who and what Christ is. They are content to know that Christ died for their sins and not passionate to know the One who died.

> "But these are not God's thoughts, nor are they the thoughts of those who know the joy of communion with Him. Such go from strength to strength in the knowledge of the grace and work of Jesus. Have they known Him as the paschal lamb in Egypt? They seek then to know Him as the offering within the tabernacle. Have they learnt Him in His different relations as offering? They seek to know Him in all His offices as priest. Do they know Him as priest? They seek Him as prophet, as manna, as water, as guide, as everything. May the Lord only fill us with His Spirit: then we cannot but follow on to know more of Jesus" (Andrew Jukes, *The Law of the Offerings*).

4. The offerings emphasize the perfection and sufficiency of Christ's sacrifice.

We see this in the spotlessness of the sacrifice (Lev. 1:3), and the blood sprinkled seven times (Lev. 4:6). In these and many other ways, Leviticus is teaching that "Christ is all I need."

> Hebrews 10:10 By the which will we are sanctified through the offering of the body of Jesus Christ once *for all.*

> Hebrews 10:14 For by one offering he hath perfected for ever them that are sanctified.

5. The five offerings picture salvation in all of its aspects.

Christ is our sanctification, justification, hope, glory, life (1 Cor. 1:30; Eph. 1:3; 1 Tim. 1:1).

> "We need to always most thankfully receive His inestimable benefit. In other words, we must by faith accept Christ as our five-fold offering, on the basis of which alone we are saved and have our standing before

> God. Morning by morning as we awaken let it be with the consciousness that in the burnt offering and meat offering of Christ we are accepted and blessed of God, that in His peace offering we have the right to commune with Him, that through His sin and trespass offering every defect is remedied and every fault will find pardon" (James Gray, *Concise Bible Commentary*).

6. The offerings teach that all men are sinners under God's judgment of death.

The words "kill" and "slay" appear 29 times in Leviticus in reference to the sacrifices. The animal had to die, because it signified the wages of sin and Christ dying in the sinner's place.

> "In the day that thou eatest thereof thou shalt surely die" (Ge. 2:17).
>
> "The wages of sin is death" (Rom. 6:23).
>
> "The soul that sinneth it shall die" (Ezek. 18:4).
>
> "Death passed upon all men, for that all have sinned" (Rom. 5:12).
>
> "... when sin is finished it bringeth forth death" (Jam. 1:15).
>
> "It is appointed to men once to die (Heb. 9:27).

And the sinner's just death is not merely physical death. It is also that most frightful second death consisting of eternal conscious torment in the lake of fire.

> Revelation 20:14-15 And death and hell were cast into the lake of fire. This is the second death. 15 And whosoever was not found written in the book of life was cast into the lake of fire.

7. The offerings teach that salvation is only through the atonement that Christ made on the cross.

This is the main teaching of the sacrifices. The price by which Jesus purchased our salvation was His death and blood. The word "blood" appears 79 times in reference to the offerings, signifying the shedding of Christ's blood. The Bible says that without the shedding of blood is no remission (Heb. 9:22). The words "kill" and "slay" appear 29 times in reference to the Leviticus offerings, signifying Christ's death.

8. The offerings teach that though God has provided the Sacrifice and Jesus has died for the sins of the world, men must individually receive Him.

Each individual had to enter the one door of the tabernacle court and bring the correct sacrifice to the brazen altar before God in the prescribed way.

This signifies that each sinner must come to God and acknowledge his sin and put his faith in Jesus Christ as the only Lord and Saviour. When the worshiper put his hands on the sacrifice he was signifying his need of it and his identification with it (Lev. 1:4). This is symbolic of repentance and faith.

9. The offerings teach fellowship and devotion.

Salvation is not merely a matter of being forgiven of sin; it is a matter of being devoted to God, walking with Him in fellowship, and serving Him.

Thus, there was not only the sin offering but also the burnt offering, the peace offering, and the meal offering.

Salvation is not a mere ticket to heaven whereby one prays a sinner's prayer and then lives his or her life as before. Salvation is to come into an intimate relationship with God through Christ as an adopted son and to serve Him as a disciple, a priest, an ambassador, a soldier.

The believer is to give his best to Christ. This was signified by the wave offering, whereby the breast and right shoulder of the peace offering were to be waved before the Lord (Lev. 9:21). The breast signified the passion and devotion of one's heart, and the shoulder signified one's strength and fervor of service.

God wants His people to walk in fellowship with Him through Christ. The New Testament invites the believer to abide in Christ (John 15:4) and to walk in fellowship with the Father and the Son (1 John 1:3). We are invited to draw near (Heb. 10:22). We are encouraged to come boldly before the throne of grace (Heb. 4:16).

10. The offerings teach holiness.

God requires holiness of life.

The Hebrew word *qodesh*, which is translated "holy" and "holiness," is used more than 150 times in Leviticus.

> Leviticus 19:2 Speak unto all the congregation of the children of Israel, and say unto them, Ye shall be holy: for I the LORD your God *am* holy.

> Leviticus 20:7 Sanctify yourselves therefore, and be ye holy: for I *am* the LORD your God.

The same emphasis is found in the New Testament.

> 1 Peter 1:15-16 But as he which hath called you is holy, so be ye holy in all manner of conversation; 16 Because it is written, Be ye holy; for I am holy.

The believer's holiness has a three-fold aspect. We *are* holy before God because of our eternal position in Christ (Eph. 1:3-4); we *are being made* holy in practice through Christian growth (Eph. 4:22-24); and we *will be perfected* in holiness when we receive the fullness of our redemption (Eph. 5:27).

We *are sanctified* in eternal position (1 Cor. 6:11; Heb. 10:10, 14). We are *being sanctified* in Christian living (1 Th. 4:3-4; 2 Tim. 2:21). We *will be sanctified wholly* in perfection (1 Th. 5:23).

11. The offerings teach separation.

God's people are to make a distinction between the clean and the unclean, and their leaders are to teach this (Lev. 10:8-11). This is the main teaching of the dietary rules in

Leviticus 11 (Lev. 11:47) and the law of leprosy in Leviticus 13-14 (Lev. 14:53-57).

We find this teaching reflected in the New Testament's commands about strict separation from sin and error. Compare Romans 16:17; 2 Corinthians 6:14-18; Ephesians 5:11; 1 Thessalonians 5:22; 1 Timothy 6:13-14; 1 John 2:16-18.

12. The offerings teach Christian service.

There is a lot of work to do in the service of the Lord, as signified by the fact that the work of the priests was multi-faceted and never ending.

The phrase "the priest shall" appears 121 times in Leviticus.

They had to set up the tabernacle, take it down, transport it, service the lampstand and the incense altar and the table of shewbread. They had to prepare oil and incense, make bread, and keep the laver filled with water. They offered all of the sacrifices on the brazen altar. They carried the bodies of sacrificial animals outside of the camp for burning. They removed the ashes of the sacrifices from the altar every morning. They had to keep the fire of the altar burning. They dealt with leprosy (Lev. 13-14). They valued property (Lev. 27:12, 14). They were teachers (Lev. 10:11). They were preservers of Scripture (De. 31:24-26).

Likewise there is much work to do in the Christian life.

> 1 Corinthians 15:58 Therefore, my beloved brethren, be ye stedfast, unmoveable, always abounding in the work of the Lord, forasmuch as ye know that your labour is not in vain in the Lord.

Our responsibilities are much greater than those of Old Testament priests, because the church's objective is to preach the gospel to every person in every nation and disciple every believer (Mat. 28:19-20; Mk. 16:15).

Every believer has spiritual gifts and ministries and there is no place for laziness in the Lord's service.

THE TYPOLOGY OF THE OFFERINGS

The Typology of the Animals

1. The animals were "without blemish" (Lev. 1:3).

This signifies Christ's sinless character, "as a lamb without blemish and without spot" (1 Pet. 1:19).

2. The bullock or ox depicts Christ as the strong, faithful Servant of God who came to accomplish God's will.

> Philippians 2:5-8 Let this mind be in you, which was also in Christ Jesus: 6 Who, being in the form of God, thought it not robbery to be equal with God: 7 But made himself of no reputation, and took upon him the form of a servant, and was made in the likeness of men: 8 And being found in fashion as a man, he humbled himself, and became obedient unto death, even the death of the cross.

This is the theme of the Gospel of Mark. Christ summarized it as follows: "For even the Son of man came not to be ministered unto, but to minister, and to give his life a ransom for many" (Mk. 10:45).

> "The bullock is typical of the Lord Jesus Christ in His life of perfect service, as well as in His atoning death. The bullock ploughed the land, brought home the sheaves from the harvest field, trod out the corn for the household" (Thomas Newberry, *Types of the Levitical Offerings*).

3. The sheep or lamb depicts Christ as the holy Lamb of God willing to suffer on the Cross.

> Isaiah 53:7 He was oppressed, and he was afflicted, yet he opened not his mouth: he is brought as a lamb to the slaughter, and as a sheep before her shearers is dumb, so he openeth not his mouth.

4. The goat depicts Christ taking the sinner's place in judgment.

The goat was a sin offering (Lev. 4:24; 9:15; 16:9; Num. 15:27; 28:22; 29:22; Eze. 43:25). It depicts Christ "in the likeness of sinful flesh" (Rom. 8:3) and "made sin for us" (2 Cor. 5:21). It depicts Christ made a curse for us (Gal. 3:13), bearing our sins (1 Pet. 2:24; Isa. 53:6).

The Scapegoat outside the camp

The scapegoat of the Day of Atonement (Lev. 16:8-10) depicted the complete salvation that Jesus purchased. As the goat was released into a wilderness to bear away the nation's sin, so our sin is forever gone because Christ bore it in full on the cross.

5. The sheep and goat together depict the two-fold aspect of what Christ did on the cross.

"For not only was sin laid upon Him as the spotless Lamb, but, under the emblem of a goat, sin was imputed to Him so that on the cross, whilst He bare and put away the iniquity of our outward transgressions, He also met our deeper need in atoning, not simply for what we have done, but for what we are; or, as Scripture expresses it, 'He made HIM sin for us, who knew no sin; that we might become the righteousness of God in Him' (2 Cor. 5:21)" (Thomas Newberry, *Types of the Levitical Offerings*).

6. The ram is a male sheep and depicts the same thing as the goat.

It was a ram that God supplied as a sacrifice in the place of Isaac (Ge. 22:11-13). The ram's horns signify Christ's power and authority as the Son of God.

7. The dove or pigeon depicts Christ as the poor man's Saviour.

These depict the One willing to lay aside His riches to become poor that He might make sinners rich (2 Cor. 8:9). Since Joseph and Mary offered doves or pigeons as a sacrifice, we know that they were poor (Lk. 2:22-24).

The Typology of the Details of the Offerings

1. The animals were brought into the court area to the north side of the brazen altar. The sacrifice was presented "before the Lord" (Lev. 1:3).

The expression "bring ... unto the door of the tabernacle of the congregation" refers to the brazen altar inside the main entrance of the court. Compare Leviticus 4:4 with Leviticus 4:18.

> Leviticus 4:4 And he shall bring the bullock unto the door of the tabernacle of the congregation before the LORD; and shall lay his hand upon the bullock's head, and kill the bullock before the LORD.
>
> Leviticus 4:18 And he shall put *some* of the blood upon the horns of the altar which *is* before the LORD, that *is* in the tabernacle of the congregation, and shall pour out all the blood at the bottom of the altar of the burnt offering, which *is at* the door of the tabernacle of the congregation.

2. The offerer laid hands on the animal's head (Lev. 1:4).

This symbolizes identification with the sacrifice and acceptance of the sacrifice in one's place. It signifies confession of sin and personal faith in God's Sacrifice. It has a two-fold action. By the laying on of hands, the offerer's sins are transferred to the sacrifice, and the atoning value of the sacrifice is transferred to the offerer. This signifies the two-fold aspect of justification as described in the following verse:

> 2 Corinthians 5:21 For he hath made him *to be* sin for us, who knew no sin; that we might be made the righteousness of God in him.

3. The killing and shedding of blood depicts the means of salvation through the bloody death of Christ.

Note that both blood and death are required. Blood is mentioned 44 times, and death, 22 times. Compare Romans 5:9-10, which teaches that we are saved both by Christ's death and by His blood.

> Romans 5:9-10 Much more then, being now justified BY HIS BLOOD, we shall be saved from wrath through him. 10 For if, when we were enemies, we were reconciled to God BY THE DEATH of his Son, much more, being reconciled, we shall be saved by his life.

4. The priest offering the blood signifies Christ presenting His own atonement before God (Lev. 1:5). Both the offering and the priest represent Christ.

5. The sprinkling of the blood (Lev. 1:5) signifies Christ's salvation being received by the nations.

> Isaiah 52:14-15 As many were astonied at thee; his visage was so marred more than any man, and his form more than the sons of men: 15 So shall he sprinkle many nations; the kings shall shut their mouths at him: for *that* which had not been told them shall they see; and *that* which they had not heard shall they consider.

As the sprinkled blood spreads out in a pattern and covers a large area, so the gospel goes forth to all nations and to redeem people from every tribe and tongue. And it will continue to provide redemption for countless multitudes in the Tribulation and beyond (Rev. 7:9).

6. The sprinkling of the blood seven times (Lev. 4:6; 8:11) signifies completeness and perfection, as in the seven days of creation and the seven seals of Revelation. It depicts the perfection of Christ's sacrifice (Heb. 10:14).

7. The pouring of the blood (Lev. 4:7, 18, 25, 30, 34) signifies Christ pouring out all of His life's blood for our sins by means of the beating, the crucifixion, and the terrible wound in his side (John 19:34). Isaiah prophesied that he "poured out his soul unto death" (Isa. 53:12). Jesus said, "This is my blood of the new testament WHICH IS SHED for many for the remission of sins" (Mat. 26:28).

8. The burning of part of the sacrifice outside the camp (Lev. 4:11-12) signifies Christ as rejected by His own people Israel and being crucified outside of the city of Jerusalem as a common criminal.

> Hebrews 13:11-12 For the bodies of those beasts, whose blood is brought into the sanctuary by the high priest for sin, are burned without the camp. 12 Wherefore Jesus also, that he might sanctify the people with his own blood, suffered without the gate.

It depicts Christ bearing man's sin, being made sin for us, and therefore being unworthy to remain in the camp.

9. The fine flour depicts the perfect righteous humanity of Christ (Lev. 2:1).

"It was flour that had been thoroughly ground, there were no lumps in it. There was no unevenness in it. It sets forth the perfect, balanced humanity of the Lord" (I.M. Haldeman).

Christ was holy and compassionate. He was humble and bold. He was patient and firm. He offered salvation and warned of judgment. He comforted and He rebuked. He said, "Neither do I condemn you," but He also said, "Go, and sin no more" (John 8:11). He loved and honored his parents (Luke 2:51), but He put God first (Luke 2:48-49), and He put spiritual relationships before natural ones (Mat. 12:47-50). He kept every law of God in perfect harmony with other laws.

In contrast, all other men are unbalanced. Noah was strong in faith but weak in regard to wine. David was passionate toward God but weak toward his family and grievously failed in the matter of Bathsheba.

Every man falls short of the glory of God, but Christ is the glory of God.

> "God's glory was the test, and that was manifested in perfection everywhere. He was not more perfect in rebuking sin and hypocrisy than in pardoning and healing the sin-sick soul. Grace did not eclipse righteousness, nor righteousness grace. Patience was ever coupled with promptness; firmness with gentleness. As the hymn says, 'Thy name encircles every grace, that God as Man could show; there only could He fully trace a life divine below (Samuel Ridout, *Lectures on the Tabernacle*).

10. The anointing with oil symbolizes Christ as the Anointed One of God.

> Acts 10:38 How God anointed Jesus of Nazareth with the Holy Ghost and with power: who went about doing good, and healing all that were oppressed of the devil; for God was with him.

This is the meaning of the terms *Messiah* (Hebrew) and *Christ* (Greek).

> Isaiah 11:2-5 And the spirit of the LORD shall rest upon him, the spirit of wisdom and understanding, the spirit of counsel and might, the spirit of knowledge and of the fear of the LORD; 3 And shall make him of quick understanding in the fear of the LORD: and he shall not judge after the sight of his eyes, neither reprove after the

hearing of his ears: 4 But with righteousness shall he judge the poor, and reprove with equity for the meek of the earth: and he shall smite the earth with the rod of his mouth, and with the breath of his lips shall he slay the wicked. 5 And righteousness shall be the girdle of his loins, and faithfulness the girdle of his reins.

Isaiah 42:1-4 Behold my servant, whom I uphold; mine elect, *in whom* my soul delighteth; I have put my spirit upon him: he shall bring forth judgment to the Gentiles. 2 He shall not cry, nor lift up, nor cause his voice to be heard in the street. 3 A bruised reed shall he not break, and the smoking flax shall he not quench: he shall bring forth judgment unto truth. 4 He shall not fail nor be discouraged, till he have set judgment in the earth: and the isles shall wait for his law.

Isaiah 61:1-3 The Spirit of the Lord GOD *is* upon me; because the LORD hath anointed me to preach good tidings unto the meek; he hath sent me to bind up the brokenhearted, to proclaim liberty to the captives, and the opening of the prison to *them that are* bound; 2 To proclaim the acceptable year of the LORD, and the day of vengeance of our God; to comfort all that mourn; 3 To appoint unto them that mourn in Zion, to give unto them beauty for ashes, the oil of joy for mourning, the garment of praise for the spirit of heaviness; that they might be called trees of righteousness, the planting of the LORD, that he might be glorified.

The anointing with oil also symbolizes the believer-priest anointed by the Holy Spirit for salvation and service.

2 Corinthians 1:21-22 Now he which stablisheth us with you in Christ, and hath anointed us, *is* God; 22 Who hath also sealed us, and given the earnest of the Spirit in our hearts.

1 John 2:27 But the anointing which ye have received of him abideth in you, and ye need not that any man teach you: but as the same anointing teacheth you of all things,

> and is truth, and is no lie, and even as it hath taught you, ye shall abide in him.

11. The frankincense depicts that which is exclusively set apart to God.

> Leviticus 2:16 And the priest shall burn the memorial of it, *part* of the beaten corn thereof, and *part* of the oil thereof, with all the frankincense thereof: *it is* an offering made by fire UNTO THE LORD.

> Leviticus 24:7 And thou shalt put pure frankincense upon *each* row, that it may be on the bread for a memorial, *even* an offering made by fire UNTO THE LORD.

The frankincense signifies God's satisfaction with Christ. As the sweet fragrance of the frankincense wafted up before the Lord's presence in the tabernacle, so Christ is well-pleasing to the Father. He has delighted in the Son from all eternity.

The frankincense reminds us that "Christ is God's (1 Cor. 3:23). Only the Father knows the Son fully (Mat. 11:27).

> "Frankincense was a sweet gum. When fire was applied it gave forth a fragrance that pleased. That represents the attitude of the Son of God to the Father (John 4:34; 8:29). ... The more He was tried the more it was manifest that He sought to please the Father and fulfill His will. Behold Him there in the garden. ... 'If it be possible let this cup pass from me.' ... He sees the cup; He sees the dregs. He sees the bottom of it, the unspeakable horror and woe and hell and wordless anguish of the cross--all in that cup; and all His soul, and al the fire of the perfectness of hate against sin and shame in His soul cry out and throb in Him, till every essence of His perfect humanity revolts; and all He is of God and all the claims He has on the Father, and the assurance that should He press for it the Father who has always answered Him will answer Him now--all this drives in a sharp, stinging torment of justified pain--innocence, purity, holiness, sinlessness, flow upward like a tidal wave of demand to the very throne of God; if He let it

roll on in prayer it must be answered and He must be delivered--the cup will be put aside. But listen to the most wonderful, 'nevertheless' that ever came from human lips. 'Nevertheless, not as I will, but as thou wilt.' Surely, there is frankincense in that!" (I.M. Haldeman).

12. Leaven symbolizes evil or error. The lack of leaven in the offerings depicts Christ's sinless nature.

> Luke 12:1 In the mean time, when there were gathered together an innumerable multitude of people, insomuch that they trode one upon another, he began to say unto his disciples first of all, Beware ye of the leaven of the Pharisees, which is hypocrisy.

> 1 Corinthians 5:8 Therefore let us keep the feast, not with old leaven, neither with the leaven of malice and wickedness; but with the unleavened *bread* of sincerity and truth.

13. Salt (Lev. 2:13) refers to holiness and truth that act as a preservative and purifier in personal lives and in society.

> Matthew 5:13-14 Ye are the salt of the earth: but if the salt have lost his savour, wherewith shall it be salted? it is thenceforth good for nothing, but to be cast out, and to be trodden under foot of men. 14 Ye are the light of the world. A city that is set on an hill cannot be hid.

> Mark 9:50 Salt *is* good: but if the salt have lost his saltness, wherewith will ye season it? Have salt in yourselves, and have peace one with another.

> Colossians 4:6 Let your speech *be* alway with grace, seasoned with salt, that ye may know how ye ought to answer every man.

Salt has many other meanings with which we will deal in the studies on the meal offering.

14. The absence of honey in the offerings signifies at least three things (Lev. 2:11).

Honey is nature's sweetener and refers to the most pleasant things of this world; honey signifies that which is attractive and appealing in nature; it signifies man's natural goodness.

> Numbers 14:8 If the LORD delight in us, then he will bring us into this land, and give it us; a land which floweth with milk and honey.
>
> 1 Samuel 14:29 Then said Jonathan, My father hath troubled the land: see, I pray you, how mine eyes have been enlightened, because I tasted a little of this honey.
>
> Psalms 19:10 More to be desired *are they* than gold, yea, than much fine gold: sweeter also than honey and the honeycomb.
>
> Psalms 81:15 The haters of the LORD should have submitted themselves unto him: but their time should have endured for ever.
>
> Proverbs 24:13 My son, eat thou honey, because *it is* good; and the honeycomb, *which is* sweet to thy taste.

The absence of honey in the offerings *teaches us about Christ's nature*. He was not of this world. He was the Lord from heaven and His righteousness was not the imperfect natural goodness that fallen man can produce but was the perfect righteousness of God.

> "Natural affection, precious and excellent as it is in its place, will not bear the test of divine holiness in any individual born after the flesh. That human excellency which was manifested in Christ, and constituted Him the chiefest among ten thousand and altogether lovely, was not merely human, it was also spiritual and divine. In Him divine affections were manifested in human form" (Thomas Newberry, *Types of the Levitical Offerings*).

The absence of honey *signifies that Christ was above all human relations*. Christ honored His mother and father, but when He was 12 years old and they questioned why He stayed behind in Jerusalem and gave them a fright when they could not find Him, He replied, "Wist ye not that I must be about my Father's business?" (Luke 2:49). When his mother and brethren sent word that they wanted to see Him while He was teaching, He replied that His mother and brethren are those who do the will of God (Mat. 12:48-50).

The absence of honey in the offerings also *teaches us about Christian living*. We must die unto the flesh and live unto the Spirit. The Christian life is not a natural life; it is a supernatural life. We don't grow by perfecting the old flesh. We grow by reckoning that the old man is dead and living to the new man in Christ.

> Romans 6:6-11 Knowing this, that our old man is crucified with *him*, that the body of sin might be destroyed, that henceforth we should not serve sin. 7 For he that is dead is freed from sin. 8 Now if we be dead with Christ, we believe that we shall also live with him: 9 Knowing that Christ being raised from the dead dieth no more; death hath no more dominion over him. 10 For in that he died, he died unto sin once: but in that he liveth, he liveth unto God. 11 Likewise reckon ye also yourselves to be dead indeed unto sin, but alive unto God through Jesus Christ our Lord.

We don't perfect the old man; we put off the old man and put on the new.

> Ephesians 4:22-24 That ye put off concerning the former conversation the old man, which is corrupt according to the deceitful lusts; 23 And be renewed in the spirit of your mind; 24 And that ye put on the new man, which after God is created in righteousness and true holiness.

INTRODUCTORY LESSONS ABOUT THE OFFERINGS

1. The description of the offerings is given twice. *In Leviticus 1:1 - 6:7*, God gives instructions to the people. *In Leviticus 6:8 - 7:21*, God gives further instructions to the priests. The latter are called "the law of" the offerings (Lev. 6:9, 14, 25; 7:1, 11).

2. The typical meaning of the offerings in brief is as follows:

The *burnt offering* depicts Christ's complete devotion to God and God's acceptance of Him. The burnt offering is burnt wholly on the altar (Lev. 1:9). It signifies Christ offering "himself without spot to God" (Heb. 9:14). It signifies Christ as God's (1 Cor. 3:23).

The *meal offering* depicts Christ in His human sinless perfection tested by suffering. It signifies Christ as "in all points tempted like as *we are, yet* without sin" (Heb. 4:15).

The *peace offering* depicts Christ reconciling man with God through the offering of Himself. It signifies Christ as "having made peace through the blood of his cross" (Col. 1:20). And it signifies the believer enjoying peace with God through Christ (Rom. 5:1).

The *sin offering* depicts Christ as our sin-bearer. It signifies Christ as "the lamb of God, which taketh away the sin of the world" (John 1:29), as the One who bore "the iniquity of us all" (Isa. 53:6).

The *trespass offering* depicts Christ as the one who "is faithful and just to forgive us *our* sins, and to cleanse us from all unrighteousness" (1 John 1:9).

3. Sweet savour offerings vs. non-sweet savour

The burnt offerings, meal offerings, and peace offerings of Leviticus 1-3 are "sweet savour" offerings unto God (Lev. 1:9, 13, 18, 2:2, 9, 12; 3:5, 16). The word "sin" is not mentioned in Leviticus 1-3. These offerings depict the sweet savour that Christ is before the Father, both in His life and in His death.

The sin and trespass offerings are *not* sweet savour offerings. These offerings depict Christ bearing our sin, Christ being made sin for us to make atonement for sin.

4. The offerings begin with God

When describing the offerings, the Bible does not begin with the sin offering. It begins with the burnt offering and the meal offering. There are at least two reasons for this.

Salvation is first of all about God. He is the creator of all. He sits on the throne of the universe. Every soul belongs to Him. It is His law that has been broken; He is the One that must be propitiated with an acceptable sacrifice. There is nothing man can do or offer to provide this. Man cannot propitiate God; God must provide the propitiation Himself.

Salvation was a transaction by God the Son to God the Father through God the Spirit (Heb. 9:14). Christ, the holy Son of God, is the acceptable sacrifice that God required. He came to do the Father's will and was well pleasing and accepted both in His life and in His death. When He died, it was an offering to the Father.

Christ's resurrection is the ultimate testimony of God's acceptance. Had Christ not satisfied God's holy law 100%, He would have remained in the grave. The sins of all of mankind were placed on Christ, and had even one sin been left unatoned He would still be dead, for the wages of sin is death.

The burnt offering and the meal offering precede the peace offering and sin offering, because unless Christ had been perfect before God, no atonement could have been made for man's sin and no peace or reconciliation could have been achieved.

5. The offerings could not take away sin; they only pointed to Christ (Heb. 10:1-12).

> Hebrews 10:1 For the law having a shadow of good things to come, *and* not the very image of the things, can never with those sacrifices which they offered year by year continually make the comers thereunto perfect.

Those who believed under the law, such as David, understood this.

Salvation was always by faith without works and was never through the law and its sacrifices.

> Psalms 51:16-17 For thou desirest not sacrifice; else would I give *it*: thou delightest not in burnt offering. 17 The sacrifices of God *are* a broken spirit: a broken and a contrite heart, O God, thou wilt not despise.

> Romans 4:5-7 But to him that worketh not, but believeth on him that justifieth the ungodly, his faith is counted for righteousness. 6 Even as David also describeth the blessedness of the man, unto whom God imputeth righteousness without works, 7 *Saying*, Blessed *are* they whose iniquities are forgiven, and whose sins are covered.

A STUDY OF THE INDIVIDUAL OFFERINGS

THE BURNT OFFERING

> Leviticus 1:1-17 And the LORD called unto Moses, and spake unto him out of the tabernacle of the congregation, saying, 2 Speak unto the children of Israel, and say unto them, If any man of you bring an offering unto the LORD, ye shall bring your offering of the cattle, *even* of the herd, and of the flock. 3 If his offering *be* a burnt sacrifice of the herd, let him offer a male without blemish: he shall offer it of his own voluntary will at the door of the tabernacle of the congregation before the LORD. 4 And he shall put his hand upon the head of the burnt offering; and it shall be accepted for him to make atonement for him. 5 And he shall kill the bullock before the LORD: and the priests, Aaron's sons, shall bring the blood, and sprinkle the blood round about upon the altar that *is by* the door of the tabernacle of the congregation. 6 And he shall flay the burnt offering, and cut it into his pieces. 7 And the sons of Aaron the priest shall put fire upon the altar, and lay the wood in order upon the fire: 8 And the priests, Aaron's sons, shall lay the parts, the head, and the fat, in order upon the wood that *is* on the fire which *is* upon the altar: 9 But his inwards and his legs shall he wash in water: and the

> priest shall burn all on the altar, *to be* a burnt sacrifice, an offering made by fire, of a sweet savour unto the LORD. 10 And if his offering *be* of the flocks, *namely*, of the sheep, or of the goats, for a burnt sacrifice; he shall bring it a male without blemish. 11 And he shall kill it on the side of the altar northward before the LORD: and the priests, Aaron's sons, shall sprinkle his blood round about upon the altar. 12 And he shall cut it into his pieces, with his head and his fat: and the priest shall lay them in order on the wood that *is* on the fire which *is* upon the altar: 13 But he shall wash the inwards and the legs with water: and the priest shall bring *it* all, and burn *it* upon the altar: it *is* a burnt sacrifice, an offering made by fire, of a sweet savour unto the LORD. 14 And if the burnt sacrifice for his offering to the LORD *be* of fowls, then he shall bring his offering of turtledoves, or of young pigeons. 15 And the priest shall bring it unto the altar, and wring off his head, and burn *it* on the altar; and the blood thereof shall be wrung out at the side of the altar: 16 And he shall pluck away his crop with his feathers, and cast it beside the altar on the east part, by the place of the ashes: 17 And he shall cleave it with the wings thereof, *but* shall not divide *it* asunder: and the priest shall burn it upon the altar, upon the wood that *is* upon the fire: it *is* a burnt sacrifice, an offering made by fire, of a sweet savour unto the LORD.

The burnt offering pictures Christ's complete devotion to the Father in His life and death, and the believer's acceptance *in Him*. These two things are seen in Ephesians 5:2. Christ gave Himself FOR US and Christ gave Himself TO GOD.

> Ephesians 5:2 And walk in love, as Christ also hath loved us, and hath given himself for us an offering and a sacrifice to God for a sweetsmelling savour.

The burnt offering also depicts the believer-priest's devotion to God *in Christ*.

First, the burnt offering pictures Christ's complete devotion to the Father and God's complete acceptance of Him, delight in Him, and exaltation of Him.

> Philippians 2:5-11 Let this mind be in you, which was also in Christ Jesus: 6 Who, being in the form of God, thought it not robbery to be equal with God: 7 But made himself of no reputation, and took upon him the form of a servant, and was made in the likeness of men: 8 And being found in fashion as a man, he humbled himself, and became obedient unto death, even the death of the cross. 9 Wherefore God also hath highly exalted him, and given him a name which is above every name: 10 That at the name of Jesus every knee should bow, of *things* in heaven, and *things* in earth, and *things* under the earth; 11 And *that* every tongue should confess that Jesus Christ *is* Lord, to the glory of God the Father.

Christ is the Second Man who fulfills the plan that God had for man from the beginning but which Adam could not fulfill.

> 1 Corinthians 15:47 The first man *is* of the earth, earthy: the second man *is* the Lord from heaven.

Christ is the Man who fulfills God's plan that man be put in authority over the entire creation.

> Hebrews 2:5-9 For unto the angels hath he not put in subjection the world to come, whereof we speak. 6 But one in a certain place testified, saying, What is man, that thou art mindful of him? or the son of man, that thou visitest him? 7 Thou madest him a little lower than the angels; thou crownedst him with glory and honour, and didst set him over the works of thy hands: 8 Thou hast put all things in subjection under his feet. For in that he put all in subjection under him, he left nothing *that is* not put under him. But now we see not yet all things put under him. 9 But we see Jesus, who was made a little lower than the angels for the suffering of death, crowned with glory and honour; that he by the grace of God should taste death for every man.

Christ is the Head of the new creation, the firstborn from the dead.

Colossians 1:18 And he is the head of the body, the church: who is the beginning, the firstborn from the dead; that in all *things* he might have the preeminence.

Revelation 3:14 And unto the angel of the church of the Laodiceans write; These things saith the Amen, the faithful and true witness, the beginning of the creation of God;

Christ is the one man in heaven and in earth who is worthy to open the book of God's eternal kingdom and to bring it to pass.

Revelation 5:1-5 And I saw in the right hand of him that sat on the throne a book written within and on the backside, sealed with seven seals. 2 And I saw a strong angel proclaiming with a loud voice, Who is worthy to open the book, and to loose the seals thereof? 3 And no man in heaven, nor in earth, neither under the earth, was able to open the book, neither to look thereon. 4 And I wept much, because no man was found worthy to open and to read the book, neither to look thereon. 5 And one of the elders saith unto me, Weep not: behold, the Lion of the tribe of Juda, the Root of David, hath prevailed to open the book, and to loose the seven seals thereof.

The book in God's hand is the book of Revelation chapters 6-22. It is the record of how God will judge this world, bring in Christ's kingdom, and create the new heaven and the new earth "wherein dwelleth righteousness."

Christ, the God-Man, is God's Man. This is the mystery of the Trinity.

The Father has delighted in the Son from all eternity. Jesus is in the bosom of the Father, referring to His position as the eternal Son, one with God and dwelling in the most intimate affections of God (John 1:18). In John 17:5, Jesus spoke of the glory that He had with the Father before the world was.

In Proverbs 8, the Son of God is depicted poetically as wisdom. He was with Jehovah from eternity (Prov. 8:22-23). He was the Father's delight (Prov. 8:30).

The Father delighted in the Son when He was on earth. Twice He said from heaven, "This is my beloved son, in whom I am well pleased" (Mat. 3:17; 12:18).

And the Father will delight in the Son forever. Consider Psalm 45.

> Psalms 45:1-6 To the chief Musician upon Shoshannim, for the sons of Korah, Maschil, A Song of loves. My heart is inditing a good matter: I speak of the things which I have made touching the king: my tongue *is* the pen of a ready writer. 2 Thou art fairer than the children of men: grace is poured into thy lips: therefore God hath blessed thee for ever. 3 Gird thy sword upon *thy* thigh, O *most* mighty, with thy glory and thy majesty. 4 And in thy majesty ride prosperously because of truth and meekness *and* righteousness; and thy right hand shall teach thee terrible things. 5 Thine arrows *are* sharp in the heart of the king's enemies; *whereby* the people fall under thee. 6 Thy throne, O God, *is* for ever and ever: the sceptre of thy kingdom *is* a right sceptre.

Here God the Father is writing about God the Son. This is stated plainly in Hebrews.

> Hebrews 1:8-9 But unto the Son *he saith*, Thy throne, O God, *is* for ever and ever: a sceptre of righteousness *is* the sceptre of thy kingdom. 9 Thou hast loved righteousness, and hated iniquity; therefore God, *even* thy God, hath anointed thee with the oil of gladness above thy fellows.

In this amazing Psalm, the Father expresses delight in the Son (Psa. 45:2) and promises Him an eternal kingdom (verse 6). Christ's millennial kingdom is then described:

> Psalms 45:7-17 Thou lovest righteousness, and hatest wickedness: therefore God, thy God, hath anointed thee with the oil of gladness above thy fellows. 8 All thy garments *smell* of myrrh, and aloes, *and* cassia, out of the ivory palaces, whereby they have made thee glad. 9 Kings' daughters *were* among thy honourable women: upon thy right hand did stand the queen in gold of Ophir. 10

> Hearken, O daughter, and consider, and incline thine ear; forget also thine own people, and thy father's house; 11 So shall the king greatly desire thy beauty: for he *is* thy Lord; and worship thou him. 12 And the daughter of Tyre *shall be there* with a gift; *even* the rich among the people shall intreat thy favour. 13 The king's daughter *is* all glorious within: her clothing *is* of wrought gold. 14 She shall be brought unto the king in raiment of needlework: the virgins her companions that follow her shall be brought unto thee. 15 With gladness and rejoicing shall they be brought: they shall enter into the king's palace. 16 Instead of thy fathers shall be thy children, whom thou mayest make princes in all the earth. 17 I will make thy name to be remembered in all generations: therefore shall the people praise thee for ever and ever.

Christ will be anointed with the oil of gladness (v. 17). Joy will flow from Him throughout the kingdom. He will wear garments that smell of rare perfumes and will dwell in beautiful palaces (vv. 8-9). The church, His wife, will be clothed in the finest gold (v. 9). For this reason, she is instructed to forget her own people and her father's house (v. 10), which is what the believer does when he turns his back on this world and receives Christ and becomes a pilgrim on the way to his heavenly country. The church's husband is also her God (v. 11). The kings of the earth will bring gifts to Christ and seek His blessing (v. 12). Christ will appoint His people as governors throughout the earth (v. 16). He will be praised forever (v. 17).

This reminds us that the millennial kingdom is only the beginning of Christ's eternal reign. There will be a new heaven and a new earth and the New Jerusalem (Rev. 21-22).

Through all of this the Father delights in the Son. The Son is indeed the Father's burnt offering!

Consider some more lessons about the burnt offering from the perspective of Christ's complete devotion to the Father and God's complete acceptance of Him.

1. This aspect of the burnt offering is depicted in three ways:

First, the offering was displayed "BEFORE THE LORD" (Lev. 1:3). Before it was killed, it was shown before the Lord, and it had to be "without blemish." What a beautiful picture of Christ coming into the world and living a sinless life in devotion to the Father.

Second, the burnt offering was a "sweet savour UNTO THE LORD" (Lev. 1:9).

Third, the offering was entirely consumed on the altar to God ("the priest shall burn all on the altar," Lev. 1:9).

2. All of these form a picture of the perfect life that Christ lived on earth as described in the Gospels.

The Father was perfectly pleased with the Son, both in life and in death (Mat. 3:17; 17:5). Christ is the perfect Man who fulfilled God's law. He loved God with all of His heart, soul, and mind (Mat. 22:37-38). Christ was totally devoted to the Father and totally committed to doing His will even unto death (Mat. 26:39; Jn. 4:34; 5:30; 6:38; 8:50; 17:4; 18:11; Phil. 2:8).

Psalm 40:6-8 describes the Messiah's passion for God the Father. Verse 6, which says "mine ears hast thou opened," refers to the custom of puncturing a hole in a servant's ear when he determined to stay with his master instead of gaining his freedom (Exodus 21:5-6).

This is the loving passion that took Jesus to the cross. As the servant of old loved his master, his wife, and his children so much that he gave up his personal liberty, Christ loved the Father and the redeemed so much that He gave Himself without reservation.

> "Man's duty to God is not the giving up of one faculty, but the entire surrender of all. So Christ sums up the First Commandment, all the mind, all the soul, all the affections. ... I cannot doubt that the type refers to this in

speaking so particularly of the parts of the Burnt-offering; for 'the head,' 'the fat,' 'the legs,' 'the inwards,' are all distinctly enumerated. 'The head' is the well-known emblem of the thoughts; 'the legs' the emblem of the walk; and 'the inwards' the constant and familiar symbol of the feelings and affections of the heart. The meaning of 'the fat' ... represents the energy not of one limb or faculty, but the general health and vigour of the whole. ... In Jesus these were all surrendered, and all without spot or blemish. Had there been but one thought in the mind of Jesus which was not perfectly given to God; had there been but one affection in the heart of Jesus which was not yielded to His Father's will — had there been one step in the walk of Jesus which was taken not for God, but for His own pleasure — then He could not have offered Himself or been accepted as 'a whole burnt-offering to Jehovah.' But Jesus gave up all: He reserved nothing. All was burnt, all consumed upon the altar. There isn't anything more remarkable than this in the perfect offering of our blessed Master. Everything He did or said was for God. From first to last, self had no place: His Father's work, His Father's will, were everything. The first words recorded of Him as a child are, 'I must be about my Father's business.' His last words on the cross, 'It is finished,' proclaim how that business and that labour were fulfilled and cared for. ... It is vain to endeavour to describe His perfectness; words cannot express it: God only knows it. Of this, however, I am fully assured — the more we are in communion with God, the more we shall estimate it. ... But the Burnt-offering was for God's acceptance, not for man's. He at least could estimate the full value of the offering" (Andrew Jukes, *The Law of the Offerings*).

3. The burnt offering was burnt in the fire, depicting the manifold testings and sufferings that Christ endured in this world.

Leviticus 1:9 ... the priest shall burn all on the altar, *to be* a burnt sacrifice, an offering made by fire, of a sweet savour unto the LORD.

Even being in this wicked world was a severe trial for a perfectly holy man. But far more than that, He endured the trial of being rejected by His own family, by His own neighbors, and by His own nation. He endured the trial of testing by the vile, blasphemous devil. He endured the trial of being mocked by the Pharisees and Sadducees. He endured the trial of being misunderstood and misjudged. He endured the trial of appearing before the lying Sanhedrin, the scheming Herod, and the gutless Pilate, of being mocked by the heartless Roman soldiers, of being brutally beaten, of being paraded through the streets of Jerusalem, of being nailed to a terrible cross and displayed before the laughing soldiers and the mocking crowds.

> "When He was there, all the waves and the billows of the judgment of God rolled over His head. When He was made sin for us, who knew no sin; when He was there, bearing the whole weight of our judgment, in His infinite grace, what came out? Nothing but infinite perfection, nothing but a sweet savor to God, nothing but what God found infinite delight in. He was tested to the utmost, and the more He was tested the more sweet savor came out. The more we are tested, very often, the more our imperfections come out. The more He was tested, the more His perfections came out--the more the sweet savor came out before God" (R.F. Kingscote, *Christ as Seen in the Offerings*).

4. The burnt offering could be a bullock, a sheep, or a goat (Lev. 1:2, 5, 10).

This represents Christ in three ways, as we have seen. The bullock or ox depicts Christ as the strong, faithful servant of God who came to accomplish God's will (Mark 10:45; Phil. 2:5-8). The sheep or lamb depicts Christ surrendering to the suffering of the Cross (Isa. 53:7; Acts 8:32-35). The goat depicts Christ taking the sinner's place in judgment. It depicts Christ "in the likeness of sinful flesh" (Rom. 8:3), "made sin for us" (2 Cor. 5:21), made a curse for us (Gal. 3:13), bearing our sins (1 Pet. 2:24; Isa. 53:6), wounded for our transgressions (Isa. 53:5).

The different animals also represent the different perspective of or comprehension of Christ by individual believers.

When we are first saved, we don't know Christ very well; we only know that He is Lord and Saviour, and we rejoice in that. As we grow spiritually, we grow in our understanding of Him.

We see this in Peter's life. In Mark 4:41 he declared, "What manner of man is this?" But by the time that Peter wrote his first epistle, he knew Jesus as "the Lamb of God who purchased us with His blood" (1 Pet. 1:19), "the living stone" (2:4), "the chief corner stone" (2:6), the one "who did no sin" (2:22), "the shepherd and bishop of our souls" (2:25), the resurrected and ascended Christ to whom all powers are subject (3:21-22), the "chief Shepherd" who is coming again (5:4).

> "What we see typified in these variations is not a greater or lesser acceptance but a greater or lesser apprehension on the part of the offerer, To put it in another way: every believer stands accepted before God in the perfection and fragrance of the sacrifice of Christ which never varies and is the same for all. What does vary is the measure in which we appreciate the value of His work" (Ernest Wilson, *Blood Sacrifices of the Old Testament*).

5. The offering was cut apart before it was burnt on the altar.

> Leviticus 1:6-8 And he shall flay the burnt offering, and cut it into his pieces. 7 And the sons of Aaron the priest shall put fire upon the altar, and lay the wood in order upon the fire: 8 And the priests, Aaron's sons, shall lay the parts, the head, and the fat, in order upon the wood that *is* on the fire which *is* upon the altar.

This depicts Christ's perfection in thought and life, open before the eyes of God and perfectly acceptable. All things are naked and opened unto His eyes (Heb. 4:13). Only God the Father knows the Son perfectly (Mat. 11:27). The head signifies Christ's mind; the fat, His energy and passion (fat stores energy and regulates temperature); the inwards, His heart and emotions; the legs, His actions.

> "He yielded Himself up to death, all the hidden springs of His life were laid bare, and all was seen to be for God. The shoulder which speaks of strength; the fat within and without, which speaks of the energy of the will--in man, that which fills him with pride and rebellion; and the vitals, His thoughts, motives and desires: all that He was sent up in death in the sweet savor to God that perfect holiness could desire" (Samuel Ridout, *Lectures on the Tabernacle*).

6. The washing of the sacrifice depicts Christ's sinlessness.

> Leviticus 1:9 But his inwards and his legs shall he wash in water: and the priest shall burn all on the altar, *to be* a burnt sacrifice, an offering made by fire, of a sweet savour unto the LORD.

The sacrifice was doubly perfect. First, it was without blemish; second, it was washed. This signifies Christ's complete, absolute purity.

The washing of the inwards signifies His sinlessness in thought, and the washing of the legs signifies His sinlessness in action.

There was nothing that man could find wrong in Christ's external life, and there was nothing that God could find wrong even in His most secret thoughts, affections, and motives.

> "As a ray of sunlight remains pure, whatever objects it might shine upon, so the pathway of the Lord Jesus was unsullied by any of the scenes through which He passed" (Thomas Newberry).

7. The fire of the burnt offering never went out.

> Leviticus 6:12-13 And the fire upon the altar shall be burning in it; it shall not be put out: and the priest shall burn wood on it every morning, and lay the burnt offering in order upon it; and he shall burn thereon the fat of the peace offerings. 13 The fire shall ever be burning upon the altar; it shall never go out.

This is a beautiful picture of the eternal nature of Christ's sacrifice. He is risen from the dead and "ever liveth to make intercession for them" (Heb. 7:25).

Christ's sacrifice will continue to provide a perfect standing for the believer throughout eternity. This should cast all fear from the believer's heart. As the hymn says,

My love is ofttimes low,

My joy still ebbs and flows;

But peace with Him remains the same:

No change Jehovah knows.

> "*Never go out.* What does that imply? When we have been in the glory of God for innumerable ages, we shall be there on the same ground as that upon which we are now accepted--namely, the value of the work of Christ before God. When God brings in the new heavens and the new earth, wherein dwells righteousness, the foundation of the sweet savor of the sacrifice of Christ before God is as fresh as ever, and in that we are accepted. Does that sweet savor ever alter? Never. Therefore the believer's acceptance never alters" (R.F. Kingscote).

8. The fire of the burnt offering burned all night.

> Leviticus 6:9 Command Aaron and his sons, saying, This *is* the law of the burnt offering: It *is* the burnt offering, because of the burning upon the altar all night unto the morning, and the fire of the altar shall be burning in it.

First, this pictures the unceasing efficacy of Christ's sacrifice through the long night of this present world.

There is no night in heaven, and there will be no night in the New Jerusalem. All will be brightness and joy and blessing. But in this present life there are hardships of every kind and faith is continually tested. Thank God that no matter what happens, Christ never sleeps or slumbers. That He will never leave nor forsake His own is a promise founded on the perfect and eternal efficacy of the sacrifice that Christ made on the cross.

Second, the fire burning all night reminds us of the promise of the Lord to be with the churches unto the end of the age.

> Matthew 28:20 ... and, lo, I am with you alway, *even* unto the end of the world. Amen.

The apostasy that has increased throughout the age (2 Tim. 3:13) will explode in intensity at the end of the age (2 Timothy 3-4), yet Christ will never forsake His people.

He promised that the church at Philadelphia will be kept "from the hour of temptation, which shall come upon all the world" (Rev. 3:9-11). This promise was never experienced by the historic church at Philadelphia. It is a promise that looks down the long corridor of time to the faithful Bible-believing congregations of the last hours of the church age, congregations that are struggling in the midst of terrible apostasy and compromise, congregations that live in the perilous times described in 2 Timothy 3. It is a promise that Jesus will be with them through the darkest part of the night and will then appear as the morning star to take them unto Himself in the glorious Rapture of the saints before the Tribulation comes upon all the world.

All of this can be seen in the ancient fire of the burnt offering "burning all night unto the morning" (Lev. 6:9).

9. The burnt offering was offered by "any man" and "of his own voluntary will" (Lev. 1:2-3).

This signifies the universal offer of the gospel. Jesus Christ, Jehovah's Burnt Offering, is available to "whosoever believeth" (John 3:15, 16; 12:46; Acts 10:43; Romans 9:33).

The burnt offering secondly pictures the believer's acceptance in Christ.

> Leviticus 1:3-4 If his offering *be* a burnt sacrifice of the herd, let him offer a male without blemish: he shall offer it of his own voluntary will at the door of the tabernacle of the congregation before the LORD. 4 And he shall put his hand upon the head of the burnt offering; and it shall be accepted for him to make atonement for him.

There were two portions of the burnt offering: one portion was burnt on the altar as a sweet savour unto the Lord. That is God's portion, as we have seen.

The other portion was eaten by the priests (Lev. 2:2-3). That signifies man's part in Christ.

1. The priest's part of the offering signifies the believer feasting on Christ in this life and forever.

In this sense, the meal offering depicts the same thing as the manna that Israel ate in the wilderness and the shewbread that the priests ate in the tabernacle.

The unbeliever "eats" Christ for salvation by believing on Him as Lord and Saviour (John 6:35, 47-48). The believer "eats" Christ by abiding in Him and taking on His yoke of service and learning of Him.

> John 15:3-4 Now ye are clean through the word which I have spoken unto you. 4 Abide in me, and I in you. As the branch cannot bear fruit of itself, except it abide in the vine; no more can ye, except ye abide in me.

> Matthew 11:28-30 Come unto me, all *ye* that labour and are heavy laden, and I will give you rest. 29 Take my yoke upon you, and learn of me; for I am meek and lowly in heart: and ye shall find rest unto your souls. 30 For my yoke *is* easy, and my burden is light.

Revelation 3:20 Behold, I stand at the door, and knock: if any man hear my voice, and open the door, I will come in to him, and will sup with him, and he with me.

We have the same picture in the Lord's Supper. The bread depicts Christ's body which was broken for us. Christ's objective in giving Himself on the cross was not only to provide forgiveness of sins and eternal life to lost sinners but also to fellowship with them forever.

1 Corinthians 1:9 God *is* faithful, by whom ye were called unto the fellowship of his Son Jesus Christ our Lord.

1 John 1:3 That which we have seen and heard declare we unto you, that ye also may have fellowship with us: and truly our fellowship *is* with the Father, and with his Son Jesus Christ.

"May the Lord enable us in the power of the Holy Spirit to feed on Himself. Surely that is what the Lord speaks to us of in the message to the church at Pergamos in Revelation 2: 'To him that overcometh will I give to eat of the hidden manna.' What is the 'hidden manna'? There in glory we shall, in the power of the Holy Spirit, look back and enter fully into God's delight in the perfections of the blessed Lord in His humiliation upon earth, and it is surely our portion now" (R.F. Kingscote).

2. The burnt offering teaches us that the believer's acceptance is complete before God, because God's acceptance of Christ is complete, and we are in Him.

We are "accepted in the beloved" (Eph. 1:6). Christ is our righteousness and our holiness (1 Cor. 1:30).

Christ is everything that the believer is not. God made man in His own image. He made him to be holy and righteousness, but man rebelled and became corrupt. As a consequence, every human life is unacceptable to God. He cannot accept the sinner or anything that the sinner does because he doesn't have the perfect righteousness God requires. Our most sincere devotion to God and our most earnest service to God is imperfect (Isa. 64:6).

It is only in Christ that we find the divine perfection, the holy righteousness, that we lack. In our natural selves, we "come short of the glory of God" (Rom. 3:23). To offend in even one point of God's law is to be guilty of all (James 2:10). How guilty we are, then!

God's law says that hidden sins of the heart, though unseen by man, are sins nonetheless and condemn us before God. Covetousness, sexual lust, hatred, and such are sins of the heart, invisible to our fellow man but seen by God (Mat. 5:27-28).

When measured by this standard, we are without any hope of pleasing God in our own selves. We fall so horribly short of the glory of God. It is the distance between heaven and hell.

But Christ is the very glory of God, and in Christ we are what we cannot be in ourselves. He is the perfect Man, and we are accepted in Him. God is not pleased with the sinner, but He is "well pleased" with Jesus, and when we exercise saving faith in Christ, we are placed in Christ by God and before God, and He is pleased with us because of Christ!

That is the theme of Ephesians 1-3. Ten times the words "in Christ" appear (Eph. 1:1, 3, 10, 12, 20; 2:6, 10, 13; 3:6, 11). Our eternal salvation is "in Christ" (Eph. 1:3). God's eternal purposes are "in Christ" (Eph. 1:10; 3:11). Everything having to do with God is "in Christ."

This is the wonderful message of the burnt offering.

The burnt offering is all about devotion and obedience and surrender. Devotion is what God *requires of* man and what God *desires from* man. In the first great law, God demands that we love Him with "all thy heart, and with all thy soul, and with all thy mind" (Mat. 22:37-38).

We fall terribly and miserably short of this.

Though God had tenderly made them and placed them in a paradise and provided them with every legitimate pleasure and placed them in authority over the earth, Adam and Eve did not love their Creator enough even to keep one simple law, and their children are no better.

But Jesus lived the first and great commandment to perfection. He was wholly and perfectly and passionately devoted to pleasing the Father, even unto the shameful death of the cross, and the Father twice testified, "This is my beloved Son, in whom I am well pleased" (Mat. 3:17; 17:5).

The second great law of God demands, "Thou shalt love thy neighbour as t hyself" (Mat. 22:39). We fallen sons of Adam fail to keep this commandment in a thousand ways. At our very best, everything we do is tainted with our unholy selfishness, but Christ loved His neighbour as Himself indeed. He even loved His enemies and died to save them from eternal judgment.

3. The offerer laid hands on the sacrifice (Lev. 1:4; 3:2, 8, 13; 4:15, 24, 29, 33).

The significance is twofold. It signifies the transfer of the sinner's guilt to the sacrifice. And it signifies the transference of the value of Christ's atonement to the believing sinner. This depicts the two aspects of justification (2 Cor. 5:21).

The words "it shall be accepted FOR HIM" (Lev. 1:4) signify these wonderful truths.

> "The offerer was fully identified with the value of the sacrifice before God. As we read, 'And it shall be accepted for him,' or instead of him. Oh, how simple and how blessed that is! The sacrifice of Christ accepted by God for us, according to all the value that He puts upon it--Christ accepted instead of us. Instead of being before God with our sins and hatred to Him, instead of our disobedience and lack of devotedness, we are accepted according to all the value of that work on the cross, where our sins were all

atoned for and where Christ's obedience, devotedness and love to the Father were fully manifested" (R.F. Kingscote).

The burnt offering also depicts the believer's devotion to God in Christ.

Just as the burnt offering was wholly consumed on the altar, the believer is exhorted to present his body unto God as a living sacrifice, holy, acceptable to God (Romans 12:1-2).

We can do this because we have been redeemed and cleansed, and we stand in Christ.

As the offering was entirely burnt on the altar ("burn all on the altar," Lev. 1:9), so the believer is to wholly surrender to God and His will. This is what the hymn "Is Your All on the Altar" speaks of. Consider the second stanza and the chorus:

> Would you walk with the Lord,
> In the light of His word,
> And have peace and contentment alway?
> You must do His sweet will,
> To be free from all ill,
> On the altar your all you must lay.
>
> Is your all on the altar of sacrifice laid?
> Your heart does the Spirit control?
> You can only be blest,
> And have peace and sweet rest,
> As you yield Him your body and soul.

The fire of the burnt offering burning all night (Lev. 6:9) is a call for the believer to be daily and continually devoted to God throughout the dark night of this world.

Thank God, "the night is far spent, the day is at hand" and soon this present wretched night will be swallowed up in eternal day.

In the meantime, let us be devoted to the Lord's righteous service.

> Romans 13:12-14 The night is far spent, the day is at hand: let us therefore cast off the works of darkness, and let us

> put on the armour of light. 13 Let us walk honestly, as in the day; not in rioting and drunkenness, not in chambering and wantonness, not in strife and envying. 14 But put ye on the Lord Jesus Christ, and make not provision for the flesh, to *fulfil* the lusts *thereof.*

Each morning the priest removed the ashes and rebuilt the fire and placed another burnt offering on it.

> Leviticus 6:8-13 And the LORD spake unto Moses, saying, 9 Command Aaron and his sons, saying, This *is* the law of the burnt offering: It *is* the burnt offering, because of the burning upon the altar all night unto the morning, and the fire of the altar shall be burning in it. 10 And the priest shall put on his linen garment, and his linen breeches shall he put upon his flesh, and take up the ashes which the fire hath consumed with the burnt offering on the altar, and he shall put them beside the altar. 11 And he shall put off his garments, and put on other garments, and carry forth the ashes without the camp unto a clean place. 12 And the fire upon the altar shall be burning in it; it shall not be put out: and the priest shall burn wood on it every morning, and lay the burnt offering in order upon it; and he shall burn thereon the fat of the peace offerings. 13 The fire shall ever be burning upon the altar; it shall never go out.

This is a beautiful picture of the believer's daily devotion to the Lord. Each day is a new day and requires a fresh dedication of oneself to Christ, a fresh private time in God's Word and prayer.

It is not in our own power that we do this. It is not in our own power that we walk with the Lord through the day. We offer ourselves *through Him.* He is our life and our sanctification (Gal. 2:20).

We must not live the Christian life by our feelings or by our situation. The Levitical priest removed the ashes and offered a fresh sacrifice each morning regardless of his feelings. He did this out of obedience to God and he did it by faith, and this is how the believer must live his Christian life.

We offer ourselves afresh to God each morning, not because of how we might feel that day, but because God has given us great promises and we believe those promises. We believe that the mercies of God are new every morning and this is because of the perfect sacrifice of Christ (Lam. 3:23).

We are invited to come boldly to the throne of grace for mercy and help (Heb. 4:16). Our boldness in coming is not based on our feelings but on our confidence in the atoning value of Christ's blood.

> "Let's follow the example of the priest and each morning get rid of the old ashes, stir up the fire, and offer a burnt offering to the Lord. The phrase 'stir up' in 2 Timothy 1:6 means 'stir up the flame into life again.' Is the flame burning high on the altar of your heart, or are you getting lukewarm (Rev. 3:15-16) or cold (Mat. 24:12)?" (Warren Wiersbe).

THE MEAL OFFERING

> Leviticus 2:1-16 And when any will offer a meat offering unto the LORD, his offering shall be *of* fine flour; and he shall pour oil upon it, and put frankincense thereon: 2 And he shall bring it to Aaron's sons the priests: and he shall take thereout his handful of the flour thereof, and of the oil thereof, with all the frankincense thereof; and the priest shall burn the memorial of it upon the altar, *to be* an offering made by fire, of a sweet savour unto the LORD: 3 And the remnant of the meat offering *shall be* Aaron's and his sons': *it is* a thing most holy of the offerings of the LORD made by fire. 4 And if thou bring an oblation of a meat offering baken in the oven, *it shall be* unleavened cakes of fine flour mingled with oil, or unleavened wafers anointed with oil. 5 And if thy oblation *be* a meat offering *baken* in a pan, it shall be *of* fine flour unleavened, mingled with oil. 6 Thou shalt part it in pieces, and pour oil thereon: it *is* a meat offering. 7 And if thy oblation *be* a meat offering *baken* in the fryingpan, it shall be made *of* fine flour with oil. 8 And thou shalt bring the meat offering

> that is made of these things unto the LORD: and when it is presented unto the priest, he shall bring it unto the altar. 9 And the priest shall take from the meat offering a memorial thereof, and shall burn *it* upon the altar: *it is* an offering made by fire, of a sweet savour unto the LORD. 10 And that which is left of the meat offering *shall be* Aaron's and his sons': *it is* a thing most holy of the offerings of the LORD made by fire. 11 No meat offering, which ye shall bring unto the LORD, shall be made with leaven: for ye shall burn no leaven, nor any honey, in any offering of the LORD made by fire. 12 As for the oblation of the firstfruits, ye shall offer them unto the LORD: but they shall not be burnt on the altar for a sweet savour. 13 And every oblation of thy meat offering shalt thou season with salt; neither shalt thou suffer the salt of the covenant of thy God to be lacking from thy meat offering: with all thine offerings thou shalt offer salt. 14 And if thou offer a meat offering of thy firstfruits unto the LORD, thou shalt offer for the meat offering of thy firstfruits green ears of corn dried by the fire, *even* corn beaten out of full ears. 15 And thou shalt put oil upon it, and lay frankincense thereon: it *is* a meat offering. 16 And the priest shall burn the memorial of it, *part* of the beaten corn thereof, and *part* of the oil thereof, with all the frankincense thereof: *it is* an offering made by fire unto the LORD.

The *meal offering* depicts Christ in His human sinless perfection tested by suffering. It signifies Christ as "in all points tempted like as *we are, yet* without sin" (Heb. 4:15).

1. The fine flour without leaven (Lev. 2:1, 11) represents Christ's sinless, balanced humanity.

The offering was not merely flour; it was *fine* flour. It was the finest flour sifted repeatedly to remove every imperfection and to make it uniform throughout. The fine ingredients were blended to perfection.

What a lovely picture of Christ's beautiful humanity. Not only is there no hint of sin, but also every character trait is balanced within the whole Person. As we see the Gospels, there are no flaws, no weaknesses, no imbalances in Christ.

2. The burning on the fire (Lev. 2:2), signifies the manifold suffering that Christ experienced in this sin-cursed world.

"The meat offering speaks to us of the perfect, sinless humanity of the Lord Jesus--what He was as a man here on earth, but as offered to God; 'an offering,' as it states in chapter 2, 'made by fire.' This fire represents testing judgment, and surely the blessed Lord was tested in all His path through this world, as also on the cross and by death itself. But the more He was tested, the more was brought out His infinite perfection before God. Every thought, every word and every action was a sweet savor to God. The Lord was perfect in every step of His way through this world--perfect in obedience, perfect in dependence, perfect in meekness, perfect in kindness, perfect in sympathy, perfect in humility; in fact, there is not a single grace you can think of that the Lord Jesus did not exhibit in all its perfection during His life upon earth. This the meat offering typifies. All the frankincense was to be burned with the meat offering, and the sweet perfume of that frankincense speaks to us of all the graces of the Lord Jesus, everything being perfectly acceptable to God--a sweet-smelling savor" (R.F. Kingscote).

3. The presentation of the offering to the Lord and the burning of it unto the Lord as a sweet savour signifies God the Father's acceptance of Christ and His delight in Christ, as we have seen in the burnt offering.

It also speaks of the perfection of our acceptance in Christ. Insofar as God is pleased with the Son, so far He is pleased with those who are in the Son.

As R.F. Kingscote says in his excellent studies on the offerings:

> "The better we know God's thoughts about Christ, the better we know God's thoughts about us, who are in Christ.

According to that verse in 1 John 4, 'As He is, so are we in this world.' There is not a single grace, not a single beauty, not a single perfection of the Lord Jesus that we see brought out in the Gospels respecting which we, as believers, may not say, 'That is mine.' Do you ask how this can be? I reply, Is not Christ your life? 'When Christ, who is our life, shall appear' (Col. 3: 4). Do you want to see what your life is in its perfection? You must not look at yourselves or your fellow-Christians; you must look at Christ here on earth. 'For the life was manifested'--shown out (1 John 1: 2). What life? The eternal life. That is the life you and I possess as believers. ... You must not look at me to find it out, because very often a great deal that is not the life of Christ comes out; very often the sin, the Adam-nature, shows itself. No, if you wish to see the eternal life that I possess perfectly manifested, you must look at the Lord Jesus Christ as a man on earth" (*Christ as Seen in the Offerings*).

4. Baked in the oven (Lev. 2:4), in a shallow pan (Lev. 2:5), and in a frying pan (Lev. 2:7) signify Christ's testing and suffering.

The oven signifies Christ's private sufferings, seen only by God the Father.

The *shallow or flat pan* (Hebrew *machabath*) signifies Christ's public sufferings.

The *frying pan or stewing pan* which had short sides (Hebrew *marchesheth*) signifies Christ's sufferings that were both public and private, particularly on the cross where He suffered both the curse of God, the pain of crucifixion, and the mocking of man.

"You may have noticed the different intensity of the trials to which the Lord as man was subject here. This was typified by the different ways in which the meat offering was prepared. In one case it was baked in an oven (v. 4). In another case it was baked in a pan--a flat slice or plate (v. 5). In a third case it was baked in a frying pan. These

> different modes of offering the meat offering by fire no doubt set forth the different degrees of intensity in the trials to which the Lord was subject here. The 'oven' may refer to the hidden path of His life, that which men could not see, that which was between Himself and God alone. How blessed to be allowed to enter into all this! It will be the joy of our souls in that day of glory that is coming when we are with Him to be going over and retracing the pathway of that blessed Lord who so humbled Himself in this world--the One who, in coming to do the will of God, also, in the love and grace of His heart, gave Himself for our sins, becoming a man in order to do it" (Kingscote).

5. The absence of honey signifies at least two things in relation to Christ, as we have seen.

> Leviticus 2:11 No meat offering, which ye shall bring unto the LORD, shall be made with leaven: for ye shall burn no leaven, nor any honey, in any offering of the LORD made by fire.

The absence of honey *teaches us about Christ's nature.* He was not of this world. He was the Lord from heaven, and His righteousness was not the imperfect natural goodness that fallen man can produce but was the perfect righteousness of God.

The absence of honey *signifies that Christ was above all human relations.* Christ honored His mother and father but He honored God first (Luke 2:49; Mat. 12:48-50).

6. The *oil mingled with the meal* represents Christ's Incarnation (Lev. 2:4).

Christ was conceived of the Spirit (Luke 1:35). He was wholly permeated with the Spirit of God in every fiber of His being, as the flour was permeated with the oil.

7. The *oil anointing the meal* (Lev. 2:1) signifies Jesus was the Anointed One, the Messiah, the Christ (Acts 10:38). He was anointed by the Spirit at His baptism (Luke 3:32).

8. The *oil saturating the meal* signifies Christ filled with the Spirit (Lev. 2:7).

> Luke 4:1 And Jesus being full of the Holy Ghost returned from Jordan, and was led by the Spirit into the wilderness,

> John 3:34 For he whom God hath sent speaketh the words of God: for God giveth not the Spirit by measure *unto him*.

9. The salt with the offering depicts Christ in several ways.

> Leviticus 2:13 And every oblation of thy meat offering shalt thou season with salt; neither shalt thou suffer the salt of the covenant of thy God to be lacking from thy meat offering: with all thine offerings thou shalt offer salt.

By comparing Scripture with Scripture, we can see that salt has many meanings and implications.

The first meaning of salt in Scripture, as a spiritual type, refers to holiness and truth that act as a preservative and purifier in personal lives and society.

> Matthew 5:13-14 Ye are the salt of the earth: but if the salt have lost his savour, wherewith shall it be salted? it is thenceforth good for nothing, but to be cast out, and to be trodden under foot of men. 14 Ye are the light of the world. A city that is set on an hill cannot be hid.

> Mark 9:50 Salt *is* good: but if the salt have lost his saltness, wherewith will ye season it? Have salt in yourselves, and have peace one with another.

> Colossians 4:6 Let your speech *be* alway with grace, seasoned with salt, that ye may know how ye ought to answer every man.

God gave the holy law to Israel so she could be the salt of the earth, but Israel failed. She turned the law into a path of self-righteousness and thus destroyed its message. Christ is the salt that Israel never was. By His life and teaching, He showed forth the holy requirements of God and exposed all men as sinners (Mat. 5:19-20). He then drew them to Himself for salvation, as in the cases of Nicodemus and Zacchaeus and the woman at the well. After Christ ascended to heaven, He sent His Spirit to continue the work of teaching, conviction, and drawing (John 12:32; 16:7-8). This is the work of "salt."

Salt refers to a preservative influence.

> Matthew 5:13 Ye are the salt of the earth: but if the salt have lost his savour, wherewith shall it be salted? it is thenceforth good for nothing, but to be cast out, and to be trodden under foot of men.

Salt stops corruption, as when salted meat is preserved by not allowing it to rot. Likewise the Spirit of Christ is a preservative influence in society even in this wicked world, as God's Spirit strove with men before the Flood. The only reason there is any safety, any law and order, in this sin-cursed world is that the Spirit of Christ exercises a retraining influence. All authority is of God (Rom. 13:1).

Christ is also the preservative in the lives of believers, living His life in them, convicting them of sin, keeping them from sin. This is a major theme of John's First Epistle (1 John 2:3-6; 3:3-9; 5:18).

Salt refers to flavoring.

> Job 6:6 Can that which is unsavoury be eaten without salt? or is there *any* taste in the white of an egg?

As a spice, salt increases the pleasure of eating, and Christ is certainly the spice of life! Without him everything is bland and ultimately meaningless, but with Him everything is delightful.

The Christian life should also be salty in this way. By our sound doctrine and godly living, we should sweeten our environment.

Salt refers to wholesome words that edify.

> Colossians 4:6 Let your speech *be* alway with grace, seasoned with salt, that ye may know how ye ought to answer every man.

No one ever spoke such edifying words as Jesus. He is the eternal Word of God, and every word that proceeds from His mouth is salty. Some of His words are recorded for us in the Gospels, and we can examine every one and see its spiritual beauty. His words are infinite and can be studied forever without exhausting their meaning and import.

We think of John 3:16, which Jesus spoke to Nicodemus. The meaning of this one short statement and the blessing of it will never be exhausted.

Every word from Christ's lips was perfect truth seasoned with grace. There was nothing wrong or frivolous or insignificant. Every word fit the situation. We think of the words that He spoke to the adulterous woman, caught in the very act, "And Jesus said unto her, Neither do I condemn thee: go, and sin no more" (John 8:11).

The believer has the unspeakable privilege to hear Christ's words and to meditate on them forever.

> "After two thousand years not a word He spoke needs to be forgiven, forgotten, modified, corrected or erased; after two thousand years they remain in the very essence of spirit, the very pulse of life, the very concrete of cleanness, impassable barriers against corruption, against sin in thought as well as deed" (I.M. Haldeman).

Salt refers to God's sure covenants.

> 2 Chronicles 13:5 Ought ye not to know that the LORD God of Israel gave the kingdom over Israel to David for ever, *even* to him and to his sons by a covenant of salt?

Christ is the salt of all of God's covenants and promises. He is the heart and soul of them. They are founded upon Him and His sacrifice. In Christ, all of the promises of God are yea and amen (2 Cor. 1:20)!

Salt refers to healing.

> 2 Kings 2:20-21 And he said, Bring me a new cruse, and put salt therein. And they brought *it* to him. 21 And he went forth unto the spring of the waters, and cast the salt in there, and said, Thus saith the LORD, I have healed these waters; there shall not be from thence any more death or barren *land.*

Christ is the great Healer. He comes with healing in his wings (Mal. 4:2). He healed every type of disease during His earthly life. By His stripes we are healed of our sin sickness (1 Pet. 2:24). Ultimately, He will heal the universe with eternal healing, and there will never again be suffering or death (Rev. 21:4).

Salt refers to judgment.

> Deuteronomy 29:23 *And that* the whole land thereof *is* brimstone, and salt, *and* burning, *that* it is not sown, nor beareth, nor any grass groweth therein, like the overthrow of Sodom, and Gomorrah, Admah, and Zeboim, which the LORD overthrew in his anger, and in his wrath:

> Judges 9:45 And Abimelech fought against the city all that day; and he took the city, and slew the people that *was* therein, and beat down the city, and sowed it with salt.

Christ is the judge of the world (John 5:22). The wrath of the Lamb will be displayed in eternal fiery judgment upon every soul that rejects Him (2 Th. 1:7-9; Jude 14-15; Rev. 20:11-15).

Salt represents the holiness of life which Christ had and which is necessary to save man from judgment.

> Mark 9:43-50 And if thy hand offend thee, cut it off: it is better for thee to enter into life maimed, than having two hands to go into hell, into the fire that never shall be quenched: 44 Where their worm dieth not, and the fire is not quenched. 45 And if thy foot offend thee, cut it off: it is better for thee to enter halt into life, than having two feet to be cast into hell, into the fire that never shall be quenched:

46 Where their worm dieth not, and the fire is not quenched. 47 And if thine eye offend thee, pluck it out: it is better for thee to enter into the kingdom of God with one eye, than having two eyes to be cast into hell fire: 48 Where their worm dieth not, and the fire is not quenched. 49 For every one shall be salted with fire, and every sacrifice shall be salted with salt. 50 Salt *is* good: but if the salt have lost his saltness, wherewith will ye season it? Have salt in yourselves, and have peace one with another.

As we have seen, the most prominent meaning of salt in Scripture refers to holiness and truth that act as a preservative and purifier in personal lives and in society (Mat. 5:13-14; Mk. 9:50; Col. 4:6).

The Altar of Sacrifice - © *GoodSalt*

In Mark 9:43-50 Christ taught the requirement for salvation, which is sinless perfection. To avoid hell requires having no sin. He taught this in the most dramatic way. He said to avoid offense or sin, one must cut off the hand and foot and pluck out the eye. But elsewhere Jesus taught that the root of sin is in the heart (Mat. 15:18-19). Multiple amputees and blind men sin. How can cutting off one's limbs remove man's sin, then? It can't. Jesus was using a dramatic illustration to show how impossible it is for man to avoid hell by his own efforts. Christ was using the terrible holiness of the law to show men their lost condition and their need of salvation, which is the divine purpose of the law (Rom. 3:19-21; Gal. 3:24). Christ alone has the holiness demanded by God's law, and we are saved by His sinless offering that was made in our place.

This is what the salt of Mark 9:49 points to. Unless he is safe in Christ, every sinner will be salted with the fire of eternal judgment because he has broken God's holy laws. Thank God, the salt of judgment fell on Christ when He died in our place. Salvation is available.

THE PEACE OFFERING

See Leviticus 3:1-17; 7:13-34

1. The peace offering has two major meanings:

First, the *peace offering* depicts Christ reconciling man with God through the offering of Himself. It signifies Christ as "having made peace through the blood of his cross" (Col. 1:20).

Christ is the Prince of Peace (Isa. 9:6). He preaches peace to every sinner through the gospel.

> Ephesians 2:17 And came and preached peace to you which were afar off, and to them that were nigh.

Second, the peace offering typifies the believer enjoying this peace with God.

> Romans 5:1 Therefore being justified by faith, we have peace with God through our Lord Jesus Christ:

The peace offering "is a picture of God and the sinner at peace with each other, all issues between them perfectly settled. It is peace upon the basis of a mutually accepted sacrifice. It is the picture of reconciliation" (I.M. Haldeman).

This is perhaps why the peace offering could be male or female (Lev. 3:1). Our perception of Christ is not perfect, and our worship is not perfect. Only the Father knows the Son perfectly (Mat. 11:27).

And this is perhaps why the peace offering included leaven.

> Leviticus 7:13-14 Besides the cakes, he shall offer *for* his offering LEAVENED BREAD with the sacrifice of thanksgiving of his peace offerings. 14 And of it he shall offer one out of the whole oblation *for* an heave offering unto the LORD, *and* it shall be the priest's that sprinkleth the blood of the peace offerings.

Observe that the leaven was not offered to God on the altar; it was eaten by the priest. The believer's worship of God in this present world is deeply imperfect.

The only other offering that included leaven was the wave offering of the feast of weeks or Pentecost (Lev. 23:15-17). This offering depicted the church.

> "Here is a deep mystery, for God had said that no leaven was to be burned on the altar in any offering, (Lev. 2:11). The answer is that the leavened cakes were not offered on the altar, but were eaten by the offerer. It is a recognition of the sinful nature of every human participant in the worship of God" (Ernest Wilson, *Blood Sacrifices of the Old Testament*).

2. The peace offering was shared by God and the high priest and the priests.

> Leviticus 7:31-32 And the priest shall burn the fat upon the altar: but the breast shall be Aaron's and his sons'. 32 And the right shoulder shall ye give unto the priest *for* an heave offering of the sacrifices of your peace offerings.

Each had a part. This is a picture of the communion of the saints with God. All believers are one in Christ and our fellowship is with the Father and the Son (1 John 1:3).

God the Father's pleasure is fulfilled in the Son.

> Isaiah 53:11-12 He shall see of the travail of his soul, *and* shall be satisfied: by his knowledge shall my righteous servant justify many; for he shall bear their iniquities. 12 Therefore will I divide him *a portion* with the great, and he shall divide the spoil with the strong; because he hath poured out his soul unto death: and he was numbered with the transgressors; and he bare the sin of many, and made intercession for the transgressors.

The Father is delighted with the Son and with those that He accepts in the Son.

> John 14:23 Jesus answered and said unto him, If a man love me, he will keep my words: and my Father will love him, and we will come unto him, and make our abode with him.

Christ, our High Priest, delights in the Father and is presently enjoying the glory with the Father that He has had from eternity (John 17:5).

Christ also delights in the results of the redemption He has purchased.

> Hebrews 12:2 Looking unto Jesus the author and finisher of *our* faith; who for the joy that was set before him endured the cross, despising the shame, and is set down at the right hand of the throne of God.

He delights with His redeemed people today, and He will delight in them forever. We will be with Him in paradise (John 14:1-3). We will shine as the sun in His kingdom (Mat. 13:43). We will eat and drink with Him (Mat. 26:29).

The mutual sharing of the peace offering is also depicted in the bread of the Lord's Supper.

> 1 Corinthians 10:16-17 The cup of blessing which we bless, is it not the communion of the blood of Christ? The bread

which we break, is it not the communion of the body of Christ? 17 For we *being* many are one bread, *and* one body: for we are all partakers of that one bread.

This is the picture of all of the redeemed feasting forever with God the Son. Eating the bread means that together with all of the redeemed the believer receives Jesus as the Sacrifice of God which is the atonement for the sins of the world and which will be the spiritual foundation of the new heaven and the new earth.

It means that together with all of the redeemed, the believer contemplates Christ and delights in Him and grows into His likeness. It means that together with all of the redeemed the believer partakes of Christ's life and blessing. It means that together with all of the redeemed the believer praises Christ as worthy to receive power, and riches, and wisdom, and strength, and honour, and glory, and blessing (Rev. 5:11-13).

3. The priest's part of the peace offering was the breast.

Leviticus 7:31 And the priest shall burn the fat upon the altar: but the breast shall be Aaron's and his sons'.

This signifies Christ's love. That is the part that His people most delight in, and that is the part that is given to us to enjoy! This signifies the same thing as the breastplate and the jewels that were worn over the high priest's heart. God did not give His only begotten Son out of a sense of duty, nor did the Son give Himself out of a mere sense of duty. The sacrifice of Christ was an act of incomprehensible love.

John 3:16 For God so loved the world, that he gave his only begotten Son, that whosoever believeth in him should not perish, but have everlasting life.

Romans 5:8 But God commendeth his love toward us, in that, while we were yet sinners, Christ died for us.

Ephesians 5:2 And walk in love, as Christ also hath loved us, and hath given himself for us an offering and a sacrifice to God for a sweetsmelling savour.

Titus 3:4-5 But after that the kindness and love of God our Saviour toward man appeared, 5 Not by works of righteousness which we have done, but according to his mercy he saved us, by the washing of regeneration, and renewing of the Holy Ghost.

1 John 3:16 Hereby perceive we the love *of God*, because he laid down his life for us: and we ought to lay down *our* lives for the brethren.

1 John 4:9-10 In this was manifested the love of God toward us, because that God sent his only begotten Son into the world, that we might live through him. 10 Herein is love, not that we loved God, but that he loved us, and sent his Son *to be* the propitiation for our sins.

God *is* love (1 John 4:16). He is the God of love (2 Cor. 13:11).

At the last supper, the Lord expressed His love in these words, "This is my body, which is given FOR YOU" (Luke 22:19).

4. That the priest was given a part of the offerings also teaches that those who serve in the Lord's work should be rewarded.

Leviticus 6:17 I have given it *unto them for* their portion of my offerings made by fire...

Leviticus 7:35 This *is the portion* of the anointing of Aaron, and of the anointing of his sons, out of the offerings of the LORD made by fire...

1 Corinthians 9:13-14 Do ye not know that they which minister about holy things live *of the things* of the temple? and they which wait at the altar are partakers with the altar? 14 Even so hath the Lord ordained that they which preach the gospel should live of the gospel.

THE SIN OFFERING

See Leviticus 4:1-35.

The *sin offering* depicts Christ as our sin-bearer. It signifies Christ as "the lamb of God, which taketh away the sin of the world" (John 1:29), as the One who bore "the iniquity of us all" (Isa. 53:6).

1. The offering provided forgiveness for all classes of people--priests (Lev. 4:3), congregation (Lev. 4:13), rulers (Lev. 4:22), and common people (Lev. 4:27).

This reminds us that all men can be saved and all must approach God in the same way, through Christ's one sacrifice.

2. The offering provided forgiveness for sins of ignorance.

> Leviticus 4:2 Speak unto the children of Israel, saying, If a soul shall sin through ignorance against any of the commandments of the LORD *concerning things* which ought not to be done, and shall do against any of them.

In one sense the unsaved sinner is ignorant of God and truth, whereas in another sense he is not ignorant. The lost sinner has enough light to know that there is a great God and to know that there is right and wrong (Rom. 1:19-20; 2:14-16). Men know the truth about the holy God in their heart of hearts, but they suppress that truth because they love unrighteousness (Rom. 3:18).

For this reason every sinner is without excuse before God and is therefore under God's condemnation (John 3:18-20).

But it is also true that the unsaved sinner is ignorant in the sense that he doesn't know much about God and he doesn't know how great his sin is before God and how much God hates sin. He doesn't know how terribly lost and condemned he is. He doesn't know that he is an enemy of God.

But even when man was in this condition, Christ loved him and died for his sins (Rom. 5:8).

3. The offering provided forgiveness for sins "against any of the commandments of the LORD" (Lev. 4:2).

This reminds us that we are guilty of breaking the entire law of God, for to break one commandment is to break all (James 2:10). And it reminds us that Christ died for all of our sins. He died to satisfy every infraction that has ever been made against any of God's laws.

4. The offerings were "without blemish" (Le. 4:3).

This signifies Christ's sinless humanity and His acceptance before God to die in the sinner's place.

5. The offerer placed his hands on the offering (Lev. 4:4).

This signifies the two-fold action of saving faith: the transfer of the believer's sins to Christ and the transfer of the value of Christ's atonement to the believer (2 Cor. 5:21).

6. The sacrifice was killed before the Lord and its blood was shed.

> Leviticus 4:4-5 And he shall bring the bullock unto the door of the tabernacle of the congregation before the LORD; and shall lay his hand upon the bullock's head, and kill the bullock before the LORD. 5 And the priest that is anointed shall take of the bullock's blood, and bring it to the tabernacle of the congregation:

This points directly to Christ's cross, where the Son of God suffered before the Father and made the acceptable sacrifice by His own blood and death.

7. The blood was taken into the tabernacle and sprinkled seven times before the veil.

> Leviticus 4:6 And the priest shall dip his finger in the blood, and sprinkle of the blood seven times before the LORD, before the vail of the sanctuary.

The sprinkling before God signifies that it is God that man has offended with his sin; it is God's law that we have broken; and it is God who must be satisfied or propitiated.

The number seven signifies perfection, as in the seven days of creation and the seven seals of Revelation. We have perfect redemption before God through His blood (Heb. 9:12; 10:14).

Nine times in Leviticus 4-6 we hear the sweet words "IT SHALL BE FORGIVEN" (Lev. 4:20, 26, 31, 35; 5:10, 13, 16, 18; 6:7). Biblical salvation is a know-so salvation.

8. Some of the blood was placed on the horns of the incense altar.

> Leviticus 4:7 And the priest shall put *some* of the blood upon the horns of the altar of sweet incense before the LORD, which *is* in the tabernacle of the congregation...

This signifies the high priestly intercession of Christ based on His shed blood. Because He ever lives to make intercession for His people, Christ can save them to the uttermost (Heb. 7:25).

8. The rest of the blood was poured out at the bottom of the brazen altar.

> Leviticus 4:7 And the priest shall ... pour all the blood of the bullock at the bottom of the altar of the burnt offering, which *is at* the door of the tabernacle of the congregation.

The pouring out signifies Christ's blood poured out for our sins by the beatings and the crucifixion wounds and the piercing of His side.

9. The fat and the kidneys and the flanks and the caul above the liver were burned on the altar as a sweet savour unto God (Lev. 4:8-10, 31).

> Leviticus 4:8-10 And he shall take off from it all the fat of the bullock for the sin offering; the fat that covereth the inwards, and all the fat that *is* upon the inwards, 9 And the two kidneys, and the fat that *is* upon them, which *is* by the flanks, and the caul above the liver, with the kidneys, it shall he take away, 10 As it was taken off from the bullock of the sacrifice of peace offerings: and the priest shall burn them upon the altar of the burnt offering.

This signifies Christ's inner righteousness that made Him an acceptable sacrifice to God.

10. The rest of the bullock was burned outside the camp.

> Leviticus 4:11-12 And the skin of the bullock, and all his flesh, with his head, and with his legs, and his inwards, and his dung, 12 Even the whole bullock shall he carry forth without the camp unto a clean place, where the ashes are poured out, and burn him on the wood with fire: where the ashes are poured out shall he be burnt.

This signifies Christ as rejected by His own people Israel and crucified outside of the city of Jerusalem as a common criminal (Heb. 13:11-12). It depicts Christ bearing man's sin, being made sin for us, and therefore being unworthy to remain in the camp.

The carrying of the sacrifice out of the camp away from God's presence in the tabernacle also depicts the sin being taken away out of God's sight.

The burning to ashes signifies the completeness of the sacrifice. As there was nothing left of the sacrifice but ashes, and these were soon covered over by more ashes, so our sins are gone as if they were cast into the depths of the sea (Mic. 7:19).

The burning of the sin sacrifice over the ashes of the burnt offering (Lev. 4:12; 6:10-11) depicts God's acceptance of Christ, both in His life and in His death.

THE TRESPASS OFFERING

See Leviticus 5-6.

The *trespass offering* depicts Christ as the One who "is faithful and just to forgive us *our* sins, and to cleanse us from all unrighteousness" (1 John 1:9).

> "In the sin offering you have a sacrifice for the nature of sin. In the trespass offering you have a sacrifice for the sins of nature. In one case God is dealing with the root of sin.

> In the other He is dealing with the fruit of sin. The blood of Christ not only meets the root, 'sin in the flesh,' it meets and provides for the fruit, the sins produced by the nature of sin in us. After the believer has owned and accepted the Lord; after he is assured, not only that he has been forgiven and justified, but that he has received a new and spiritual nature, he awakes with a shock to discover the nature of sin still in him. The defilement must be removed and the consciousness of communion and fellowship restored. The provision for this and the manner thereof is set forth in the trespass offering" (I.M. Haldeman).

Following are some lessons from the trespass offering:

1. The trespass offering depicts Christ as the believer's high priest standing between God and man.

> Leviticus 5:5-6, 8-9 And it shall be, when he shall be guilty in one of these *things*, that he shall confess that he hath sinned in that *thing*: 6 And he shall bring his trespass offering unto the LORD for his sin which he hath sinned, a female from the flock, a lamb or a kid of the goats, for a sin offering; and the priest shall make an atonement for him concerning his sin. ... And he shall bring them unto the priest, who shall offer *that* which *is* for the sin offering first, and wring off his head from his neck, but shall not divide *it* asunder: 9 And he shall sprinkle of the blood of the sin offering upon the side of the altar; and the rest of the blood shall be wrung out at the bottom of the altar: it *is* a sin offering.

When the believer confesses his sin, Christ intercedes for him on the basis of the sacrifice He made on the cross.

2. The trespass offering was to be made for every type of trespass, even hearing swearing and not speaking against it, or touching an unclean thing.

> Leviticus 5:1-2 And if a soul sin, and hear the voice of swearing, and *is* a witness, whether he hath seen or known *of it*; if he do not utter *it*, then he shall bear his iniquity. 2 Or if a soul touch any unclean thing, whether *it be* a

carcase of an unclean beast, or a carcase of unclean cattle, or the carcase of unclean creeping things, and *if* it be hidden from him; he also shall be unclean, and guilty.

Likewise the Christian life is to be lived in the strictest separation from evil. God's people are not to overlook "little sins."

1 Corinthians 11:2 Now I praise you, brethren, that ye remember me in ALL things, and keep the ordinances, as I delivered *them* to you.

Ephesians 5:11 And have NO fellowship with the unfruitful works of darkness, but rather reprove *them*.

1 Thessalonians 5:22 Abstain from ALL appearance of evil.

Titus 2:14 Who gave himself for us, that he might redeem us from ALL iniquity, and purify unto himself a peculiar people, zealous of good works.

1 Peter 2:1 Wherefore laying aside ALL malice, and ALL guile, and hypocrisies, and envies, and ALL evil speakings.

2 Peter 3:11 *Seeing* then *that* all these things shall be dissolved, what manner *of persons* ought ye to be in *ALL* holy conversation and godliness.

3. To sin against our fellow man is to sin against the Lord.

Leviticus 6:2 If a soul sin, and commit a trespass against the LORD, and lie unto his neighbour in that which was delivered him to keep, or in fellowship, or in a thing taken away by violence, or hath deceived his neighbour;

When the prodigal son repented, he understood that by sinning against his father he had sinned against God.

Luke 5:18 And, behold, men brought in a bed a man which was taken with a palsy: and they sought *means* to bring him in, and to lay *him* before him.

Jesus taught that if I trespass against someone, I should make it right and be reconciled to my brother before I make offerings to God.

Matthew 5:23-24 Therefore if thou bring thy gift to the altar, and there rememberest that thy brother hath ought against thee; 24 Leave there thy gift before the altar, and go thy way; first be reconciled to thy brother, and then come and offer thy gift.

The law of the trespass teaches the same thing. If someone sinned against his neighbor, he was to make restitution first and then offer his trespass offering to the Lord.

Leviticus 6:4-6 Then it shall be, because he hath sinned, and is guilty, that he shall restore that which he took violently away, or the thing which he hath deceitfully gotten, or that which was delivered him to keep, or the lost thing which he found, 5 Or all that about which he hath sworn falsely; he shall even restore it in the principal, and shall add the fifth part more thereto, *and* give it unto him to whom it appertaineth, in the day of his trespass offering. 6 And he shall bring his trespass offering unto the LORD, a ram without blemish out of the flock, with thy estimation, for a trespass offering, unto the priest:

4. Lying is mentioned three times.

Leviticus 6:2-3 If a soul sin, and commit a trespass against the LORD, and lie unto his neighbour in that which was delivered him to keep, or in fellowship, or in a thing taken away by violence, or hath deceived his neighbour; 3 Or have found that which was lost, and lieth concerning it, and sweareth falsely; in any of all these that a man doeth, sinning therein:

Lying is a serious sin before God, who is the God of truth. He hates lying (Prov. 6:16-17). Deceit is in man's fallen heart (Mark 7:21-22), but God's people are to put away lying and speak truth every man with his neighbour (Eph. 4:25).

Paul instructed Titus to rebuke liars sharply (Titus 1:12-13).

We had to hire a lawyer to take care of our business with a foreign government, and he lies continually. He promises to do something and invariably he doesn't do it or doesn't do it on time, and then he lies about why he couldn't do it: he was sick or his mother was sick or his motorcycle broke, etc. He thinks the lie makes everything right, but it is obvious that he has no fear of God. He claims to be a Christian, but he has no Christian character. He seemingly has no guilt about the lies and never repents. He should read Revelation 21:8.

5. We are responsible for the things we borrow and the things people commit to our keeping.

> Leviticus 6:2 If a soul sin, and commit a trespass against the LORD, and lie unto his neighbour in that which was delivered him to keep, or in fellowship, or in a thing taken away by violence, or hath deceived his neighbour;

One reason why people lie is that they get themselves into difficult situations and they try to lie their way out. They borrow money and can't repay or don't want to repay, so they lie. They borrow something and break it, and instead of admitting that they did this and offering to pay for the breakage, they make up a lie to shift blame. Or they try to return the item without telling the person what happened, which is a form of lying.

The law of trespassing applies to an employee. When a person is employed by someone, he is responsible for his employer's money and property. If someone "borrows" money or goods from his employer without asking, he is stealing.

Many employees are like the steward that Jesus told about in His parable who wasted his master's goods. When he was caught, instead of repenting, he stole even more (Luke 16:1-7).

The believer rather should be like Joseph. His master put everything into his hands (Ge. 39:4), but Joseph did not cheat him in any way. Another example of a godly employee is Abraham's eldest servant who "ruled over all that he had" (Ge. 24:2). He could easily have taken things for himself. He could have said to himself, "Abraham is rich; he doesn't need all of this; he won't miss some of these things," but nowhere do we read of this servant abusing his position of responsibility. He was honest and dependable and honorable in all of his dealings with Abraham, and you can be sure that his reward is great in heaven.

The law of Leviticus 6:2 also applies to borrowing money and not repaying. To promise to repay a debt and then fail to do it is to lie. It is a sin against my fellow man. In America, a person can file for bankruptcy and escape paying some of his debts. Though this is legal, it is not godly. The Lord holds me responsible to keep my word and to pay all of my debts. If something unforeseen happens I might have to try to renegotiate the loan and spread the repayment out longer than agreed, but I must repay it.

In the 1970s, the associate pastor of Highland Park Baptist Church in Chattanooga, Tennessee, was J.R. Faulkner. He told of how that he got into debt and couldn't repay, so he sold his automobile and walked until he could pay the debt in full. That is the godly way of living.

6. If we find something that is lost, we are obligated before God to try to find the owner and to return it.

> Leviticus 6:3 Or have found that which was lost, and lieth concerning it, and sweareth falsely; in any of all these that a man doeth, sinning therein:

The popular idea, "Finders keepers, losers weepers," is not a godly principle.

A couple of times something that I was transporting fell off my motorcycle in Nepal, and bystanders grabbed it and ran away instead of calling out for me to stop.

The believer should not act like this. He should know that God will meet all of his needs and that God will reward him for being honest and compassionate.

7. The trespass offering was a continual thing.

Because the offering was to be made for all types of sins, the trespass offering would have been made frequently.

This is the same lesson that we learn from the laver of the tabernacle. The priests had to wash every time they went into the service of the Lord. They got defiled with every step.

This means that we must not grow weary in bringing our trespasses to the Lord for cleansing. And it means that we must not think that God gets weary of forgiving. God is not surprised by our sin. He doesn't want us to sin, but He has made perfect provision for our sin (1 John 2:1-2). He knows our frame (Psa. 103:14), and He knows the sins that so easily beset us (Heb. 12:1).

If God instructs us to forbear and forgive one another, and He does (Col. 3:13), and if He instructs us to forgive a brother seven times in a day, and He does (Luke 17:4), how much more does He forebear with and forgive us?

8. Birds or meal could be offered in place of a lamb.

> Leviticus 5:7 And if he be not able to bring a lamb, then he shall bring for his trespass, which he hath committed, two turtledoves, or two young pigeons, unto the LORD; one for a sin offering, and the other for a burnt offering.
>
> Leviticus 5:11 But if he be not able to bring two turtledoves, or two young pigeons, then he that sinned shall bring for his offering the tenth part of an ephah of fine flour for a sin offering; he shall put no oil upon it, neither shall he put *any* frankincense thereon: for it *is* a sin offering.

This teaches us that forgiveness is available to every believer of every class and situation: rich or poor, educated or uneducated, young or old.

9. The burnt offering in connection with the sin offering depicts the believer's renewed consecration to the Lord.

> Leviticus 5:7-10 And if he be not able to bring a lamb, then he shall bring for his trespass, which he hath committed, two turtledoves, or two young pigeons, unto the LORD; one for a sin offering, and the other for a burnt offering. 8 And he shall bring them unto the priest, who shall offer *that* which *is* for the sin offering first, and wring off his head from his neck, but shall not divide *it* asunder: 9 And he shall sprinkle of the blood of the sin offering upon the side of the altar; and the rest of the blood shall be wrung out at the bottom of the altar: it *is* a sin offering. 10 And he shall offer the second *for* a burnt offering, according to the manner: and the priest shall make an atonement for him for his sin which he hath sinned, and it shall be forgiven him.

It is not God's will that we merely confess our sins; we are to seek to be cleansed of all unrighteousness (1 John 1:9). We are to press toward the mark of God's perfect calling (Phi. 3:14).

10. Restitution should be made when appropriate (Lev. 6:1-5; Mat. 5:23-24).

> Leviticus 6:1-5 And the LORD spake unto Moses, saying, 2 If a soul sin, and commit a trespass against the LORD, and lie unto his neighbour in that which was delivered him to keep, or in fellowship, or in a thing taken away by violence, or hath deceived his neighbour; 3 Or have found that which was lost, and lieth concerning it, and sweareth falsely; in any of all these that a man doeth, sinning therein: 4 Then it shall be, because he hath sinned, and is guilty, that he shall restore that which he took violently away, or the thing which he hath deceitfully gotten, or that which was delivered him to keep, or the lost thing which he found, 5 Or all that about which he hath sworn falsely; he shall even restore it in the principal, and shall add the fifth part more thereto, *and* give it unto him to whom it appertaineth, in the day of his trespass offering.

If I have sinned against my fellow man, it is not enough to confess my sin to God. Christ's royal law is, "Thou shalt love thy neighbour as thyself" (Jam. 2:8).

This means that we should not sin against our fellow man in any way (Rom. 13:9-10). We should not cause him any type of injury. We should not lie to him or slander him or backbite him (Gal. 5:14-15) or steal from him or borrow and not repay or cheat him or covet his goods or steal the affections of a wife or a husband or rebel against God-given authority.

When we do such things, we should try to make it right. It is not enough to seek forgiveness from God.

> Matthew 5:23-24 Therefore if thou bring thy gift to the altar, and there rememberest that thy brother hath ought against thee; 24 Leave there thy gift before the altar, and go thy way; first be reconciled to thy brother, and then come and offer thy gift.

If someone steals from me, I want him to get right with God, but I also want him to repay me that which he has stolen!

The Prodigal Son made restitution when he returned home and apologized to his father and told him that he was no longer worthy to be a son (Luke 15:18-19). This was evidence of true repentance.

After I trusted the Lord and was saved at age 23, I tried to make restitution to people against whom I had sinned. The first was my dad and mom whom I had hurt deeply by my rebellion and foolishness. I went directly home after I was converted and asked their forgiveness.

Another person I made restitution to was the owner of a hamburger restaurant where I had worked as the night manager. I had stolen money from the cash register, and after I came to the Lord I saved up my money, found out where he lived, and visited him. I told him how the Lord had changed my life. I confessed my sin to him and told him that I wanted to pay my debt. I can't remember the details of what happened. He was a fairly wealthy man and I don't think he took the money, but I did my best to make things right.

There was a sergeant in my army unit in Vietnam who loaned me a camera lens and instead of returning it I took it with me when I returned to America. After I came to Christ, I contacted the Army Record Center in St. Louis and tried to find the man so I could return the lens or repay him. I was unable to locate him, but I wanted to find him and I wanted to make things right.

Of course, restitution does not apply only to those against whom we have sinned before we are saved. It should continue to be exercised in the Christian life whenever necessary.

Strange Fire

> Leviticus 10:1-5 And Nadab and Abihu, the sons of Aaron, took either of them his censer, and put fire therein, and put incense thereon, and offered strange fire before the LORD, which he commanded them not. 2 And there went out fire from the LORD, and devoured them, and they died before the LORD. 3 Then Moses said unto Aaron, This *is it* that the LORD spake, saying, I will be sanctified in them that come nigh me, and before all the people I will be glorified. And Aaron held his peace. 4 And Moses called Mishael and Elzaphan, the sons of Uzziel the uncle of Aaron, and said unto them, Come near, carry your brethren from before the sanctuary out of the camp. 5 So they went near, and carried them in their coats out of the camp; as Moses had said.

The sin of "strange fire" was presumption and disobedience in the service of God.

1. Nadab and Abihu offered incense contrary to God's commandment.

The occasion of this sin was the setting up of the tabernacle. The preceding passage emphasizes that everything had been done "as the Lord commanded." This expression is repeated at least 12 times in Leviticus chapters 8 and 9. Moses and Aaron did everything precisely "according to the manner" of God's prescribed order (Lev. 9:15).

But Nadab and Abihu did something contrary to God's instructions.

They offered incense which only the high priest was to offer. Aaron was charged with burning incense on the golden altar in the morning and evening (Ex. 30:7-9). Aaron also was charged with burning incense in the holy of holies on the Day of Atonement (Lev. 16:12-13). No permission was given for other priests to burn incense.

They probably entered into the holy of holies. We learn this from the fact that right after their deaths, God gives the instructions about the Day of Atonement (Lev. 16:1-2). Here God says that only the high priest can enter the holy of holies and only on one day in the year.

They probably used fire from some source other than the brazen altar. Their sin is called "strange fire" (Lev. 10:1). Just before this God had consumed the offering on the altar of sacrifice (Lev. 9:24). The divine fire burning on the altar represented the cross where the judgment of God fell upon Christ as the foundation for man's saving relationship with the Almighty. For Nadab and Abihu to bring fire into the tabernacle from another source would have been abominable to God because they ignored the importance of the fire that symbolized the ONE and ONLY sacrifice and altar acceptable to God. This was the same sin that was committed by Cain, when he offered vegetables instead of a lamb (Ge. 4:3-4).

It is also probable that Nadab and Abihu were intoxicated. The account of their sin is followed immediately by a proscription against priests drinking alcoholic beverages during their ministration (Lev. 10:8-11). The priests were to teach the people the difference between the holy and the unholy, but alcoholic drink affects the heart and morality. It perverts one's sense of justice.

> Proverbs 23:29-35 Who hath woe? who hath sorrow? who hath contentions? who hath babbling? who hath wounds without cause? who hath redness of eyes? 30 They that tarry long at the wine; they that go to seek mixed wine. 31 Look not thou upon the wine when it is red, when it giveth his colour in the cup, *when* it moveth itself aright. 32 At the last it biteth like a serpent, and stingeth like an adder. 33 Thine eyes shall behold strange women, and thine heart shall utter perverse things. 34 Yea, thou shalt be as he that lieth down in the midst of the sea, or as he that lieth upon the top of a mast. 35 They have stricken me, *shalt thou say,*

and I was not sick; they have beaten me, *and* I felt *it* not: when shall I awake? I will seek it yet again.

Proverbs 31:4-5 *It is* not for kings, O Lemuel, *it is* not for kings to drink wine; nor for princes strong drink: 5 Lest they drink, and forget the law, and pervert the judgment of any of the afflicted.

Isaiah 28:7 But they also have erred through wine, and through strong drink are out of the way; the priest and the prophet have erred through strong drink, they are swallowed up of wine, they are out of the way through strong drink; they err in vision, they stumble *in* judgment.

Hosea 4:11 Whoredom and wine and new wine take away the heart.

2. Nadab and Abihu were acting out of presumption, and God used this occasion to fortify the importance of obeying His Word in all points.

God made examples of these men at the beginning of the era of Moses' law, just as He made examples of Ananias and Sapphira at the beginning of the church age (Acts 5). These are given for our warning and admonition (1 Cor. 10:6, 11).

Presumption is proud, stubborn, self-willed rebellion against God's commands. It is defined in the following passage.

Numbers 15:30-36 But the soul that doeth *ought* presumptuously, *whether he be* born in the land, or a stranger, the same reproacheth the LORD; and that soul shall be cut off from among his people. 31 Because he hath despised the word of the LORD, and hath broken his commandment, that soul shall utterly be cut off; his iniquity *shall be* upon him. 32 And while the children of Israel were in the wilderness, they found a man that gathered sticks upon the sabbath day. 33 And they that found him gathering sticks brought him unto Moses and Aaron, and unto all the congregation. 34 And they put him in ward, because it was not declared what should be done

> to him. 35 And the LORD said unto Moses, The man shall be surely put to death: all the congregation shall stone him with stones without the camp. 36 And all the congregation brought him without the camp, and stoned him with stones, and he died; as the LORD commanded Moses.

Presumption is to despise God's Word and to blatantly disobey God's Word. God had plainly commanded that no fires be lit on the sabbath (Ex. 35:2-3), but one man ignored this and determined that he was going to build a fire. Like Nadab and Abihu, this man died for his presumptuous sin.

3. We should also note that Nadab and Abihu had a poor example in their father Aaron, who made the golden calf and was involved in Israel's debauchery (Ex. 32:1-6, 25). This doubtless encouraged them to be careless in the things of God.

Leprosy

Leviticus 13-14

The discovery of leprosy is described in chapter 13 and the cleansing of it is described in chapter 14.

Leprosy referred to various types of skin disease. It had multiple symptoms, such as hair turning white and a depression of the skin (Lev. 13:3, 20, 25), raw flesh lesions (Lev. 13:14-15), boils and white, reddish lesions (Lev. 13:18-19), spreading in the skin (Lev. 13:22, 27), white reddish sores (Lev. 13:42). Sometimes a two-week period was required before leprosy could be distinguished from other types of skin diseases (Lev. 13:4-8). Leviticus leprosy could also take the form of some type of toxic spreading mold in cloth or leather (Lev. 13:47-52).

The Old Testament tells of two people who were stricken with leprosy as a judgment of God: Miriam (Num. 12:10) and Uzziah (2 Ch. 26:19). Miriam's leprosy turned her as white as snow.

The leprosy of Leviticus was different from the leprosy known to medical science today, which is called Hansen's disease. It is named after G.H. Hansen, who in 1873 discovered the bacterium that causes the disease (*Mycobacterium leprae*). It is an infectious disease of the nervous system that results in ugly tumor-like growths on the skin, deformities of the hands, feet, and face, damage to the skin, nerves and eyes, muscle weakness, and impotency. Many indirect injuries occur because of loss of feeling due to nerve damage.

For example, one young leper man in western Nepal put his foot in a fire while he was sleeping at night and unknowingly burned himself severely. By the time that he reached the hospital where my wife worked, most of the foot fell off as she was trying to cleanse it.

Since the 1940s, the disease has been successfully treated through drugs, but there are still roughly 200,000 people afflicted with leprosy. In India there are 1,000 leper colonies.

The leprosy of Leviticus is treated as an uncleanness rather than a disease (Lev. 14:54-57). The main purpose of these chapters is to teach spiritual lessons, as follows:

Leprosy Signifies Sin

Leprosy signifies sin which has corrupted man and which reveals itself in manifold ways.

Like leprosy, sin makes the sinner unclean before God and an outcast from God's presence (Isa. 64:6).

Like leprosy, sin deforms and destroys. Sin's corruption has spread everywhere and touches everything man does, as signified by the leprosy in the body, the beard, the head, even in garments and houses (Lev. 13:2, 29, 42, 47; 14:34).

Like leprosy, sin begins small and spreads (Lev. 13:22,27). The sin that has defiled the entire human race began as a "small" matter of eating fruit that God had forbidden. David's "small" sin of lusting after Bathsheba while she was bathing resulted in adultery and murder, the ruining of David's testimony, and great injury to his family. The "small" sin of borrowing more money than one can repay has often led to other sins such as lying, cheating, stealing, even murder.

Like leprosy in ancient times, sin is incurable apart from divine intervention.

As Jesus healed lepers, He can cure the sin problem. God's salvation for sin was typified in Leviticus 13 by the sacrifices that were offered for the cleansing of the leper. Through the blood and death of a substitute victim, the sinner can be made clean and whole. We will look at these in more detail.

Other Lessons about Leprosy

1. Our great High Priest, Jesus Christ, is always observing His people and interceding for them and reproving them and cleansing them, as signified by the priest who examined the people (Lev. 13:2-3; Heb. 2:17; 4:14-16; 7:24-27).

We see Christ exercising this ministry in Revelation 2-3 where He walks among the churches and reproves sin (Rev. 2:1; 3:19).

2. As priests in a holy priesthood, believers are to be skilled in discerning sin and its effects. We are to prove all things so as to abstain from all appearance of evil (1 Th. 5:21-22). We are to exercise our senses to discern both good and evil (Heb. 5:14).

3. As priests, believers are to exercise the ministry of cleansing one another by prayer, exhortation, reproof, forgiveness, and restoration (Rom. 15:14; Gal. 6:1-2; Col. 3:13; 1 Th. 5:11; Heb. 3:13; 10:25; Jam. 5:16; 1 John 5:16).

"The spirit of chapters 13 and 14 is that there would always be the desire that the leper might be healed, cleansed, and restored to his tent and his privileges among the redeemed" (Merrill Unger).

4. There were pre-leprous conditions which could either dissipate or grow into full-blown leprosy (Lev. 13:2-8).

This signifies various types of sin and the believer's handling of sin. If "small" sins aren't dealt with and are allowed to grow, they can result in greater sins with greater consequences.

> James 1:14-15 But every man is tempted, when he is drawn away of his own lust, and enticed. 15 Then when lust hath conceived, it bringeth forth sin: and sin, when it is finished, bringeth forth death.

For example, a man who nurses lust in his heart can commit fornication and adultery in his physical life, and a man who nurses bitterness can ruin many people (Heb. 12:14-15).

5. Leprosy in the garment signifies the defilement that comes through one's environment and associations and activities (Lev. 13:47-59).

"The symbolism here represents sin working not exactly in the believer, but as closely identified with his person, such as his possessions, occupation, habits, or associations. What an illustration of the care that must be taken to avoid inlets to sin as to where he permits himself to go or what he allows himself to do, or what associations and alliances he permits himself to make. Any garment tainted with leprosy was to be burned in the fire, illustrating how rigidly sin is to be put away in a believer's associations" (Merrill Unger).

See 2 Corinthians 7:1; Ephesians 5:11; James 1:27.

6. Leprosy in the house (Lev. 14:33-53), signifies the defilement of the home and family through sin.

Marriage is the foundational institution in society and the church, being the first institution established by God on earth (Ge. 2:21-25). The husband and wife are to bear children and raise them to God's glory. Today the institution of marriage and the family are under attack as never before, and God's people need to learn biblical instructions about marriage and the home from the Bible and live it out. Every church should train the families with the objective of helping parents raise their children as disciples of Christ. We deal with this in the book *Keeping the Kids*, which is available in print and eBook formats from Way of Life Literature -- www.wayoflife.org.

7. As the priests were to look on the houses (Lev. 14:36-37, 39, 44), pastors must act as priests to watch over the families and help them.

If the leprosy of sin appears in a family, the pastors must take action. This reminds us of God's qualifications for pastors, which require that they raise their own children so that they have a good testimony (Titus 1:6). If the pastor's own family isn't right, he is a poor example to the entire church and harms the cause of Christ. It is like Eli of old who did not discipline his sons but instead allowed them to serve in God's work (1 Sam. 2:12-17). Samuel reproved his sons but he did not enforce God's Word in his family and in his ministry. He honored his sons above God (1 Sam. 2:22-25, 29; 3:13).

8. The leprous house defiled those who entered (Lev. 14:46)

Likewise when sin is not dealt with in a family, it corrupts not only the family members but also those who visit. This is one reason why parents must be very careful about their children's friends and about where they are allowed to go.

When I was growing up, it was my friends that corrupted my morals. I was a willing participant, but had my parents been more careful about my friends, it could have made a big difference. The problem was that our church wasn't strong, and none of the kids in the church families loved Christ. All of them were worldly. It was in the home of a deacon where I was first introduced to rock & roll, and that music had a great defiling influence on me. The saddest part is that I'm not sure there were any better churches in our area.

9. Defiled stones had to be removed (Lev. 14:40-41).

This depicts the removal of sin by repentance. It depicts the cleansing of the home of worldly evils. So many parents are careless about what they allow in their homes. They allow their children to have things such as violent and sensual video games, science fiction novels, occult novels such as Harry Potter, and cell phones and laptops and tablet devices that are used for unwholesome activities. The result is the pollution of the children's minds so that the voice of the Holy Spirit is crowded out by the more "exciting" things of the world and the flesh.

10. If the leprosy wasn't healed, it would result in the destruction of the whole house (Lev. 14:44-45).

How many homes have been ruined by sin that was not repented of!

11. Leprosy of the head was the worse type of leprosy.

In this case alone was the man called "utterly unclean" (Lev. 13:44).

This signifies error in thinking. Heresy refers to a self-willed choice of error. It is not a sin of ignorance but a sin of willful rejection of the truth (Titus 3:10-11). The New Testament warns repeatedly about the danger of false teaching (e.g., Acts 20:28-31) and human philosophy (Col. 2:8).

12. Full-blown leprosy caused the individual to be put out of the camp (Lev. 13:45-46), signifying the defiling effect of sin.

In the Christian life, sin puts the believer out of fellowship with God and man (1 John 1:5-7) and can result in being disciplined by the church (1 Cor. 5). There is even a sin unto death (1 John 5:17).

13. Complete cleansing was available, signifying the full salvation the believing sinner has in Christ.

First, there were the two birds, the one killed and its blood shed and the other released (Lev. 14:4-7). The slain bird and its blood signifies Christ's atonement on the cross, and the living bird signifies His resurrection, which was the evidence that God had accepted the sacrifice (Romans 4:25). Just as the living bird was released and flew away, the believer's sin has been carried away and, as it were, buried in the deepest sea (Micah 7:19).

"The living bird in its upward flight bore the blood heavenward upon its outstretched wings as the badge of a finished redemptive work, Hebrews 9:22" (Merrill Unger).

Then there were the three lambs of the trespass offering, the sin offering, and the burnt offering, plus the meal and the oil (Lev. 14:10-20). The multiplication of sacrifices signify Christ as our wisdom, righteousness, sanctification, and redemption (1 Cor. 1:30).

The anointing of the ear, thumb, and toe with blood and oil signifies salvation by the blood and the Spirit (Titus 3:5-6; Heb. 9:14). Having been cleansed by the blood and sanctified by the Spirit, we are to walk in newness of life.

The leper was also to cleanse himself (Lev. 14:9). Though full salvation is provided in Christ, the believer is to work out his salvation in fear and trembling (Phil. 2:12). He is to put off the old man and put on the new (Eph. 4:22-24). He is to devote himself to Christ, renewing his mind by God's Word, not being conformed to the world but pursuing God's perfect will (Rom. 12:1-2). God has provided "all things that pertain unto life and godliness," but we must appropriate this and live it out (2 Peter 1:3-11).

The Day of Atonement

Leviticus 16

The Day of Atonement is one of the preeminent types of Christ and salvation in the Old Testament.

The Jews call it by the Hebrew name *Yom Kippur*, but it is an empty ritual at present, for they have no temple, no high priest, and no national sacrifices.

The meaning of the Day of Atonement is given in the context:

> Leviticus 16:30 For on that day shall *the priest* make an atonement for you, to cleanse you, *that* ye may be clean from all your sins before the LORD.

It was a day when an atonement was made to cleanse the nation from her sins before the Lord.

The Day of Atonement points to the cross where Jesus purchased eternal redemption by His death and blood. God the father is the offended party who receives the atonement. Christ is the High Priest who offers the atonement. The people are only observers and benefactors. The high priest does everything for them. Their part is to do no work at all and to afflict their souls.

The Hebrew word for atonement is "kaphar," meaning to cover. It is first mentioned as the covering of Noah's ark (Ge. 6:14). The Old Testament offerings did not take away sin. They only covered sin until Jesus came and died on the cross. This is evident by the fact that they had to be repeated. See Romans 3:25. On the cross, sins were not merely covered, they were removed.

1. One day each year the high priest went into the holy of holies to offer blood upon the mercy seat, depicting Christ as the great High Priest making one offering for sin for ever (Heb. 9:7-14).

High Priest on the Day of Atonement

2. The offerings were made "before the LORD."

This is mentioned seven times (Lev. 16:1, 6, 10, 12, 13, 18, 30). The offering was made in the holy of holies before the ark of the covenant where God dwelt (Lev. 16:2; Ex. 25:21-22). It is God that man has offended with his sin. It is God's holy law that man has broken. It is God that must be propitiated or satisfied. Every infraction must be punished. Every sin has a wage, which is death (Rom. 6:23). To break one of God's laws is to be guilty of breaking all of them (Jam. 2:10).

3. The high priest first offered a sin offering for himself (Lev. 16:6).

We are reminded that the Levitical high priest was himself a sinner in need of cleansing. But Christ had no need to make an offering for Himself.

The cleansing of the high priest teaches us that only a perfect man could stand before God and make the atonement for mankind. Only Jesus fits this standard. When a search was made for a man who was worthy to open the book of God's redemption of creation in Revelation 5, only the sinless Lamb of God was found worthy (Rev. 5:1-9).

4. When the sin offering was made, the high priest was attired only in his ordinary priestly garment, not in his finery (Lev. 16:4). This depicts how that Christ laid aside His glory when He came to earth to perform the work of atonement. See Philippians 2:5-8.

5. The high priest was alone in the tabernacle during the atonement (Lev. 16:17).

This signifies that Christ performed redemption by Himself (Heb. 1:3). Salvation is 100% of God. It was planned of God and worked out by God. It is a gift that Christ purchased with His own blood.

The high priest alone in the holy of holies also signifies Christ offering Himself before God. The cross was a transaction between God the Father and God the Son, with the Son offering Himself as a sinless sacrifice to the Father to make atonement for man's sins, and with the Father accepting the sacrifice. This was done "through the eternal Spirit."

> Hebrews 9:14 How much more shall the blood of Christ, who through the eternal Spirit offered himself without spot to God, purge your conscience from dead works to serve the living God?

Christ gave himself "as a sacrifice to God" (Eph. 5:2). This required the terrible deed of the holy Son of God being made sin for us and the Father turning away from the Son. Darkness covered the world on that occasion to hide this holy transaction from the eyes of men (Luke 23:44), just as the high priest was hidden from the eyes of men when he was in the tabernacle on the Day of Atonement.

6. The cloud of incense was to cover the ark of the covenant so that the high priest would not die (Lev. 16:12-13).

The incense depicts Christ's intercessory prayers. With Him God is well pleased (Mat. 3:17; 17:5), and His prayers are always heard (John 11:42). Christ prayed on the cross, "Father, forgive them; for they know not what they do" (Lk. 23:34).

We looked more extensively at Christ's intercessory ministry in the studies on the incense altar in the tabernacle.

7. The high priest sprinkled the blood seven times, signifying the fulness of Christ's atonement (Lev. 16:14-15).

Seven is the number of perfection, as in the seven days of creation and the seven seals of Revelation. Christ saves His people to the uttermost! We have eternal redemption and eternal perfection before God through His blood (Heb. 9:12; 10:14).

8. The blood of the sin offering was put on the horns of the brazen altar (Lev. 16:18).

The blood-anointed horns signify the power of the cross of Christ to take away sin. The horns picture Christ's authority as the eternal Son of God. He has all power in heaven and in earth (Mat. 28:18). All things have been put under His feet (Eph. 1:22). The fact that this is the One who made the sacrifice teaches us that it was perfectly acceptable before God and perfectly efficacious.

9. The scapegoat represents the completeness of Christ's atonement (Lev. 16:10, 21-22).

The goat bore "upon him ALL their iniquities unto a land not inhabited" (Lev. 16;22). The word "all" appears four times in this passage (Lev. 16:21-22). The goat carrying all of the iniquities was sent away into the wilderness, just as the believer's sins are taken away forever through the blood of Christ. The scapegoat pictures complete remission of sin. Compare Micah 7:19.

The scapegoat was sent away by the hand of a "fit man" (Lev. 16:21). The fit man, of course, represents Christ who is God's Anointed! He bore our sins in His own body on the tree and took them away forever.

Aaron first laid his hands on the scapegoat before sending it away (Lev. 16:21). This signifies the Lord Himself making the atonement.

> "This was the only occasion upon which that procedure was followed. When an individual Israelite offered a sin offering, he himself was to lay his hand upon its head, (Lev. 4: 27, 29). Here it is Aaron. The typical lesson in the latter case is well expressed in Isaiah 53:6, 'the Lord hath laid on him the iniquity of us all.' In the former it is the individual sinner identifying himself with his substitute." (William Rodgers, cited by Ernest Wilson, *Blood Sacrifices of the Old Testament*).

10. A burnt offering was made after the completion of the sin offering (Lev. 16:24).

This pictures Christ's resurrection and His eternal position as the beloved of the Father and as the One in whom every believer is accepted by the Father.

One day He will come and receive His people to Himself. The following verse describes the reality of the burnt offering

> Hebrews 9:28 So Christ was once offered to bear the sins of many; and unto them that look for him shall he appear the second time without sin unto salvation.

11. The Day of Atonement was a day in which the people did no work (Lev. 16:29). This signifies the grace of salvation as a free gift.

12. On the Day of Atonement the people afflicted their souls (Lev. 16:29).

This signifies repentance which is necessary for salvation. Paul preached repentance toward God and faith toward the Lord Jesus Christ (Acts 20:21). God commands all men everywhere to repent (Acts 17:30).

Repentance is to turn to God from one's idols and false religion and self-centered, sinful lifestyle. It is not a change of life; it is a change of mind that results in a change of life.

13. The Day of Atonement is also prophetic, pointing to the wonderful day in the end times when Israel will repent and receive her Messiah and be converted (Zechariah 12:10 - 13:1).

The Nazarite Vow

Numbers 6

The Nazarite vow was a vow of total consecration to be holy unto the Lord (Num. 6:2, 8).

Major Teachings

The major teachings of the Nazarite vow are three-fold.

First, God desires that His people be wholly dedicated to Him in holy service. The Nazarite vow is the Old Testament equivalent of the following passage.

> Romans 12:1-2 I beseech you therefore, brethren, by the mercies of God, that ye present your bodies a living sacrifice, holy, acceptable unto God, *which is* your reasonable service. 2 And be not conformed to this world: but be ye transformed by the renewing of your mind, that ye may prove what *is* that good, and acceptable, and perfect, will of God.

Second, no man can be saved through keeping God's law. The standard is too high, and we are too polluted by sin. Even if the Nazarite was successful in keeping the law for a time, the moment he failed he was condemned and his work was lost (Nu. 9:9, 12).

This reminds us of James 2:10, which says that if we break God's law in one point we are guilty of all. It reminds us of Galatians 3:10, which says that we are cursed if we do not continue in all of the works of the law. It reminds us of Christ's teaching in the Sermon on the Mount that we are obligated to keep God's holy law from the heart as well as by our actions (Mat. 5:21-22, 27-28).

Third, even our holiest devotion is accepted only in Christ. No matter how zealous and strict the Nazarite was, he had to be purified by the sacrifices, which signify Christ (Num. 6:13-20). Likewise the believer is accepted only in Christ. The offerings were multiple to signify the various aspects of Christ's life and atonement and the various aspects of our salvation in Him (1 Cor. 1:30).

(For more about the meaning of the following see the previous studies on the offerings.)

The sacrificial animals were "without blemish." This signifies Christ's character, "as a lamb without blemish and without spot" (1 Pet. 1:19).

The killing and shedding of blood depicts the means of salvation through the bloody death of Christ. Compare Romans 5:9-10, which teaches that we are saved both by Christ's death and by His blood.

The lamb of the *sin offering* represents Christ dying for our sins (Isa. 53:7).

The *burnt offering* depicts Christ's complete devotion to God and God's acceptance of Him. The burnt offering was burnt wholly on the altar (Lev. 1:9). It signifies Christ offering "himself without spot to God" (Heb. 9:14).

The *peace offering* depicts Christ reconciling man with God through the offering of Himself. It signifies Christ as "having made peace through the blood of his cross" (Col. 1:20).

The *meal offering* depicts Christ in His human perfection tested by suffering. It signifies Christ "in all points tempted like as *we are, yet* without sin" (Heb. 4:15). Christ is the Second Man who is the perfection that the first man Adam failed to be. The believer is accepted in Him. The fine flour without leaven represents Christ's sinless, perfectly balanced humanity. The flour mingled with oil signifies Christ's virgin birth and holy life (Luke 1:35). The wafer anointed with oil signifies His anointing by the Holy Spirit at baptism (Luke 3:32). He is the Messiah, the Christ, the Anointed One of God (Luke 4:17-21; Acts 10:38).

All of these offerings were brought before Jehovah God, offered to Him, and waved before Him (Nu. 6:16-17, 20). This signifies the sinless Christ and His sacrifice on the cross as accepted by God in the place of sinners. In Christ, God is well pleased. It is God that man has offended by his sin; it is God's law that we have broken; and Christ satisfies God as the full payment.

Miscellaneous Lessons

1. The Nazarite vow was a free-will vow.

The believer is God's by right of creation and by right of redemption ("bought with a price," 1 Cor. 6:20), but God desires that our devotion to Him be from the heart. Paul *beseeched* the believers to give themselves to God as living sacrifices because it is our reasonable service in light of what Christ has done for us (Rom. 12:1). The word "beseech" is from the Greek *parakaleo*, which is also translated "desire," "exhort," "intreat," and "pray."

2. The rule of the Nazarite was prescribed by God.

Likewise the dedicated believer must walk according to God's Word and not according to the tradition of men or according to his own thinking. We are not to be Pharisees who add layers of tradition to God's Word (Mark 7:7-13). We are not to be monks who are holy by means of an ascetic lifestyle--living in caves, enduring long fasts, sleep deprivation, self-beatings, and otherwise "neglecting of the body" (Col. 2:23).

3. The rule of the Nazarite was a life of strict separation to God (Num. 6:3-8).

The neglect of wine signified separation from the lusts of the flesh (Gal. 5:16-21; 1 John 2:15-16).

The separation from every product of the vine--the grape, even raisins and husks--signified the strictness of the separation. Compare 2 Corinthians 7:1; Ephesians 5:11; 1 Thessalonians 5:22; Titus 2:14.

The separation even from a father, mother, brother, or sister who died signifies the believer's love for Christ being greater than his love for his closest and dearest human relations (Mat. 8:21-22; 10:37-38).

The neglect of cutting the hair signifies separation from vanity and the wholehearted pursuit of that which is holy and eternal (Mat. 6:33; Col. 3:1-4; 1 Tim. 2:9; 4:8; 1 Pet. 3:3-4). It also signifies bearing Christ's reproach in this world, since long hair on a man is a shame (1 Cor. 11:14; Heb. 13:13).

4. Touching any forbidden thing defiled the Nazarite (Nu. 6:9-12).

This reminds us that we live in a polluted world filled with spiritual danger. We must therefore live very carefully (Rom. 13:13-14; Eph. 5:15; 1 Pet. 5:8).

5. When the Nazarite was defiled, he had to be purified (Nu. 6:9-11).

In the Christian life, this signifies confession of sin and cleansing through Christ's blood (1 John 1:6-9).

6. The Nazarite vow was for a specified period of time.

In contrast, the New Testament believer is to be wholly devoted to Christ all his life.

The Red Heifer

Numbers 19

The Context

The heifer was sacrificed and its ashes were used to make the water of separation (Num. 19:9, 17-18). This signifies the believer's eternal salvation and his daily purification from sin in this present world.

Israel was traveling through the wilderness, which is a picture of the believer's journey through this sinful world. Just as Israel got defiled by contact with the dead (Num. 19:16), so the believer is defiled by contact with the evil things of this present world.

The water of separation provided cleansing so that the Lord's people could maintain fellowship with God. Likewise the Lord has provided purification in the Christian life through confession of sin.

> 1 John 1:8-10 If we say that we have no sin, we deceive ourselves, and the truth is not in us. 9 If we confess our sins, he is faithful and just to forgive us *our* sins, and to cleanse us from all unrighteousness. 10 If we say that we have not sinned, we make him a liar, and his word is not in us.

The making of the water of separation

> Numbers 19:1-10 And the LORD spake unto Moses and unto Aaron, saying, 2 This *is* the ordinance of the law which the LORD hath commanded, saying, Speak unto the children of Israel, that they bring thee a red heifer without spot, wherein *is* no blemish, *and* upon which never came yoke: 3 And ye shall give her unto Eleazar the priest, that he may bring her forth without the camp, and *one* shall slay her before his face: 4 And Eleazar the priest shall take

> of her blood with his finger, and sprinkle of her blood directly before the tabernacle of the congregation seven times: 5 And *one* shall burn the heifer in his sight; her skin, and her flesh, and her blood, with her dung, shall he burn: 6 And the priest shall take cedar wood, and hyssop, and scarlet, and cast *it* into the midst of the burning of the heifer. 7 Then the priest shall wash his clothes, and he shall bathe his flesh in water, and afterward he shall come into the camp, and the priest shall be unclean until the even. 8 And he that burneth her shall wash his clothes in water, and bathe his flesh in water, and shall be unclean until the even. 9 And a man *that is* clean shall gather up the ashes of the heifer, and lay *them* up without the camp in a clean place, and it shall be kept for the congregation of the children of Israel for a water of separation: it *is* a purification for sin. 10 And he that gathereth the ashes of the heifer shall wash his clothes, and be unclean until the even: and it shall be unto the children of Israel, and unto the stranger that sojourneth among them, for a statute for ever.

The red heifer pictures Christ dying and shedding His blood for our sin.

The heifer was "without spot" (Num. 19:2), depicting Christ's sinless character.

It had never born the yoke, depicting Christ as never having been under the yoke of sin.

The redness of the heifer, the color of blood, further signifies Christ's atonement, just as the ram's skins dyed red that covered the tabernacle.

1. The heifer was killed and its blood was sprinkled before the tabernacle seven times (Num. 19:3-4).

This depicts Christ's death and blood shed for our sins. The seven-fold sprinkling depicts perfection as in the seven days of creation and the seven seals of Revelation. It depicts the perfection of Christ's sacrifice to save ("by one offering he hath perfected for ever," Heb. 10:14). The blood was only applied one time, signifying the eternal security of the believer. The sprinkling depicts the broadness of availability and effectualness of Christ's atonement. He died that all men might be saved.

2. The heifer was killed and burned in the sight of the priest ("before his face," Num. 19:3, "in his sight," Num. 19:5)

This signifies that God the Father was pleased with Christ both in His perfect life and in His atoning death. His sacrifice was acceptable to God.

3. The heifer was burned without the camp (Num. 19:3).

This signifies Christ rejected by His own people Israel and crucified outside of the city of Jerusalem as a common criminal (Heb. 13:11-12). It depicts Christ bearing man's sin, being made sin for us, and therefore being unworthy to remain in the camp. It was the unclean who had to go outside the camp (Lev. 13:46).

4. The heifer was wholly burned (Num. 19:5).

This signifies Christ's complete devotion to God the Father and the complete sacrifice of Himself for man's sins.

5. Cedar wood, hyssop, and scarlet were put into the burning sacrifice (Num. 19:6).

This signifies all of the glory of this present world which is condemned by God and crucified with Christ. The cedar and hyssop are the largest and smallest members of the vegetable kingdom (1 Kings 4:33).

The scarlet signifies earthly wealth, royalty, and power (Rev. 17:4; 18:16). This world is under God's curse and will be judged at Christ's return (Isa. 2:12-17). Those who do not turn their backs to it and receive Christ will perish with it. Christ was condemned in our place on the cross, and the believer who receives Him is crucified to the world and alive to Christ (Gal. 6:14; 2 Cor. 5:14-15). This is the picture of baptism: dying with Christ and being raised with Christ

(Rom. 6:3-4). The believer is dead to the world in Christ, and he is exhorted *not* to love this present world system and its wickedness (1 John 2:16-17). To love this world is to commit spiritual adultery, because this world is at enmity with God (James 4:4).

The application of the water of separation

The water of separation was required whenever an Israelite came into contact with anything pertaining to the dead (Num. 19:11, 14-16).

This is a powerful illustration of the corrupting influence of sin. Defilement came even by being in a tent where someone died. It came even from touching one bone of a dead person.

In this dispensation, we know that it is not the dead body or dead bones that defile; it is sin in all of its aspects that defiles. The law of touching the dead was a type that teaches us to walk carefully in this world. We are to avoid even the appearance of evil (1 Th. 5:22).

1. When the Israelite was defiled by coming into contact with the dead, he was cleansed by the sprinkling of the water of separation.

Note that the heifer was not sacrificed again and the blood was not sprinkled again. The application of the blood happens once when we believe and its effect is eternal. The water of separation was not a repetition of the sacrifice; it was the memorial of the sacrifice.

2. The running water that flowed through the ashes to create the water of purification (Num. 19:17) signifies the Holy Spirit (John 7:38-39).

Living in the believer, the Holy Spirit convicts the believer of his sin and applies the sacrifice of Christ to the believer's heart to put away the consciousness of guilt. He teaches us the value of Christ's sacrifice. The Holy Spirit testifies of

Christ and glorifies Christ (John 15:26; 16:14). This is the Spirit's role as Comforter (John 14:16). What is more comforting than for the believer to learn of Christ's love and to grow in his understanding of the great efficacy of Christ's sacrifice for his sin? What is more comforting than to be taught that God has forgiven our sin and continues to forgive our sin and will forever forgive our sin?

3. The running water signifies Christ Himself as our ever living Intercessor (Heb. 7:25).

"In Numbers 19:16-19 is a beautiful picture of what is done when a child of God commits a sin or gets defiled by coming in contact with evil in his pathway through this world. When an Israelite contracted defilement, was the blood sprinkled on him again? No. What was sprinkled on him? Not blood, but ashes and water. What do they imply? The ashes were simply the memorial of that blood which was shed and that body which was burned outside the camp--the remembrance of Christ's sufferings and death. ... All the Trinity, so to speak, is engaged with the restoration of our souls when we have sinned. God the Son, the Lord Jesus, is there as our advocate with the Father; God the Holy Spirit, in answer to Christ's advocacy, brings home the sin to our conscience, leading us to confession; and God the Father forgives us. He is faithful and just to forgive us on the ground of that previous blood shed once for all" (R. F. Kingscote, *Christ as Seen in the Offerings*).